D1351722

Palgrave Socio-Legal Studies

Series Editor
Dave Cowan, School of Law, University of Bristol, Bristol, UK

The Palgrave Socio-Legal Studies series is a developing series of monographs and textbooks featuring cutting edge work which, in the best tradition of socio-legal studies, reach out to a wide international audience.

Editorial Board
Dame Hazel Genn, University College London, UK
Fiona Haines, University of Melbourne, Australia
Herbert Kritzer, University of Minnesota, USA
Linda Mulcahy, University of Oxford, UK
Rosemary Hunter, University of Kent
Carl Stychin, University of London, UK
Mariana Valverde, University of Toronto, Canada
Sally Wheeler, Australian National University College of Law, Australia

More information about this series at
https://link.springer.com/bookseries/14679

Joe McGrath · Ciaran Walker

New Accountability in Financial Services

Changing Individual Behaviour and Culture

Joe McGrath
Sutherland School of Law
University College Dublin
Dublin, Ireland

Ciaran Walker
Eversheds Sutherland
Dublin, Ireland

Palgrave Socio-Legal Studies
ISBN 978-3-030-88714-8   ISBN 978-3-030-88715-5   (eBook)
https://doi.org/10.1007/978-3-030-88715-5

© The Editor(s) (if applicable) and The Author(s), under exclusive license to Springer Nature
Switzerland AG 2022
This work is subject to copyright. All rights are solely and exclusively licensed by the Publisher, whether
the whole or part of the material is concerned, specifically the rights of translation, reprinting, reuse
of illustrations, recitation, broadcasting, reproduction on microfilms or in any other physical way, and
transmission or information storage and retrieval, electronic adaptation, computer software, or by similar
or dissimilar methodology now known or hereafter developed.
The use of general descriptive names, registered names, trademarks, service marks, etc. in this publication
does not imply, even in the absence of a specific statement, that such names are exempt from the relevant
protective laws and regulations and therefore free for general use.
The publisher, the authors and the editors are safe to assume that the advice and information in this book
are believed to be true and accurate at the date of publication. Neither the publisher nor the authors or
the editors give a warranty, expressed or implied, with respect to the material contained herein or for any
errors or omissions that may have been made. The publisher remains neutral with regard to jurisdictional
claims in published maps and institutional affiliations.

Cover illustration: Martin Barraud/GettyImages

This Palgrave Macmillan imprint is published by the registered company Springer Nature Switzerland AG
The registered company address is: Gewerbestrasse 11, 6330 Cham, Switzerland

Foreword to New Accountability in Financial Services

There could not be a book more topical nor timely than this monograph by Professor Joe McGrath and Ciaran Walker. We in the Irish Banking Culture Board have, since our launch in 2019, been engaged in working with our member banks to build trustworthiness in order to assist the industry in regaining public trust. Changing individual behaviour and culture lies at the very heart of what we have been working on since our launch. Individual accountability is a prerequisite for positive cultural change. Thus, this work is aimed directly at an endeavour that has profound implications for the financial services sector including banks, for customers and for the wider community.

The authors examine in detail the evolution of the regulatory process. They proceed from the argument that an interactive approach leaving sanctions as a last resort seems to work best. One might consider that, in this model, the regulator should be seen as being analogous to the modern referee whose role is no longer just to penalise infringements but is to ensure that the game is kept running smoothly and is played according to the rules, to the benefit of all.

The chapter which considers unethical behaviour as a systemic problem is a sobering and essential read which highlights the importance of embedding ethics within day-to-day business decisions. I remain convinced however that the vast majority of bank staff wish only to do a good, honest days work and serve their customers well. They deserve to work in an environment with the necessary checks and balances in place to facilitate and ensure that this is the approach adopted by all of their colleagues. The authors rightly reference the criticality of effective whistle-blowing (or "speaking-up") mechanisms in this regard.

The view is taken that focussing on individual and organisational factors is not enough. A broader approach that goes beyond regulation seems called for. This is very much in line with our board's view recently reiterated by me that regulation can change behaviour but not culture. Positive culture requires accountability and a willingness to embrace new ways of doing things. We have commenced a process for facilitating an environment where ethical conduct both personally and organisationally is encouraged and enhanced within the banking sector with the ambition that it becomes inevitable. Examples of that approach may be found in the IBCB's DECIDE framework for ethical decision-making at every level and the recently launched Guiding Principles for Change agreed by our five member banks. The banks must themselves want cultural change that ensures ethical conduct of business at all levels. It is very encouraging that the authors of this work seem in accordance with this approach. They will greatly enhance what the IBCB is trying to do with their particular perspective backed up by their intellectual rigour.

The chapter that deals with the new individual accountability regimes will surely and deservedly attract great interest in the course of the imminent discussion of the recently introduced draft legislation on the senior executive accountability regime—SEAR in Ireland. This proposed regime will be central to a full debate on the present and future shape of banking in Ireland presently being demanded by many of the stakeholders in the Irish banking sector. The comparative analysis of the Irish proposed regime with those of the UK, Australia, Hong Kong, Singapore, and Malaysia is an outstanding contribution to this debate. There is so much we can and must learn from what other jurisdictions have done.

The authors deal in a most interesting way with the professionalising of the banking industry. In this they foresee a more effective and sustainable way of ensuring that business is conducted in an ethical manner. Strict rules and regulations on the state side alone will not cut the mustard. There must be, they argue convincingly, a professionalism within the sector that creates a sense of the bank as a responsible member of society committed to conducting a sustainable business model. This again I find most encouraging and welcome support for the third Pillar of the IBCB's current work programme—The Bank in the Community—and also reflective of the ever-increasing focus on sustainability and the wider ESG agenda across business.

The authors examine how the state may set the rules whilst business implements effective systems of internal controls overseen by regulators to ensure compliance.

The authors conclude that a "New Accountability" that emphasises a positive and interdependent form of regulation is the way forward. Businesses should create and implement measures that promote the highest levels of ethical conduct. They should, as we in the IBCB have urged since our foundation, strive to create a business model where the ethical conduct of their business becomes inevitable, is closely monitored and thus maintained. In such a scenario it would be good to see the emphasis of regulation shift from what the authors describe as a command and control, sanctioning approach of regulation to ultimately a more cooperative model in which the regulator and the regulated entities work together to ensure compliance with the highest standards of ethical conduct and compliance with the rules. We must recognise that the actions of both the regulator and the regulated contribute to the overall culture within our financial services sector and I hope that an increased focus on accountability via the SEAR regime in Ireland will facilitate this alignment.

This book is an invaluable contribution to the debate on the future shape of banking in Ireland that is only just commencing. Its unique perspective can greatly inform that ongoing discussion and provide the academic rigour necessary to ensure that the financial sector that emerges from the debate is one in which the public may safely repose their trust. All involved in that debate should carefully study this fine book.

Donnybrook, Dublin

Justice John Hedigan
Chair of the Irish Banking Culture
Board

Acknowledgements

We would like to thank numerous people who kindly helped us with this project. In the first instance, we are grateful to Claire Hill (University of Minnesota) who organised a roundtable discussion to help us workshop an early draft of this monograph. We are indebted to each participant: Blanaid Clarke (Trinity College Dublin), Colin Scott (University College Dublin), Eugene Soltes (Harvard Business School), and David Zaring (Wharton Business School), all of whom helped us hone, sharpen, and polish the argument. We benefited greatly from their expertise which allowed us to significantly improve the manuscript.

A number of other colleagues and friends were also incredibly helpful in developing our thinking in the monograph and generously read sections of the text. We thank: Alan Brener (University College London), Susan Buckton (ANZ), Simon Collins (Eversheds Sutherland), Mary Donnelly (University College Cork), Deirdre Healy (University College Dublin), Jennifer Hill (Monash University), Tom Noone (Federal Reserve Bank of New York), Nicholas Lord (University of Manchester), Iain MacNeil (University of Glasgow), Gerard McCormack (University of Leeds), Ian Ramsay (University of Melbourne), Wieke Scholten (Samhoud), Andy Schmulow (University of Wollongong), Ruth Steinholtz (AretéWork LLP), and Duncan Watt (Eversheds Sutherland). Special thanks are also due to Karen Lynch Shally (University of Maynooth) for reading the entire manuscript. All remaining errors are those of the authors.

Institutional support from our employers, University College Dublin and Eversheds Sutherland, respectively, was also generous and forthcoming. We are grateful for the many conversations with our students and colleagues that positively informed our research.

Thanks are also due to the entire publishing team at Palgrave, particularly Josie Taylor for her support and advice throughout. Julie Friesner kindly proofed the text and provided copy editing assistance.

We are also grateful to Mr. Justice John Hedigan, the Chair of the Irish Banking Culture Board, for his kind and thoughtful foreword.

Finally, Joe thanks his partner, Alfredo, for his encouragement, good humour, and for providing welcome distractions. Ciaran thanks his wife, Jill, for her constant support and inspiration.

Contents

About the Authors

Joe McGrath is an Irish Research Council Scholar, a Fulbright Scholar, and an Assistant Professor of Law at the Sutherland School of Law, University College Dublin. His first monograph, *Corporate and White-Collar Crime in Ireland: A New Architecture of Regulatory Enforcement*, was published by Manchester University Press. He also edited and co-authored the book entitled *White-Collar Crime in Ireland: Law and Policy*. It was published by Clarus Press. He has published in the leading international peer-reviewed journals in his fields, including *Crime Law and Social Change*, the *European Journal of Criminology*, *Justice Quarterly*, and *Punishment and Society*, amongst others. In 2019, he was a Visiting Professor at the University of Minnesota School of Law in 2019 and the Inaugural Visiting Scholar at the Federal Reserve Bank of Minneapolis.

Ciaran Walker is a Consultant in the Financial Services Regulation & Governance group at the Dublin office of the global law firm Eversheds Sutherland. He advises local and international financial services firms on issues relating, for example, to governance and individual accountability. He also regularly lectures and speaks at conferences internationally on governance, culture, and individual accountability issues. He lectures on the Advanced Diploma in Corporate, White-Collar and Regulatory Crime at the Honorable Society of King's Inns. He contributed a chapter to the book *White-Collar Crime in Ireland: Law and Policy*. His recent paper, on *"The role of the Board of financial services firms in improving their firm's culture"*, was published in the University of Seattle Law Review. Prior to joining Eversheds Sutherland, he was Deputy Head of Enforcement at the Central Bank of Ireland.

1

Changing Individual Behaviour and Culture: An Introduction and Overview

1 Overview of New Accountability

This monograph is a critical examination of recently introduced individual accountability regimes (IARs) that apply to the financial services industry in the UK and Australia, together with a forthcoming new IAR in Ireland. Whilst individuals in financial services have, for some time, been subject to various forms of individual accountability under criminal law, corporate law and general regulatory law, the new IARs discussed in this monograph introduce important new elements of individual accountability.

The three jurisdictions have been chosen as they are all common law jurisdictions that have implemented, or are in the process of implementing, broadly similar IARs. Focusing on these three jurisdictions provides an opportunity to analyse the earlier adopter (the UK), the contemporary developer (Australia), and, potentially, the future innovator (Ireland). Exercising sensitivity for the social, cultural, historical, and legal contexts that shape compliance and enforcement,[1] the monograph analyses the conditions giving

---

[1] Pakes, F. (2019). *Comparative Criminal Justice*. Routledge; Healy, D., & McGrath, J. (2020). 'Comparing Apples with Oranges Disguised as Apples' (But Still Producing Fruit): The Methodological Challenges in Conducting White-Collar Crime Research and a Way Forward. *Irish Jurist*, 63(63), 61–81; McGrath, J., & Healy, D. (2021). Same Differences? Reflections on the Comparative Method in White-Collar Crime Research in Ireland and the United States. In Lord, N., et al. eds., *What Is European About White-Collar and Corporate Crime in Europe: Current Perspectives and Debates*. Bristol University Press, 221–236.

© The Author(s), under exclusive license to Springer Nature Switzerland AG 2022
J. McGrath and C. Walker, *New Accountability in Financial Services*,
Palgrave Socio-Legal Studies,
https://doi.org/10.1007/978-3-030-88715-5_1

rise to the development of these regimes; provides a framework for analysing their effectiveness; and proposes additional measures which may help to normalise good behaviours in the financial services sector. This analysis is informed by criminological theory, which sheds light on the causes and effects of corporate irresponsibility; regulatory theory, which casts doubt on the utility of sanctions except as a last resort; and behavioural science, which offers insights into how ethics and culture, not just law and markets, can constrain irresponsible behaviour in the financial services sector.

The new IARs are significant because they are intended to tackle the pervasive problem of misconduct in financial services. This is a global issue, which has the "potential to create systemic risks by undermining trust in both financial institutions and markets" internationally.[2] In 2013, the UK Parliamentary Commission on Banking Standards (PCBS) issued a report (PCBS Report), which considered in detail the issues of misconduct in banking in the UK and made recommendations for reform.[3] It determined that one of the core features giving rise to misconduct in the banking industry had been a "striking limitation on the sense of personal responsibility and accountability of the leaders within the industry for the widespread failings and abuses over which they presided. Ignorance was offered as the main excuse. It was not always accidental".[4]

The report found that "too many bankers, especially at the most senior levels, have operated in an environment with insufficient personal responsibility" and that "[i]ndividual incentives have not been consistent with high-collective standards, often the opposite".[5] It stated:

> Senior executives were aware that they could not be punished for what they could not see and promptly donned the blindfolds. Where they could not claim ignorance, they fell back on the claim that everyone was party to a decision, so that no individual could be held squarely to blame—the Murder on the Orient Express Defence.[6]

The PCBS Report recommendations led to the introduction of a new Senior Managers and Certification Regime (SMCR) which came into force from

---

[2] Letter from Mark Carney, Chairman Financial Stability Board to G20 Leaders, 30 August 2016, available at: https://www.fsb.org/wp-content/uploads/p20160831.pdf.

[3] UK Parliamentary Commission on Banking Standards. (2013). *Changing Banking for Good* (Vol. I). The Stationery Office Limited. https://publications.parliament.uk/pa/jt201314/jtselect/jtpcbs/27/27.pdf (Vol. II available at: https://www.parliament.uk/globalassets/documents/banking-commission/Banking-final-report-vol-ii.pdf).

[4] PCBS Report, Vol. I, para. 14.

[5] Ibid., p. 8.

[6] Ibid., para. 14.

March 2016 in the UK.[7] A broadly similar regime, known as the Banking Executive Accountability Regime (BEAR),[8] came into force in Australia from July 2018 and it is expected that it will soon be replaced by an expanded regime, the Financial Accountability Regime (FAR). It is also anticipated that legislation will soon be adopted to introduce a new individual accountability framework, including a Senior Executive Accountability Regime (SEAR) in Ireland.[9]

The aim of each of these new IARs is to establish a culture of individual accountability, particularly at a more senior level, for (mis)conduct within financial services firms, and thereby lead to improvements in ethical culture in this industry.[10] Whilst the three regimes differ from each other in various respects, they each have the following core features. First, they require that holders of specified senior roles in certain types of financial services firms identify and document their areas of individual accountability within their firm; these areas of identified individual accountability must be mapped across the firm to ensure that they cover all of the main aspects of the operations of the firm. This is intended to address the issue of (wilful) blindness to issues of misconduct by senior managers. Second, they each codify individual conduct standards. Third, they enable senior individuals to be held individually to account for breaches of regulatory requirements that occur in their respective areas of individual responsibility, in particular where it is established that they have not taken "reasonable steps" to ensure regulatory requirements are met.

Early indications from surveys of senior managers in the financial services industry in the UK and Australia suggest that the new IARs in these jurisdictions have had a positive impact. A 2019 survey carried out on behalf of a UK industry body, for example, found that the introduction of the SMCR has

---

[7] Part 4 of the Financial Services (Banking Reform) Act 2013 amended Part V of the Financial Services and Markets Act 2000 to provide the legislative framework for the SMCR in the UK. Pursuant to Section 147 of this Act, the SMCR applies to the whole of the UK i.e. England and Wales, Scotland and Northern Ireland.

[8] The BEAR was adopted in February 2018, on the basis of the Treasury Laws Amendment (Banking Executive Accountability and Related Measures) Act 2018, which inserting a new Part IIAA in the Australian Banking Act 1959.

[9] On 27 July 2021, the Irish government published the General Scheme of a Central Bank (Individual Accountability Framework) Bill 2021, available at: https://www.gov.ie/en/publication/d28d9-general-scheme-central-bank-individual-accountability-framework-bill/. A somewhat similar individual accountability regime to the SMCR has been introduced in Hong Kong and Singapore and another one, also similar, is being introduced in Malaysia. This monograph is not intended to focus on these latter three individual accountability regimes, but does briefly describe their key relevant features in Chapter 5.

[10] See, e.g., Davidson, J., Getting Conduct and Culture Right—The Role of the Regulator, UK Financial Conduct Authority, 13 July 2016, available at: https://www.fca.org.uk/news/speeches/getting-culture-and-conduct-right-role-regulator.

"focused minds" of senior managers on issues of accountability and that "there has been a meaningful and tangible change in culture, behaviour, and attitudes towards risk within firms".[11] Broadly similar conclusions were reached in a December 2020 report on implementation of BEAR in Australia.[12]

Nevertheless, as discussed in this monograph, regulators are heavily reliant on regulated firms to ensure the effective implementation of the new IARs. For example, regulators are reliant to an important extent on firms to vet the fitness and probity of their employees on an ongoing basis throughout their employment with the firm. In areas such as this, regulators do not prescribe in great detail how firms should comply with regulatory requirements. Instead, they rely on regulated firms to develop their own systems for ensuring compliance (and demonstrating that compliance). This is a well-established type of approach to regulation which has been described in the regulatory literature as "meta-regulation".[13] To a certain extent, this type of regulatory approach is a necessary and practical approach to achieving regulatory objectives.

The extent to which regulators rely on firms, however, can also be a weakness. For example, there is a risk that at least some firms might focus on compliance with the form, but not substance, of the new IARs. The aforementioned UK survey, for example, noted that some respondents stated that the changes introduced by the SMCR had "created too much complexity and engendered a focus on recording decisions and actions, rather than looking at culture more holistically".[14] Furthermore, the question of what "reasonable steps" senior managers are required to take to comply with the conduct standards imposed on them is open to a wide range of interpretations. The standards of behaviour required of individuals are quite high level. These include the requirements to "act with integrity" and "act with due skill, care, and diligence". Whilst these requirements will be helpful in targeting egregious behaviours, they are open to interpretation. The interpretation of these norms by individuals will likely depend, to an important extent, on how they are understood and applied in practice within the individual's firm and wider industry, on the basis of a "what is common is moral" heuristic.[15]

---

[11] SMCR: Evolution and Reform, September 2019, UK Finance, p. 8, available at: https://www.ukf inance.org.uk/system/files/SMCR%20-%20Evolution%20and%20Reform.pdf.

[12] Sheedy, E. A., & Canestrari-Soh, D. (2020). Regulating Accountability: An Early Look at the Banking Executive Accountability Regime (BEAR), available at: https://papers.ssrn.com/sol3/papers. cfm?abstract_id=3775275.

[13] Black, J. (2015). Regulatory Styles and Supervisory Strategies. In Moloney, N., Ferran, E., & Payne, J. eds., *The Oxford Handbook of Financial Regulation*. Oxford University Press, 217–253.

[14] SMCR: Evolution and Reform, September 2019, UK Finance, p. 8.

[15] Lindström, B., Jangard, S., Selbing, I., & Olsson, A. (2018). The Role of a "Common Is Moral" Heuristic in the Stability and Change of Moral Norms. *Journal of Experimental Psychology: General*, 147(2), 228–242.

Whilst the sanctioning of individuals who infringe the IAR conduct standards will serve to hold individuals to account for their failings and to elucidate, to some extent, the expected standards of individual conduct under the IARs, reliance on sanctions as a means of deterring future misconduct is likely to form only a very small part of a more comprehensive regulatory strategy. This is the case, in particular, because of the limited number of sanctions cases that will likely be concluded, given both the evidential burden that has to be overcome and the typically protracted nature of sanctions cases against individuals. In this regard, it is interesting to note that, since the SMCR came into force in the UK in March 2016, the UK regulatory authorities have imposed a sanction for breach of the SMCR individual conduct requirements in only one case.[16]

Whilst sanctioning individuals to deter future misconduct is an important part of any successful regulatory strategy, this monograph argues that the focus should be on ensuring that individuals in the financial services industry internalise the norms of behaviour expected under the IARs. As Ayres and Braithwaite note with regard to efforts to achieve compliance through rewards and punishments:

> what may be best for short-term compliance might also be counterproductive for long-term internalisation of a desire to comply. And this long-term internalisation is the more important matter in almost any domain of social control because it is usually impossible for society to organize its resources so that rewards and punishments await every act of compliance or non-compliance.[17]

In order to achieve an internalisation of ethical norms by individuals and generate positive cultural change in the financial services industry, it is critical to understand and address how norms are internalised by individuals. As stated by Black,

> behaviour, including responses to regulation, are shaped by the complex interplay of factors at the individual level (incentive structures and interests of key individuals); the level of internal organisational systems, processes and cultures;

---

[16] In that case, the FCA and PRA imposed fines totalling £642,430 on Mr Jes Staley, CEO of Barclays Group, for breach of the conduct rule requiring him to "act with due skill, care, and diligence". See, FCA Press Release, 11 May 2018, available at: https://www.fca.org.uk/news/press-rel eases/fca-and-pra-jointly-fine-mr-james-staley-announce-special-requirements.

[17] Ayres, I., & Braithwaite, J. (1992). *Responsive Regulation: Transcending the Deregulation Debate.* Oxford University Press, 49.

and at the macro-level: not only the organisation's immediate field but also the deeper normative and cognitive environment.[18]

Similarly, Omarova refers to the metaphor of the Russian nesting doll, the Matryoshka, to describe the multiple layers of the dynamics influencing individual behaviours in the financial services industry. She notes, in particular, that "[a] critically important source of firms' internal systems of norms, incentives, and behavioural patterns is the market in which these firms compete and the industry which they collectively compose".[19]

This monograph recognises that individual behaviours are shaped, whether for good or otherwise, by a complex interplay of factors at the levels of (1) the individual; (2) the firm and its culture; and (3) wider industry and external structural factors. It analyses each of these three levels of factors separately, and argues that, whilst the IARs focus on individual accountability in order to generate cultural change within firms, they are not designed to address the wider industry/structural factors that influence individual behaviours and organisational cultures. To address this, and to facilitate an internalisation of ethical norms, this monograph argues for a "trajectory towards professionalisation" of banking as an important means of positively influencing industry-wide norms of behaviour, which have a key influence on firms' and individuals' behaviours.[20]

In this regard, the former Governor of the Bank of England, Mark Carney, argues that an approach based on total regulation and large ex post sanctions is "bound to fail because it promotes a culture of complying with the letter of the law, not its spirit and because authorities will inevitably lag developments in fast-changing markets".[21] He argues that a "more comprehensive, lasting solution combines public regulation with private standards"; this would involve three components: aligning compensation with values, increasing senior management accountability and "renewing a sense of vocation in finance."[22]

Whilst the focus of much of the discussion herein relates to retail banking, simply because most of the main official reports into misconduct in financial

---

[18] Black, J. (2012), Paradoxes and Failures: "New Governance" Techniques and the Financial Crisis. *Modern Law Review*, 75, 1037–1063, 1058. See also, McGrath, J. (2020). Why Do Good People Do Bad Things: A Multi-level Analysis of Individual, Organizational, and Structural Causes of White-Collar Crime. *Seattle University Law Review*, 43, 525–553.

[19] Omarova, S. T. (2017). Ethical Finance as a Systemic Challenge: Risk, Culture, and Structure. *Cornell Journal of Law & Public Policy*, 27, 797–840, 825.

[20] The term "trajectory towards professionalisation" is used in the PCBS Report; see, e.g. Vol. I at para. 94.

[21] Carney, M. (2021). *Values: Building a Better World for All*. Signal, 204.

[22] Ibid., pp. 204–205

services in the jurisdictions that are analysed relate largely to retail banking, it should be emphasised that the arguments regarding professionalisation also apply to the various other sectors of the financial services industry.

This monograph analyses the core attributes of a profession, the extent to which banking meets these attributes in the jurisdictions under review, and considers the steps that are being taken to further professionalise banking. An effective trajectory towards professionalisation would likely involve the industry itself providing an in-depth articulation of ethical norms of behaviour going beyond minimum regulatory requirements expected of its members. This could include, for example, providing guidance on issues such as the "reasonable steps" senior managers should take for the purposes of compliance with the individual conduct standards. Interestingly, a recent report by industry on the implementation of the SMCR in the UK recommended that further guidance be developed to detail the measures which amount to "reasonable steps" and that clarity be provided on what conduct would constitute a breach of conduct rules. It noted that such guidance "is unlikely to be provided by the regulators and may be an action for industry to pursue itself".[23] There may also be benefits in regulation being adopted to the effect that industry-generated codes of conduct might serve as a potential "safe harbour" for individuals, where the individuals can demonstrate that they have acted in accordance with such codes (UK),[24] or could be legally enforceable via legislation by the regulator (Australia).[25]

A trajectory towards professionalisation could also, for example, involve putting in place a comprehensive educational structure to enable learning about expected ethical norms of behaviour in the industry and instil them within the industry, together with feedback to individuals from peers to encourage conformity with these norms. Whilst the industry itself could take on responsibility for identifying the appropriate education and training structure, the education and training itself could be provided by various accredited third-party providers. It is anticipated that this education and training structure would lead to an improvement in industry behaviours through a process of normalisation of higher ethical standards across the industry. This could involve further development of continuing professional development (CPD) courses that include modules on ethical decision-making. Personnel at all levels of the banking industry would be expected to attend these courses. This would go beyond regulatory requirements relating to CPD that tend to

---

[23] SMCR: Evolution and Reform, September 2019, UK Finance, p. 5.

[24] See, FCA Policy Statement PS 18/18, July 2018, available at: https://www.fca.org.uk/publication/policy/ps18-18.pdf.

[25] See, Financial Sector Reform (Hayne Royal Commission Response) Act 2020.

focus on requirements for customer-facing staff. The PCBS Report stated very bluntly on this issue: "A set of expected qualifications which forces bank clerks to night school for years to come, but gives a free pass to those working in wholesale banking or at more senior levels—the groups which most conspicuously failed in recent years—would ignore the lessons of the crisis".[26]

There are significant challenges in professionalising banking. These challenges include how the banking industry could be encouraged in practice to raise its standards above those that can be enforced by regulation; whether legislation is needed to facilitate this; the role of industry-funded bodies such as the UK Financial Services Culture Board and Irish Banking Culture Board; the effectiveness or otherwise of industry-wide guidance and direction; and whether there is future scope for any form of self-regulation. These challenges would need to be considered in much greater detail in due course.

Whilst this monograph identifies some steps that have been taken in the UK, Australia, and Ireland towards further professionalising banking, it is not within its scope to seek to address the challenges in detail. Rather its focus is to explain why a trajectory towards increasing professionalisation in the banking industry is important and worthwhile for the purposes of improving individual behaviour and culture in the industry.

This monograph contends that a trajectory towards professionalisation would be beneficial for several reasons. First, it would encourage and develop a professional identity for bankers that places greater emphasis on the need for them to take account of social responsibilities going beyond short-term profit-maximisation. Second, it would facilitate the internalisation of ethical norms by the industry, through a process in which the industry itself engages with and articulates norms that are likely to be more detailed and go beyond the minimum legal standards articulated by the regulator. This is particularly important because, as the Dutch financial regulator, the DNB, has noted, "peer pressure regulates behaviour".[27] Also, regulators can be reticent about developing detailed codes of conduct, because they risk providing firms with an opportunity to "game" the detailed rules. This approach, however, leaves gaps in terms of industry understandings of appropriate norms of behaviour in particular circumstances, which could be addressed by the industry itself. A third, related, reason for encouraging a trajectory towards professionalisation in banking is that the process of active engagement by the industry in the

---

[26] PCBS Report, Vol. II, para. 607.

[27] Supervision of Behaviour and Culture: Foundations, Practice & Future Developments, De Nederlandsche Bank, p. 50, available at: https://www.dnb.nl/media/1gmkp1vk/supervision-of-behaviour-and-culture_tcm46-380398-1.pdf.

articulation of norms of behaviour is more likely to make such norms salient to its members on a day-to-day basis and, therefore, more likely to have an influence on their behaviours.

Furthermore, a "trajectory towards professionalisation" could help to address, at least to some extent, the problem that has been described in a staff paper from the Federal Reserve Bank of New York as a "co-ordination failure". This is "the inability of private actors to reach a common objective that is in the collective best interest".[28] In the present case, "firms seeking to reduce misconduct risk face a coordination challenge, where short-term competitive pressures make it difficult to make long-term investments in cultural capital".[29] Individual firms may be less willing to incur the costs of investing sufficiently in improving behaviour and culture in their firm, if this risks putting them at a competitive disadvantage. This would arise where some of their competitors choose not to make such an investment and are tolerating sharp practices and misconduct that may be profitable for them. A "trajectory towards professionalisation" would enable industry co-ordination to address the problem of trust in the financial services industry and improve that trust, for the benefit of the industry as a whole.

Ultimately, the aim of a trajectory towards professionalisation would be to generate peer pressure within the banking industry for members to meet high standards of behaviour. Groups, as Ellemers argues, are our moral anchors; individuals define what is right and wrong by what others around them consider to be right and wrong.[30] Individuals typically wish to fit in with and belong to the group with which they identify.[31] As social beings, the influence of others can shape our moral climate, affect our judgements, and influence our behaviours.[32] Individuals belong by conforming to the norms of that group. Also, as noted by O'Neill, in the long run, the realities of earning or losing professional respect, or ultimately being expelled or ostracised from the profession, can have a greater impact on securing trustworthy performance than other means, including criminal sanctions.[33] She has argued for a serious effort to reinvigorate intelligent forms of accountability, including

---

[28] Chaly, S., Hennessy, J., Menand, L., Stiroh, K., & Tracy, J. (2017). Misconduct Risk, Culture, and Supervision. Federal Reserve Bank of New York, p. 9, available at: https://www.newyorkfed.org/medialibrary/media/governance-and-culture-reform/2017-whitepaper.pdf.

[29] Ibid., p. 9.

[30] Ellemers, N. (2017). *Morality and the Regulation of Social Behavior: Groups as Moral Anchors*. Psychology Press.

[31] Ellemers, N. (2012). The Group Self. *Science*, 336(6083), 848–852.

[32] Moore, C., & Gino, F. (2013). Ethically Adrift: How Others Pull Our Moral Compass from true North, and How We Can Fix It. *Research in Organizational Behavior*, 33, 53–77.

[33] O'Neill, O. (2014). Trust, Trustworthiness, and Accountability. In Morris, N., & Vines, D. eds., *Capital Failure: Rebuilding Trust in Financial Services*. Oxford University Press, 172–189, 187.

robust forms of professional accountability which "might help re-establish a basis for placing and withholding of trust intelligently". She states that "[i]f this could be achieved we might find better ways of securing certain obligations without imposing self-defeating or ineffective controls or proliferating legal sanctions".[34]

The term "new accountability" is used in this monograph to describe a new theoretical lens for the analysis of culture in financial services. Whilst the imposition of sanctions on firms and individuals for serious regulatory breaches is a necessary and important aspect of an effective accountability regime, new accountability is focused on mechanisms, in addition to the implementation of legal requirements and sanctions, which may serve to improve behaviours in financial services. Laws, enforcement actions, and lawsuits alone may not improve the trustworthiness of financial services providers.[35] In order to achieve the broader goals of culture change and improved ethical behaviours, new accountability is focused more on inculcating an ethical culture and the internalisation of ethical norms by individuals in the industry, in particular through engagement with issues pertaining to individual incentives, firm cultures, and wider industry/structural factors that influence organisational and individual behaviours. In this regard, this work builds on the existing research by scholars in the field of regulatory theory, which emphasises the importance of moving away from a sanctioning, "command and control" model of enforcement to a more "responsive" or compliance-orientated model of enforcement, in which sanctions are increasingly a last resort.[36] To be clear, however, "new accountability" does not advocate deregulation or "light touch" regulation of financial services firms. Rather, it recognises that in order to achieve the regulatory objective of behavioural change, a "command and control" regulatory approach with a focus on sanctions to deter future misconduct is unlikely to be sufficient, in itself, to achieve this objective.

---

[34] Ibid., p. 188.

[35] Held, M. (2021). Organisational Culture: One Central Banker Lawyer's Perspective. In Starling Compendium, Culture & Conduct Risk in the Banking Sector. Why It Matters and What Regulators Are Doing to Address It, p. 91, available at: https://starlingtrust.com/the-starling-compendium/.

[36] Ayres, I., & Braithwaite, J. (1992). *Responsive Regulation: Transcending the Deregulation Debate.* Oxford University Press.

2   Contribution to Existing Research in This Area

Financial services regulation is a significant area of interest for academics, researchers, policymakers, and those with an interest in corporate affairs, although much of this research predates or otherwise does not cover an examination of IARs. There is valuable legal research on the changing nature of financial services regulation in the aftermath of the financial crisis.[37] Various scholars have examined the conditions giving rise to regulatory wrongdoing,[38] the need for regulators to be seen to react to wrongdoing and adopt "expressive" responses to crises,[39] the relative merits of public and private enforcement,[40] the utility of principles-based regulation,[41] the need to counter regulatory arbitrage as a response to more intrusive regulatory strategies,[42] and the impact of regulatory sanctions and their relationship to reputational damages to financial services providers.[43]

Given the very recent emergence of individual accountability frameworks, however, with the SMCR in the UK being the first such regime, in 2016, these new IARs have been subject to very little scholarly analysis. Some excellent articles have examined how the SMCR in the UK may address collective agency problems in the financial services sector,[44] the extent to which it

---

[37] Ferran, E., Moloney, N., Hill, J. G., & Coffee Jr, J. C. (2012). *The Regulatory Aftermath of the Global Financial Crisis*. Cambridge University Press; Moloney, N., Ferran, E., & Payne, J. (Eds.). (2015). *The Oxford Handbook of Financial Regulation*. Oxford University Press.

[38] O'Brien, J. (2009). Engineering *a Financial Bloodbath: How Sub-Prime Securitisation Destroyed the Legitimacy of Financial Capitalism*. Imperial College Press.

[39] Enriques, L. (2009). Corporate Governance Reforms in Italy: What Has Been Done and What Is Left to Do. *European Business Organization Law Review*, 10(4), 477–513.

[40] Jackson, H. E., & Zhang, J. Y. (2018). Private and Public Enforcement of Securities Regulation. In Gordon, J. N., & Ringe, W. G. eds., *The Oxford Handbook of Corporate Law and Governance*. Oxford University Press.

[41] Black, J. (2007). Principles-Based Regulation: Risks, Challenges, and Opportunities. In Principles-Based Regulation, 28 March, Sydney, Australia, available at: http://eprints.lse.ac.uk/62814/; Ferran, E. (2009). Principles-Based, Risk-Based Regulation and Effective Enforcement. In Tison, M., De Wulf, H., Van der Elst, C., & Steennot, R. eds., *Perspectives in Company Law and Financial Regulation*. Cambridge University Press.

[42] Moshirian, F. (2011). The Global Financial Crisis and the Evolution of Markets, Institutions, and Regulation. *Journal of Banking & Finance*, 35(3), 502–511.

[43] Armour, J., Mayer, C., & Polo, A. (2017). Regulatory Sanctions and Reputational Damage in Financial Markets. *Journal of Financial and Quantitative Analysis*, 52(4), 1429–1448.

[44] Alexander, S. K. (2019). Regulating Risk Culture in Banks, available at SSRN: https://ssrn.com/abstract=3321163 or https://doi.org/10.2139/ssrn.3321163; Brener, A. (2019). Developing the Senior Managers Regime. In Russo, C. A., Lastra, R. M., & Blair, W. eds., *Research Handbook on Law and Ethics in Banking and Finance*. Edward Elgar Publishing.

reflects an emphasis on "regulating instead of punishing" wrongdoers,[45] its potential to overcome problems with corporate criminal liability,[46] and the potential for adoption in Ireland.[47] Scholars analysing the regime in Australia, meanwhile, have argued on the one hand that IARs merely provide minimum standards or a "hard floor" in setting out expectations of directors' responsibilities,[48] and, in the alternative, that their purpose is to create a "panopticon" level of self-regulatory oversight, extending "regulatory reach watching over the bank executives' control over the conduct of the those who work for the organisation".[49] Much of the existing research on individual accountability frameworks is, however, practitioner-oriented.[50] In particular, the majority of the published pieces in the field are policy documents produced by the regulatory agencies administering the framework and aimed at practitioners.[51] Unlike that work, this project aims to provide an authoritative socio-legal, context-sensitive account of the emergence and effectiveness of individual accountability frameworks in multiple jurisdictions.

This monograph aims to make an important substantive contribution to the growing literature on banking culture and the internalisation of norms.[52] Some scholars in this field have sought to better understand how "ways of thinking" can generate misconduct whilst others focus on how deficient accountability systems, performance-based compensation, and market

[45] MacNeil, I. (2018) Regulating Instead of Punishing: The Senior Managers Regime in the UK. In Ligetti, K., & Tosza, S. eds., *White-Collar Crime: A Comparative Perspective*. Hart Publishing.

[46] Ryder, N. (2018). "Too Scared to Prosecute and Too Scared to Jail?" A Critical and Comparative Analysis of Enforcement of Financial Crime Legislation Against Corporations in the USA and the UK. *Journal of Criminal Law*, 82(3), 245–263.

[47] Clarke, B. (2018). Individual Accountability in Irish Credit Institutions—Lessons to Be Learned from the UK's Senior Managers Regime. *Common Law World Review*, 47(1), 35–52.

[48] Manwaring, K., & Hanrahan, P. F. (2019). BEARing Responsibility for Cyber Security in Australian Financial Institutions: The Rising Tide of Directors' Personal Liability. *Journal of Banking and Finance Law and Practice*, 30(1), 20–42.

[49] Adams, M., Borsellino, G., McCalman, J., & Young, A. (2017). Australia's Proposed Banking Executive Accountability Regime: Regulatory Panopticon or Fail-Safe? *Governance Directions*, 69, 528–531, 531. https://core.ac.uk/download/pdf/96919959.pdf.

[50] de Villiers Getz, L. (2020). Connecting Senior Managers and Certification Regime Requirements with Operational Risk. *Journal of Securities Operations & Custody*, 12(3), 207–218; Jackson, O. (2018). SMCR Extension Could Be Culture Shock for Insurance Sector. *International Financial Law Review* (18 December); Symington, J. (2019). SMCR: Waking Up to Individual Accountability. *International Financial Law Review* (4 February).

[51] Allen, T. (2018). Strengthening the Link Between Seniority and Accountability: The Senior Managers and Certification Regime. *Bank of England Quarterly Bulletin*, 58(3), 1–10; Banking Executive Accountability Regime, Consultation Paper, July 2017, available at: https://treasury.gov.au/sites/default/files/2019-03/c2017-t200667-BEAR_cp.pdf; Central Bank of Ireland (2018). Behaviour and Culture of the Irish Retail Banks. CBI, available at: https://www.centralbank.ie/docs/default-source/publications/corporate-reports/behaviour-and-culture-of-the-irish-retail-banks.pdf?sfvrsn=2.

[52] Zaring, D. (2017). The International Campaign to Create Ethical Bankers. *Journal of Financial Regulation*, 3(2), 187–209.

conditions can contribute to misconduct in the financial services industry.[53] Some scholars in this tradition focus on formal legal solutions to addressing improving addressing banking culture where, for example, contractual agreements can generate a more ethical banking industry.[54] Others have sought to analyse "softer" tools for generating better banking behaviours, including codes of conduct and oaths.[55]

Unlike that work, this monograph provides a framework for evaluating IARs and locates their effectiveness in the existing literature on individual decision-making theory, organisational culture theory, and structural theory. Given the international and comparative perspective of the monograph, and the rich analysis and application of regulatory theory, it is intended to stimulate an extensive conversation on corporate regulation and governance in multiple jurisdictions, not least in those which are the focus of the study. It is also intended to provide a platform for researchers further afield with an interest in comparative research in the fields of financial regulation, corporate governance, and white-collar crime. Moreover, given the international trend towards the increased use of robust regulatory enforcement and individual accountability mechanisms, it is reasonable to assume that similar regimes will be implemented in other jurisdictions. As such, this monograph is an essential contribution to knowledge for policymakers with an interest in legislating for these frameworks, the academics who research them, and the practitioners who navigate them.

3   The Structure of This Monograph

Chapter 2 discusses relevant regulatory theory. In particular, it analyses "responsive regulation" theory, as reworked by various scholars, which focuses on the importance of harnessing not only the regulatory capacity of the State, but also that of businesses as self-regulators, and third parties who may influence and exert pressure on regulated firms. This discussion of regulatory theory provides the framework for the subsequent assessment of individual accountability.

---

[53] Soltes, E. (2016). *Why They Do It: Inside the Mind of the White-Collar Criminal*. Public Affairs; Skinner, C. P. (2015). Misconduct Risk. *Fordham Law Review*, 84, 1559–1610.

[54] Hill, C. A., & Painter, R. W. (2015). *Better Bankers, Better Banks: Promoting Good Business Through Contractual Commitment*. University of Chicago Press.

[55] de Bruin, B. (2019). Epistemic Corporate Culture: Knowledge, Common Knowledge, and Professional Oaths. *Seattle University Law Review*, 43, 807–839; Loonen, T., & Rutgers, M. (2017). Swearing to be a good banker: Perceptions of the obligatory banker's oath in The Netherlands. *Journal of Banking Regulation*, 18(1), 28–47.

Chapter 3 outlines the scale and systemic nature of misconduct in the financial services industry in the UK, Australia, and Ireland. It then critically discusses some of the causes of this misconduct, which include individual motivations, firms' culture, and wider structural factors relating to the nature of the financial services sector.

Chapter 4 argues that whilst there has been an increased public focus on sanctioning individuals in the financial services industry, the use of legal mechanisms to sanction individuals has its limits in terms of effectiveness, in particular due to the evidential requirements that have to be met and because of the protracted nature of enforcement actions. More generally, other than for the most egregious behaviours, such legal mechanisms can be limited instruments for deterring misconduct and generating culture change.

Chapter 5 critically describes the IARs in the UK, Australia, and the proposed new IAR in Ireland. It provides a framework for assessing whether they are likely to succeed in improving behaviours in the financial services industry.

Chapter 6 argues that the banking industry should embark on a "trajectory towards professionalisation". Whilst recognising the scale of this challenge, and that professions are not without their difficulties, it contends that professionalisation may help to generate ethical norms which bankers internalise and may potentially create industry-wide cultural change.

Chapter 7 is a concluding chapter that gathers together the various threads in this monograph. It reiterates the argument in favour of a trajectory towards professionalising banking, as a form of new accountability in which bankers recognise that they owe obligations to society, not merely to their firms and shareholders.

2

"Responsively" Regulating the Financial Services Sector: An Evolving Architecture

1   Introduction: Theory and Practice

This chapter analyses the theory and practice of financial regulation, examining how regulators approach issues of compliance and enforcement to achieve regulatory objectives. The starting point for this analysis is responsive regulatory theory. This theory argues that regulators work best when they adopt a tiered or pyramidal approach to enforcement—beginning with compliance-oriented strategies when faced with wrongdoing and adopting sanctioning approaches as a last resort when other responses to compel compliance have failed. The chapter then critically describes how responsive regulatory theory has been supplemented, developed, and enhanced since its original formulation.

Regulation can also be risk-based, targeting resources to address the behaviours that are the most likely to threaten the safety and soundness of the financial system. It is considered "smart" when it enlists non-state actors to generate compliance, including third parties and even the regulated themselves. Meta-regulation, in particular, encourages regulators and industry to harness the capabilities of firms to self-regulate to generate compliance, albeit with State oversight to ensure that this form of regulation is effective. It notes that regulatory power is increasingly dispersed under this model. As such, it resonates with governmentality theory (discussed in-depth in Sect. 2 of this chapter), which recognises that regulation is increasingly depoliticised, instrumental, and exercised "at a distance" from centralised State power.

© The Author(s), under exclusive license to Springer Nature
Switzerland AG 2022
J. McGrath and C. Walker, *New Accountability in Financial Services*,
Palgrave Socio-Legal Studies,
https://doi.org/10.1007/978-3-030-88715-5_2

Having critically examined these theoretical contributions and innovations, the chapter proceeds to analyse the extent to which these regulatory models have been adopted and implemented in practice. It demonstrates that regulators historically adopted a principles-based approach to regulating the financial services sector, which emphasised collaboration and trust, where recourse to formal enforcement was rare. This approach was broadly in line with responsive regulatory theory, which prioritised compliance over deterrence-oriented approaches. After the global financial crisis (GFC), however, a much more intrusive and less deferential approach was adopted. There was a shift away from principles-based regulation to a much more robust regulatory approach, as regulators demonstrated an increased willingness to sanction wrongdoers when faced with persistent non-compliance or sufficiently serious misconduct. This did not displace compliance-based approaches. It did mean, however, that there was also a more robust deployment of formal sanctions in circumstances when compliance-based approaches were inappropriate. As part of this approach, there emerged an emphasis on credible deterrence and a willingness to escalate up the enforcement pyramid in recognition that formal enforcement may be in the public interest and necessary to achieve regulatory objectives.

The GFC stimulated regulatory change across all three jurisdictions. Nevertheless, some regulatory changes in each jurisdiction were precipitated by different causal factors, with their own momentums, generating change in different ways at different paces that were sometimes gradual, tentative, and uneven. Some factors generating change were local and slow-burning; others were international, producing intense heat. The GFC, for example, burned brightly, politicising financial regulation and producing significant regulatory changes, particularly in Ireland and the UK. Some local factors, by contrast, impacted on regulatory strategies over a significant period of time. In Australia, for example, a series of financial scandals involving misconduct against consumers emerged after the GFC. Each emerging scandal contributed to the momentum that produced change. Though different, these causal forces all whetted the appetite for increased accountability in the financial services sector. The chapter does not seek to describe each of these developments in detail or compare them on a point-by-point basis in each jurisdiction for its own sake. Instead, it takes an analytical approach that plots the changing architecture of financial regulation, examining the extent to which regulatory practices map onto regulatory theory, analysing how these regulatory models have been deployed to increase accountability, demonstrating that individual accountability regimes (IARs) represent the latest iteration of meta-governance theory in practice.

2   An Evolving Regulatory Theory

This section analyses how regulators intervene to secure compliance. It begins with an analysis of responsive regulatory theory, as first espoused by Ayres and Braithwaite. Responsive regulatory theory provides the modern theoretical foundations for financial regulatory enforcement. The section shows that the more recent theoretical advancements in this field, whether they are risk-based regulation or meta-regulation, have their intellectual origins in responsive regulation. As such, these theories should not be understood as entirely distinct regulatory strategies. They overlap and build incrementally on each previous iteration. Nevertheless, as this section canvasses a significant volume of literature, these strategies are organised and structured under separate titles for the ease of the reader.

2.1   Responsive Regulation

The responsive regulatory approach advocated by Ayres and Braithwaite is "differentiated", varying in intensity and strategy as determined by the behaviour of the regulated.[1] They suggested that regulators work best when they are "benign big guns" who "speak softly" and "carry a big stick".[2] They are most effective when they are "contingently provoking and forgiving".[3] Following this approach, regulators adopt a pyramidal or tiered approach to enforcement, depicted in Fig. 1, in which they first address wrongdoing with compliance-oriented approaches and only have recourse to progressively sanctioning approaches, or deterrence-oriented approaches, when wrongdoers continue to fail to comply with the law or remediate their wrongdoing. They note that this approach is of mutual benefit to both the regulator and the regulated because corporate actors, like other persons, are a mix of contradictory values and motivations. Sometimes, corporate executives will engage in conduct which is unethical or illegal because they are motivated, for example, by profit-maximising norms. On other occasions, they are their law-abiding selves.

Though Holmes said that the law should concern itself with the conduct of the "bad man" rather than the "good man",[4] Ayres and Braithwaite note

---

[1] Westerman, P. (2013). Pyramids and the Value of Generality. *Regulation & Governance*, 7(1), 80–94, 80.

[2] Ayres, I., & Braithwaite, J. (1992). *Responsive Regulation: Transcending the Deregulation Debate.* Oxford University Press, 19.

[3] Ibid., p. 19.

[4] Holmes, O. W. (1897). The Path of the Law. *Harvard Law Review*, 10, 457.

Fig. 1 Ayres and Braithwaite's regulatory pyramid

that contingently compliance-oriented and deterrence-oriented approaches may be better in securing compliance by good and bad market actors alike.[5] Good market actors want to obey the law. If through inadvertence they are non-compliant, a sanctioning approach might undermine their good will for the law and make them want to challenge the law in court, which could be expensive for the regulator. It may also contribute to an organisational subculture that is resistant to compliance. Education and advice are particularly important because they help good market actors to obey the law, though compliance approaches alone are ineffective (and may even be counterproductive) if law breakers go unpunished.[6] Sanctioning approaches are necessary because they incapacitate bad market actors who will obey the law only if it is rational to do so, and will break the law if they can get away with it. Sanctions, it is suggested, are "more effective against small organisations rather than large ones, and better at influencing rational actors than the incompetent".[7]

Of course, market actors and people are more complex than the good and bad person binary suggests. In recognition of this, Ayres and Braithwaite note that "situations arise when the money-making self and the responsible self are forced to stare each other in the face".[8] They suggest that wrongdoing should be addressed by compliance-oriented strategies first, with progressively deterrence-oriented strategies held in abeyance for use when faced with a continued lack of cooperation. This should make those who are regulated

---

[5] Ayres, I., & Braithwaite, J. (1992). *Responsive Regulation: Transcending the Deregulation Debate.* Oxford University Press, 26.

[6] Gunningham, N. (2016). Compliance, Enforcement, and Regulatory Excellence. In Coglianese, C. ed., *Achieving Regulatory Excellence.* Brookings Institution Press, 188–207.

[7] Ibid.

[8] Ayres, I., & Braithwaite, J. (1992). *Responsive Regulation: Transcending the Deregulation Debate.* Oxford University Press, 31.

realise that compliance is in their interest because they avoid the stick of sanctions. Both compliance and deterrence-oriented approaches on their own are limited; the trick, Ayres and Braithwaite say, is to find the right balance between persuasion and punishment, simultaneously and sequentially.[9]

Forgiveness is also an important aspect of the pyramid. Just as regulated responses may escalate, they may also de-escalate when the regulated seek to comply with regulations.[10] Circumstances may arise, however, in which regulators cannot begin by engaging at the base of the pyramid, where the misconduct has been particularly serious and political and community pressure requires more intrusive intervention.[11] With regard to financial services regulation, for example, it may be the case that slow-burn prudential issues can be addressed first by compliance-oriented approaches whereas misconduct affecting customers may require an escalated intervention to provide compensation. Nevertheless, Braithwaite has suggested that even the most serious of crimes, like genocide, might best be dealt with through dialogue at the base of the pyramid.[12] The process of dialogue and ongoing discourse between regulator and regulated is important because it legitimises regulation and regulatory strategies. When regulated businesses and industries are listened to, and their concerns are taken into account, they are more likely to accept a regulatory outcome, even when it adversely affects them.[13] Procedural justice is important if substantive justice goals are to be met.

The premise underpinning responsive regulation is that regulation works best when regulators respond or adapt to the dispositions of the regulated, escalating and potentially de-escalating as needed, depending on the cooperative or intransigent disposition of those they encounter. Crucially, however, Ayres and Braithwaite also suggest that the availability of very severe sanctions makes cooperative strategies more likely, pushing more regulatory activity into the base of the pyramid.[14] Regulators must normally be disinclined to pull the trigger on the big gun of severe sanctions, doing so carefully and

---

[9] Ibid., p. 34.

[10] Braithwaite, J. (2017). Types of Responsiveness. In Drahos, P. ed., Regulatory *Theory: Foundations and Applications*. ANU Press, 117–132.

[11] Gunningham, N. (2016). Compliance, Enforcement, and Regulatory Excellence. In Coglianese, C. ed., *Achieving Regulatory Excellence*. Brookings Institution Press, 188–207.

[12] Braithwaite, J. (2017). Types of Responsiveness. In Drahos, P. ed., Regulatory *Theory: Foundations and Applications*. ANU Press, 117–132.

[13] Tyler, T. R. (2003). Procedural Justice, Legitimacy, and the Effective Rule of Law. *Crime and Justice*, 30, 283–357.

[14] Ayres, I., & Braithwaite, J. (1992). *Responsive Regulation: Transcending the Deregulation Debate*. Oxford University Press, 40–44.

only in appropriate cases where it is likely to succeed, and with the appropriate political support, presenting an image of invincibility.[15] Taking cases that result in flea bite fines is likely to undermine the credibility of the agency. Crucially, they posit that a very clear policy of escalating up and down the enforcement pyramid communicates to industry that they should engage with regulators at less intrusive stages of regulatory intervention.

Ayres and Braithwaite's work is considered "canonical" in the field of regulatory studies.[16] It found broad appeal because it sought to find an alternative to deregulation on the one hand and intense regulation in the public interest on the other. It was popular with regulators because it mapped onto their existing practices and because it gave them significant discretion to act informally on their own professional judgement. It was also popular with scholars because they could empirically test its core principles and because it was generally in keeping with neoliberal ideas which were in the ascendency at the time.[17] Nevertheless, it has its critics. Though it sought to "transcend" the deregulation debate, some scholars have suggested that it precipitated deregulatory practices.[18] The extent to which this approach resulted in light-touch regulation in practice is revisited later in this chapter.

2.2   Risk-Based Regulation

Ayres and Braithwaite considered that regulatory resources were put to best use when targeted at those who "played fast and loose" with the rules or when they couldn't effectively self-regulate.[19] They were targeted for "more interventionist direct enforcement".[20] Though they did not articulate responsive regulation as being oriented to address risky behaviours, risk-based regulation subsequently gained traction in terms not dissimilar to those originally articulated by Ayres and Braithwaite.[21] Risk-based regulation allows regulators to concentrate their limited resources on those firms and individuals that

---

[15] Ibid., pp. 44–47.

[16] Parker, C. (2013). Twenty Years of Responsive Regulation: An Appreciation and appraisal. *Regulation & Governance*, 7(1), 2–13.

[17] Mascini, P. (2013). Why Was the Enforcement Pyramid so Influential? And What Price Was Paid? *Regulation & Governance*, 7(1), 48–60.

[18] Tombs, S., & Whyte, D. (2013). Transcending the Deregulation Debate? Regulation, Risk, and the Enforcement of Health and Safety Law in the UK. *Regulation & Governance*, 7(1), 61–79.

[19] Ayres, I., & Braithwaite, J. (1992). *Responsive Regulation: Transcending the Deregulation Debate*. Oxford University Press, 129.

[20] Braithwaite, J., & Fisse, B. (1987). Self-Regulation and the Control of Corporate Crime. In Shearing, C. D., & Stenning, P. C. eds., *Private Policing*. Sage, 221–246, 245.

[21] Black, J. (2005). The Emergence of Risk-Based Regulation and the New Public Management in the UK. *Public Law* (Autumn), 512–549.

pose the greatest risks to the regulators' ability to achieve their objectives.[22] Some argued in favour of "really responsive" regulation, which considers a range of factors including changing attitudes to compliance within particular firms and the goals of the broader regulatory environment,[23] and then "really responsive risk-based regulation",[24] in which organisations themselves take ownership and manage their own risks, de-centring regulation away from the state to private interests.[25]

Financial regulators frequently adopt risk-based regulatory strategies to concentrate their resources on those firms and individuals that pose the greatest risk to the safety and soundness of the financial system.[26] Risk-based regulation, however, differs slightly from responsive regulation, as originally conceived, in that the regulatory response is influenced by the regulators' objectives rather than the cooperativeness or intransigence of the regulated.[27] Though these theories are "not comfortable bedfellows", they are compatible when risk-based approaches are used to target resources to detect problems and when responsive strategies are applied thereafter to escalate regulatory responses, as appropriate.[28] Black and Baldwin suggest that risk-based regulation remains a valuable model of regulation when regulators are sensitive to five elements: "(1) the behaviour, attitudes, and cultures of regulatory actors; (2) the institutional setting of the regulatory regime; (3) the different logics of regulatory tools and strategies (and how these interact); (4) the regime's own performance over time; and finally, (5) changes in each of these elements".[29] As will be discussed subsequently, emphasising the extent to which organisational cultures align and interact with regulatory tools and strategies is particularly important in the context of IARs because they emphasise regulatory intervention against individuals in circumstances where internal controls have failed to generate organisational change.

---

[22] Black, J. (2005). The Development of Risk-Based Regulation in Financial Services: Just 'Modelling Through'? In Black, J., Lodge, M., & Thatcher, M. eds., *Regulatory Innovation: A Comparative Analysis*. Edward Elgar, 156.

[23] Baldwin, R., & Black, J. (2008). Really Responsive Regulation. *The Modern Law Review*, 71(1), 59–94.

[24] Black J., & Baldwin, R. (2010). Really Responsive Risk-Based Regulation. *Law & Policy*, 32, 181–213.

[25] Black, J. (2002). Regulatory Conversations. *Journal of Law and Society*, 29(1), 163–196.

[26] Haines, F. (2017). Regulation and Risk. In Drahos, P. ed., Regulatory *Theory: Foundations and Applications*: ANU Press, 181–196, 189.

[27] Gunningham, N. (2016). Compliance, Enforcement, and Regulatory Excellence. In Coglianese, C. ed., *Achieving Regulatory Excellence*: Brookings Institution Press, 188–207.

[28] Ibid.

[29] Black, J., & Baldwin, R. (2010). Really Responsive Risk-Based Regulation. *Law and Policy*, 32(2), 181–213, 186.

2.3   Smart Regulation

Although the regulatory approach advocated by Ayres and Braithwaite is often considered predominantly state-led,[30] Ayres and Braithwaite specifically recognised a role for regulatory tripartism, as they called it, in which the State, businesses, and third parties played important roles in compliance and enforcement.[31] Ayres and Braithwaite envisaged "multiple registers of action".[32] They modelled a pyramid of enforcement strategies in which firms and industry were given the freedom to self-regulate first. They also recognised, however, that progressively more intrusive strategies were required if self-regulation didn't work, giving rise to enforced self-regulation and then command and control strategies as a last resort. Enforced self-regulation is the "crucial intermediate layer of the enforcement pyramid … an arrangement under which firms develop their own set of context-specific conduct rules, which are then publicly ratified and capable of public enforcement".[33] The Basel Accords on bank capital, Ford notes, are an example of such an arrangement.[34]

Smart regulation scholars built on Ayres and Braithwaite's work on regulatory tripartism, re-envisioning the regulatory pyramid as three-sided in nature.[35] The first side reflects the involvement of the State as a regulator. The second side enlists businesses themselves as self-regulators. The third side represents third parties who may act as surrogate regulators. These surrogates may include local communities, NGOs, and business associations who advise firms to cooperate with regulators and also exert pressure on companies or members to comply with regulations.[36] The recently established Irish Banking Culture Board (IBCB), whose composition includes senior representatives from Irish banks, may represent one such body, given that it is an industry-funded body whose aim is "rebuilding trust in the [banking] sector

---

[30] Grabosky, P. (2013). Beyond Responsive Regulation: The Expanding Role of Non-state Actors in the Regulatory Process. *Regulation & Governance*, 7(1), 114–123.

[31] Ayres, I., & Braithwaite, J. (1992). *Responsive Regulation: Transcending the Deregulation Debate.* Oxford University Press, 54.

[32] Ford, C. (2013). Prospects for Scalability: Relationships and Uncertainty in Responsive Regulation. *Regulation & Governance*, 7(1), 14–29, 15.

[33] Ibid., 21–22.

[34] Ibid., 22.

[35] Gunningham, N., Grabosky, P., & Sinclair, D. (1998). *Smart Regulation: Designing Environmental Policy.* Oxford University Press.

[36] Gunningham, N. (2016). Compliance, Enforcement, and Regulatory Excellence. In Coglianese, C. ed., *Achieving Regulatory Excellence.* Brookings Institution Press.

through demonstrating a change in behaviour and overall culture".[37] It may also reflect some societal engagement as the majority of the board of the IBCB are non-bank representatives. In the UK, the Financial Services Culture Board, previously known as the Banking Standards Board, has already been performing a similar role for some time.[38] Some scholars have argued in favour of giving an increased role to third parties of this kind, "to shine the disinfecting sunlight on the workings of the financial services industry and its official overseers before the disaster strikes".[39]

Smart regulation is about taking a pluralistic approach which recognises that different forms of regulators, coalescing in concert, produce better and more effective regulation. All three dimensions of the pyramid are considered crucial for effective enforcement.[40] This approach also resonates with networked regulation, in which the State works with a range of third parties, including foreign and international regulators, industry groups, NGOs, media organisations, and civil society groups, to pressure actors into compliance.[41] Smart regulation, however, additionally "implies a diagnostically reflective regulator attending to the possible synergies and contradictions a pyramid of networked escalation can throw up".[42]

The regulatory pyramid was firmly rooted in republicanism which understood freedom as non-domination.[43] Strengthening the capacities of the regulated firms empowered them to resist domination, to check abuses of power. With this goal, Braithwaite et al. later developed the enforcement pyramid into a "strength-based pyramid".[44] This model emphasised that regulators should recognise areas in which the regulated did well, commend their strong suits, appreciate circumstances where they displayed vigour in

---

[37] See, Irish Banking Culture Board website: https://www.irishbankingcultureboard.ie/vision-and-purpose/.

[38] The Banking Standards Board was established in 2015 and relaunched in 2021 as the Financial Services Culture Board. See: Financial Services Culture Board website, available at: https://financialservicescultureboard.org.uk.

[39] Omarova, S. T. (2011). Bankers, Bureaucrats, and Guardians: Toward Tripartism in Financial Services Regulation. *Journal of Corporation Law*, 37, 621–674, 624.

[40] Van Erp, J., & Huisman, W. (2010). Smart Regulation and Enforcement of Illegal Disposal of Electronic Waste. *Criminology & Public Policy*, 9, 579–590.

[41] Braithwaite, J. (2008). *Regulatory Capitalism: How It Works, Ideas for Making It Work Better*. Edward Elgar Publishing, 94–108.

[42] Braithwaite, J. (2017). Types of Responsiveness In Drahos, P. ed., Regulatory *Theory: Foundations and Applications*. ANU Press, 117–132, 123.

[43] Braithwaite, J., & Pettit, P. (1990). *Not Just Deserts: A Republican Theory of Criminal Justice*. Oxford University Press; Pettit, P. (1997). *Republicanism: A Theory of Freedom and Government*. Clarendon Press.

[44] Braithwaite, J., Makkai, T., & Braithwaite, V. (2007). *Regulating Aged Care: Ritualism and the New Pyramid*. Edward Elgar.

tackling non-compliance, support their innovations, and reward them with praise and prizes, thereby further de-emphasising sanctioning approaches. This idea is linked to "new governance" in which the regulated are permitted to experiment with their protocols and procedures to develop effective ways to promote a culture of compliance, providing non-state actors with a greater role in regulation.[45] In line with these ideas, regulators are supposed to empathise with the situation in which the regulated find themselves and allow them a chance to design solutions to boost their compliance.[46] This also provides an element of self-regulation because the regulated is given space to experiment and reach innovative working solutions that result in compliance.[47]

2.4   Meta-Regulation

Research on meta-regulation has also made an important contribution to regulatory enforcement literature, and its contribution is particularly relevant to understanding IARs. This form of regulation gives greater flexibility to businesses themselves to determine the appropriate systems of internal control, through various protocols and risk management systems, but with oversight exercised by regulators to ensure that they work properly.[48] In the literature on governmentality, discussed further below, this is sometimes called "governance at a distance".[49] It also has some continued resonance with the early work in this field by Ayres and Braithwaite, as subsequently developed, though they called it "enforced self-regulation".[50] Scott notes that responsive regulation, as originally conceived by Ayres and Braithwaite, focused on delegating responsibility to businesses themselves and other third

---

[45] Lobel, O. (2004). The Renew Deal: The Fall of Regulation and the Rise of Governance in Contemporary Leal Thought. *Minnesota Law Review*, 89, 342–470; Ford, C. L. (2005). Toward a New model for Securities Law Enforcement. *Administrative Law Review*, 57, 757–828; Black, J. (2008). Constructing and Contesting Legitimacy and Accountability in Polycentric Regulatory Regimes. *Regulation & Governance*, 2, 137–164.

[46] Rubin, E. (2005). Images of Organizations and Consequences of Regulation. *Theoretical Inquiries in Law*, 6, 347–390, 376–377; Rubin, E. (2005). The Myth of Accountability and the Anti-Administrative Impulse. *Michigan Law Review*, 103(2073), 2131–2134.

[47] Ford, C., & Hess, D. (2008). Can Corporate Monitorships Improve Corporate Compliance. *Journal of Corporation Law*, 34, 679–738.

[48] Parker, P. (2002). *The Open Corporation: Effective Self-Regulation and Democracy*. Cambridge University Press.

[49] Miller, P., & Rose, N. (2008). *Governing the Present: Administering Economic, Social, and Personal Life*. Polity, 18.

[50] Braithwaite, J. (1982). Enforced Self-Regulation: A New Strategy for Corporate Crime Control. *Michigan Law Review*, 80(7), 1466–1507; Ayres, I., & Braithwaite, J. (1992). *Responsive Regulation: Transcending the Deregulation Debate*. Oxford University Press.

parties, but that this is sometimes forgotten, and that their work has had the biggest impact and influence on regulatory activities undertaken by the State.[51] Nevertheless, meta-regulation is important because it reminds us that governments do not have a monopoly on regulation in this "post-regulatory" world in which the State's regulatory power is more dispersed and shared with other actors.[52]

As noted by Grabosky, "Market forces may themselves be powerful regulatory instruments".[53] Non-state, market-driven governance occurs when actors recognise that norms and enforcement mechanisms are insufficient for them to act legitimately so they seek to supplement them as individuals, as organisations, or through collective actions.[54] Consumer preferences for particular products, terms and conditions, and responsible behaviours, can influence corporate behaviour. Provided there is sufficient competition in the market for consumers to choose one product or service provider over another, this has the potential to discipline those out of step with consumer sentiment and generate changes in commercial practice, particularly when consumers make that choice en masse. Braithwaite has demonstrated, for example, that taxpayers promote markets in virtue over markets in vice by preferring "honest, low-fuss" tax advisors over those who aggressively pursue tax avoidance schemes.[55]

Such market-based mechanisms, when allied with compliance and sanctioning approaches in appropriate circumstances, can "institutionalise ethical reflection within firms".[56] Similarly, institutional investors also have the power to generate changes in commercial practices and have increasingly been

---

[51] Scott, C. (2017). The Regulatory State and Beyond. In Drahos, P. ed., *Regulatory Theory: Foundations and Applications*. ANU Press, 265–287, 278.

[52] Black, J. (2001). Decentring Regulation: Understanding the Role of Regulation and Self-Regulation in a "Post-Regulatory" World. *Current Legal Problems*, 54, 103–46; Scott, C. (2004). Regulation in the Age of Governance: The Rise of the Post-regulatory State. In Jordana, J., & Levi-Faur, D. eds., *The Politics of Regulation: Institutions and Regulatory Reforms for the Age of Governance*. Edward Elgar, 145–174.

[53] Grabosky, P. (2017). Meta-Regulation. In Drahos, P. ed., Regulatory *Theory: Foundations and Applications*. ANU Press, 149–162, 153.

[54] Cashore, B. (2017). Legitimacy and the Privatization of Environmental Governance: How Non-State Market-Driven (NSMD) Governance Systems Gain Rule-Making Authority. In *International Environmental Governance*. Routledge, 339–361; Auld, G., Balboa, C., Bernstein, S., Cashore, B. E. N. I. A. M. I. N., Delmas, M., & Young, O. (2009). The Emergence of Non-State Market-Driven (NSDM) Global Environmental Governance. In *Governance for the Environment: New Perspectives*, 183–218.

[55] Braithwaite, J. (2005). *Markets in Vice, Markets in Virtue*. Oxford University Press.

[56] Braithwaite, J. (2013). Flipping Markets to Virtue with Qui Tam and Restorative Justice. *Accounting, Organizations and Society*, 38(6–7), 458–468, 467.

exercising their considerable influence to improve corporate governance standards in companies, albeit with mixed results.[57] Entire industries dedicated to inspection and compliance have developed in which gatekeepers work with companies to detect, prevent, or deter wrongdoing.[58] Omarova has argued that forms of embedded self-regulation are valuable ways to manage systemic risk in the financial system, and preferable to government regulation which precipitates regulatory arbitrage in the forms of cycles of rule-making and evasion.[59] Others are sceptical that the sector can police itself effectively. They note that this requires collective action from a sector that is competitive and where gains can be made at the expense of other market participants.[60] Black suggests, however, that meta-regulation is not merely useful or valuable; it is a practical necessity. Nevertheless, whilst regulators often rely on firms to some extent to promote compliance internally, she cautions that firms will more than likely be directed to secure their own objectives rather than those of the regulator. She determines that four elements are needed for meta-regulation to succeed: the right corporate culture to promote compliance; incentivisation of public objectives (not merely profit maximisation norms); regulators with specialist skills to monitor firms; and regulators having both the inclination and political cover to confront firms when needed.[61]

Meta-regulation is related to principles-based regulation. Principles are drafted broadly, apply widely, and are considered more flexible because they can cover issues and situations not thought of by regulators in a fast-moving environment. Principles:

> can empower those they regulate, particularly senior managers, to be proactive in addressing compliance issues because they must think about how best to give effect to a broad-based principle. This may also require engagement with

[57] Gordon, J. N. (2006). The Rise of Independent Directors in the United States, 1950–2005: Of Shareholder Value and Stock Market Prices. *Stanford Law Review*, 59, 1465–1568; Gilson, R. J., & Kraakman, R. (1991). Reinventing the Outside Director: An Agenda for Institutional Investors. *Stanford Law Review*, 863–906. See also: Roose, K. (2011). Nuns Who Won't Stop Nudging. *New York Times*, available at: https://www.nytimes.com/2011/11/13/business/sisters-of-st-francis-the-quiet-shareholder-activists.html.

[58] Kraakman, R. H. (1986). Gatekeepers: The Anatomy of a Third-Party Enforcement Strategy. *Journal of Law, Economics, & Organization*, 2(1), 53–104.

[59] Omarova, S. T. (2011). Wall Street as Community of Fate: Toward Financial Industry Self-Regulation. *University of Pennsylvania Law Review*, 159(2), 411–492.

[60] Zaring, D. (2010). Fateful Bankers. *University of Pennsylvania Law Review*. PENNumbra, 159, 303–310.

[61] Black, J. (2012). Paradoxes and Failures: "New Governance" Techniques and the Financial Crisis. *The Modern Law Review*, 75(6), 1037–1063.

regulators to generate shared understandings of compliance, moving corporate strategy away from the box-ticking nature of compliance with rules.[62]

A regulatory model which emphasises principles-based regulation means that the relationship between regulator and regulated is less directive and based more on trust.[63] The principles-based approach to regulation, thus understood, resonates to varying degrees with "decentred regulation",[64] which emphasises the interactive nature of regulation between state and non-state actors; "new governance",[65] in which securing compliance is deliberative, participatory, and dynamic, where parties are empowered to experiment with how best to achieve compliance; and with "meta-regulation" in which the state requires and oversees that the regulated have internal checks and systems to ensure regulatory goals and objectives are met.[66]

The devolution of power to organisations is not, however, without difficulties, especially where those organisations seek to frustrate rather than facilitate the achievement of public policy goals. Large, complex, and powerful organisations may choose to marginalise certain objectives to keep them off internal agendas, and insufficiently resource some strategies and withdraw support for others. In general terms, they may create a negative climate in which objectives are difficult to secure. Success also depends on how regulators engage with private actors to deliver on and secure the goals of regulatory policies; regulatory agencies need to prioritise the right objectives, measure the right outputs, and intervene in the right circumstances.[67]

---

[62] McGrath, J. (2020). "Walk Softly and Carry No Stick": Culture, Opportunity, and Irresponsible Risk-Taking in the Irish Banking Sector. *European Journal of Criminology*, 17(1), 86–105, 95.

[63] Black, J. (2008). Constructing and Contesting Legitimacy and Accountability in Polycentric Regulatory Regimes. *Regulation & Governance*, 2(2), 137–164.

[64] Black, J. (2001). Decentring Regulation: Understanding the Role of Regulation and Self-Regulation in a "Post-regulatory" World. *Current Legal Problems*, 54(1), 103–146; Black, J. (2002). Regulatory Conversations. *Journal of Law and Society*, 29(1), 163–196; Scott, C. (2002). Private Regulation of the Public Sector: A Neglected Facet of Contemporary Governance. *Journal of Law and Society*, 29(1), 56–76, Scott, C. (2017). The Regulatory State and Beyond. In Drahos, P. ed., *Regulatory Theory: Foundations and Applications*. ANU Press, 265–287.

[65] Ford, C. L. (2008). New Governance, Compliance, and Principles-Based Securities Regulation. *American Business Law Journal*, 45, 1–60.

[66] Grabosky, P. (2013). Beyond Responsive Regulation: The Expanding Role of Non-state Actors in the Regulatory Process. *Regulation & Governance*, 7(1), 114–123.

[67] Russell, G., & Hodges, C. (2019). *Regulatory Delivery*. Bloomsbury Publishing.

2.5   Governmentality

The relative intensity of regulation is, of course, a political issue but Ayres and Braithwaite's regulatory pyramid was seen to depoliticise a debate in which State intervention was pitted against market controls because they sought to harness both public and private spheres to improve corporate compliance with the law. This reflects a form of governmentality which advances instrumental and technical solutions to solve and depoliticise political problems.[68] When responsive regulation was iteratively developed into meta-regulation, its relationship with governmentality was further crystalised, as both theories illustrated how power can be diffuse and exercised by actors other than the State.[69] The precise nature of the relationship between both schools of thought is, however, somewhat contested. Some argue that meta-governance is a particular type of neoliberal governmentality whilst others see governmentality as a tool or strategy employed by meta-regulators to indirectly exercise power.[70]

In any case, governmentality combines systems of thought and activity into a logic of action in which public and private interests are harnessed and where the state and its institutions do not exclusively exercise power.[71] It is not that States and political processes are unimportant, Miller and Rose assure us, but that "multiple centres of power and calculation" exist such that "'non-state' modes of exercise of power are one of the defining features of our present".[72] The foundational principles underpinning governmentality were developed by Foucault in the late 1970s. At this time, the French economy was performing poorly and economic liberalism was increasingly

---

[68] Lemke, T. (2001). "The Birth of Bio-Politics": Michel Foucault's Lecture at the Collège de France on Neo-Liberal Governmentality. *Economy and Society*, 30, 190–207; Lemke, T. (2002). Foucault, Governmentality, and Critique. *Rethinking Marxism*, 14, 49–64; Harcourt, B. E. (2011). *The Illusion of Free Markets: Punishment and the Myth of Natural Order*. Harvard University Press.

[69] Bevir, M. (2011). Governance and Governmentality After Neoliberalism. *Policy & Politics*, 39(4), 457–471.

[70] Larsson, O. (2015). The Governmentality of Meta-Governance: Identifying Theoretical and Empirical Challenges of Network Governance in the Political Field of Security and Beyond (Doctoral dissertation, Acta Universitatis Upsaliensis).

[71] Lemke, T. (2012). *Foucault, Governmentality, and Critique, Cultural Politics & the Promise of Democracy*. Paradigm; McGrath, J. (2019). Regulating White-Collar Crime in Ireland: An Analysis Using the Lens of Governmentality. *Crime, Law and Social Change*, 72(4), 445–465. Clifford Shearing et al. have characterised a governance in which power is highly distributed as "nodal", where neither government nor any other node assume priority. See: Shearing, C., & Wood, J. (2003). Nodal Governance, Democracy, and the New "Denizens". *Journal of Law and Society*, 30(3), 400–419; Burris, S., Drahos, P., & Shearing, C. (2005). Nodal Governance. *Australian Journal of Legal Philosophy*, 30–58.

[72] Miller, P., & Rose, N. (2008). *Governing the Present: Administering Economic, Social and Personal Life*. Polity, 20.

favoured, paving the way for an increased focus on non-state-centred theories of power.[73] Foucault distinguished governmentality from the exercise of sovereign power or discipline. The former was associated with demonstrating authority, controlling territory, and the protection and survival of the sovereign. The latter, disciplinary power, was brought to bear on individuals, though prisons, schools, and other formal institutions to scrutinise, normalise, and regulate their bodies and souls, rendering them compliant and productive.

Governmentality, however, is exercised not merely to influence individual behaviour but to guide group conduct and secure objectives for the general population.[74] The methods and tools through which governmentality is exercised do not replace disciplinary power but elide and intersect with it. Dean observes that when the technologies of governmentality are brought to bear on misconduct, governmentality "is a form of regulation that is not one of sovereign power exercised through law, or of a disciplinary society with its norms, or even of the general normalisation of a biopolitics of the population"; it also encompasses the "internal subjugation of individuals".[75] O'Malley explains that governmentality "shifted away from a focus simply on command and obedience, toward regarding the central issue as the optimal harnessing of these self-governing capacities".[76] As such, there is a consensual aspect to this exercise of power.[77] As Rehmann observes, "The way in which people organise their lives and the techniques they apply to themselves, to their attitudes, their bodies, and their psyche became an important component of Foucault's late conception of power".[78]

So understood, governmentality is concerned with the "conduct of conducts".[79] It is a scale of influence, extending from regulating conduct to influencing self-regulation, ultimately resulting in the internalisation

[73] Behrent, M. C. (2016). Liberalism Without Humanism: Michel Foucault and the Free Market Creed (1976–1979). In Zamora, D., & Behrent, M. C., eds., *Foucault and Neoliberalism*. Polity, 24–62.

[74] Golder, B., & Fitzpatrick, P. (2009). *Foucault's Law*. Routledge.

[75] Dean, M. (2016). Foucault, Ewald, Neoliberalism and the Left. In Zamora, D., & Behrent, M., eds., *Foucault and Neoliberalism*. Polity, 85–113.

[76] O'Malley, P. (2008). Governmentality and Risk. In Zinn, J. O., ed., *Social Theories of Risk and Uncertainty: An Introduction*. Blackwell, 52–75, 55.

[77] Dean, M. (2010). *Governmentality: Power and Rule in Modern Society*. Sage.

[78] Rehmann, J. (2016). The Unfulfilled Promises of the Late Foucault and Foucauldian Governmentality Studies. In Zamora, D., & Behrent, M. C., eds., *Foucault and Neoliberalism*. Polity, 134–158, 135.

[79] Dean, M. (2010). *Governmentality: Power and Rule in Modern Society*. Sage.

of governance norms.[80] As acknowledged by Simon, "[m]any non-State-institutions play a governance role … business has become a governmental power to a considerable extent".[81] Audits and self-certification regimes, for example, play important roles as governmental technologies in commercial and regulatory contexts, and further the goals of monitoring, checking and reporting, so that "The motif of 'control of control' is … useful in characterising a regulatory system with a greater accent on internal self-inspection".[82]

Gathering these threads together, there have been a variety of theoretical contributions that seek to guide interventions and enforcement activities to secure compliance. Though analysed under distinct headings, it is recognised that there is no single regulatory design that is the most effective and that these models are best understood as overlapping and interwoven, at least to some degree. In general, these theories have benefitted from or expanded upon responsive regulatory theory, which recognised the value of both compliance-oriented and deterrence-oriented strategies; the targeting of resources to control risk; the importance of harnessing third parties; and State oversight of self-regulation. Some strategies may be more appropriate in some contexts than others and each model exhibits strengths and weaknesses. Moreover, regulatory excellence, which boosts compliance and shores up the legitimacy of the regulator, cannot be achieved merely by choosing one model over another; success also depends on the skills, resources, and motivations of regulators and the cultural disposition of the sector that is the subject of this regulatory gaze.[83] Nevertheless, these theories are important because they articulate a framework for how regulatory intervention should work to achieve excellence. In the next section, the implementation of these regulatory models is examined.

---

[80] Rose, N. (1999). *Powers of Freedom: Reframing Political Thought*. Cambridge University Press.

[81] Simon, J. (2001). Sanctioning Government: Explaining America's Severity Revolution. *University of Miami Law Review*, 56, 217–253. 242.

[82] Power, M. (2000). The Audit Society—Second Thoughts. *International Journal of Auditing*, 4(1), 111–119, 118.

[83] Gunningham, N. (2016). Compliance, Enforcement, and Regulatory Excellence. In Coglianese, C. ed., *Achieving Regulatory Excellence*. Brookings Institution Press, 188–207.

3 Implementation in Practice: From "Light Touch" to Intrusive Regulation Generating Cultural Change

In this section, it is argued that regulators in the UK, Australia, and Ireland have adopted aspects of the aforementioned regulatory theories to varying degrees in practice. It shows that a form of responsive regulation, as amended and shaped by its various iterations, was adopted. In particular, it demonstrates that risk-based, principles-led, compliance-oriented models were initially adopted to regulate the financial services sectors. This approach was premised on trusting financial actors to comply with the law. A command and control model of regulatory governance, in which non-compliance results in sanctions, was traditionally disfavoured. Rules-based and deterrence-oriented approaches were considered bureaucratic, inflexible, and expensive. In the aftermath of the GFC, however, the compliance-based approach, in the absence of using sanctions in appropriate cases, was considered ineffective. Regulators were considered too deferential because they were generally unwilling to "pull the trigger" on the "big gun" when needed. This precipitated a transition to a much more assertive and intrusive regulatory approach and the more robust deployment of civil and criminal sanctions in practice. Regulators adopted a clear escalation policy, resulting in an upsurge in formal enforcement activity.

Regulators now evince more activity across the regulatory pyramid, including its upper levels. More recently, however, regulators have made significant efforts to improve ethical cultures in the financial services sector. As part of this, they have placed a greater emphasis on requiring financial services providers themselves to identify specific senior individuals who are responsible for particular business activities and to file these responsibility maps with the relevant financial regulator. This reflects an increased emphasis on self-regulation, subject to State oversight, in line with meta-governance theory. This is an important development, not merely because it will make it easier to sanction wrongdoing, thereby giving practical effect to the more intrusive regulatory approaches being advanced by regulators, but also because it reflects the developing regulatory impulse to generate positive cultural change within organisations. As discussed below, the goal is to "responsibilise" organisations so they ensure that their internal corporate governance structures are improved and so that bankers and other financial services providers will treat their customers better.[84]

3.1   The Historical Trajectory: Light-Touch, Principles-Based Regulation

As the UK shifted from a "clubbish" financial services sector to a more open competitive marketplace in the 1980s,[85] legislation was enacted to give regulatory powers to a private company, limited by guarantee and funded by the financial services sector, the Securities and Investments Board (SIB).[86] The SIB sat at "the apex of new regulatory structure", in which it recognised self-regulatory organisations (SROs) operating below it to "draw up rule-books governing the conduct of their members' business".[87] This structure was considered a form of "self-regulation with a statutory mandate".[88]

After Barings Bank failed in 1996, the responsibility for prudential regulation was transferred from the Bank of England to the Financial Services Authority (FSA), which replaced the SIB in 1998.[89] The FSA became a single regulator for banks and other financial services providers. In 2000, the FSA announced "a bold new approach", implementing a form of risk-based regulation that was "flexible and proactive", targeting firms for supervision that posed the largest risks to the financial system.[90] This risk-based approach was in keeping with the Hampton Review, which recommended that risk-based regulation be adopted across multiple areas of business regulation, including financial regulation.[91] The FSA also revised the pre-existing SIB Principles, which were supplemented by some specific rules, to reflect its increased responsibilities and ambit. In its "Better Regulation Action Plan", it emphasised that it was committed to principles-based regulation

---

[84] Garland, D. (1997). Governmentality and the Problem of Crime: Foucault, Criminology, Sociology. *Theoretical Criminology*, 1(2), 173–214; Garland, D. (2001). *The Culture of Control*. Oxford University Press.

[85] Moran, M. (1986). Theories of Regulation and Changes in Regulation: The Case of Financial Markets. *Political Studies*, 34(2), 185–201.

[86] The Financial Services Act 1986.

[87] Veljanovski, C., & Gray, J. (1988). Deregulating the Securities and Investments Board. *Economic Affairs*, 8(5), 31–33, 31.

[88] Black, J. (2015). Regulatory Styles and Supervisory Strategies. In Moloney, N., Ferran, E., & Payne, J. eds., *The Oxford Handbook of Financial Regulation*. Oxford University Press, 217–253, 219.

[89] Banking Act 1997.

[90] FSA, A New regulator for a New Millennium (2000). See further Black, J. (2015). Regulatory Styles and Supervisory Strategies. In Moloney, N., Ferran, E., & Payne, J. eds., *The Oxford Handbook of Financial Regulation*. Oxford University Press, 217–253.

[91] Hampton, P. (2005). *Reducing Administrative Burdens*. HM Treasury.

and was committed to "change the balance significantly towards a more principles-based approach".[92] It emphasised that principles-based regulation was "focusing on the outcomes that matter" and that "detailed rules have become an increasing burden on our own and the industry's resources".[93] Black observes that meta-regulation is "critically linked" to principles-based regulation and that meta-regulation was "adopted as a broader regulatory philosophy" in the UK as part of the principles-based regulatory approach by the FSA.[94] Black points out that principles-based regulation does not necessarily equate to light-touch regulation,[95] but effectively amounted to this in the case of the FSA's prudential regulation of banks.[96]

Prior to the GFC, financial regulation in the UK was characterised by relatively low levels of formal enforcement.[97] The FSA was avowedly "not an enforcement-led regulator" before the GFC; it rarely sanctioned banks formally via regulatory actions, fines or by seeking convictions.[98] Sanctions were merely one part of its broader toolkit and informal enforcement actions were preferred, taking place in the absence of court proceedings.[99] Black has noted that this approach was "in line with the 'tit for tat' strategy advocated in the 'responsive regulation' literature".[100] When reviewing the causes of the GFC, however, Lord Turner, the Chairman of the FSA, argued for a major shift in the FSA's supervisory approach to a more intrusive and less deferential approach to regulation, which carefully considered systemic risks to the financial system.[101] He noted that the FSA "was not with hindsight aggressive enough in demanding adjustments to business models which even at the

---

[92] FSA. (2005). Better Regulation Action Plan (Financial Services Authority).

[93] FSA. (2007). Principles Based Regulation—Focusing on the Outcomes that Matter (Financial Services Authority).

[94] Black, J. (2012). Paradoxes and Failures: 'New Governance' Techniques and the Financial Crisis. *The Modern Law Review*, 75(6), 1037–1063, 1046.

[95] Black, J. (2008). Forms and Paradoxes of Principles Based Regulation. *Capital Markets Law Journal*, 3(4), 425–457.

[96] Black, J. (2012). Paradoxes and Failures: 'New Governance' Techniques and the Financial Crisis. *The Modern Law Review*, 75(6), 1037–1063.

[97] MacNeil, I. (2007). The Evolution of Regulatory Enforcement Action in the UK Capital Markets: A Case of "Less Is More"? *Capital Markets Law Journal*, 2(4), 345–369.

[98] Cearns, K., & Ferran, E. (2008). Non-Enforcement-Led Public Oversight of Financial and Corporate Governance Disclosures and of Auditors. *Journal of Corporate Law Studies*, 8(2), 191–224, 195.

[99] Armour, J. (2008). Enforcement Strategies in UK Corporate Governance: A Roadmap and Empirical Assessment. In Pacces, A.M. eds. *The Law and Economics of Corporate Governance: Changing Perspectives*. Edward Elgar Publishing, 213–258.

[100] Black, J. (2015). Regulatory Styles and Supervisory Strategies. In Moloney, N., Ferran, E., & Payne, J. eds., *The Oxford Handbook of Financial Regulation*. Oxford University Press, 233.

[101] Turner, A, (2009). *The Turner Review—A regulatory Response to the Global Banking Crisis*. Financial Services Authority, 86.

level of the individual institution were excessively risky and which pursued simultaneously by several banks, contributed to the build-up of system-wide risks".[102]

The Walker Review of corporate governance of the UK banking industry emphasised the need to improve corporate governance standards, and make changes to the role, composition, and operation of the board, the role of institutional investors, risk management, and remuneration practices, but recommended that these changes could be achieved through amendments to the Combined Code, which is enforced on a comply or explain basis.[103] Appearing to emphasise the maintenance of a light-touch, principles-based approach, it received a cold reception in the British media which considered it a "crashing disappointment".[104] The subsequent UK Parliamentary Commission on Banking Standards Report (PCBS Report) was stinging in its criticism, determining that regulators "neglected prudential regulation", "left the UK poorly protected from systemic risk" and that "the scale and breadth of regulatory failure was … shocking".[105] The FSA was re-constituted as the Financial Conduct Authority (FCA), which addresses misconduct to maintain the integrity of the financial services market, and the Prudential Regulation Authority (PRA), a subsidiary of the Bank of England, concerned with the safety and soundness of the system under a Twin Peaks regulatory model,[106] in accordance with the Financial Services Act 2012.[107]

In Ireland, the Central Bank of Ireland (CBI) operated in a very limited regulatory capacity when it was first established in accordance with the Central Bank Act 1942 and did not acquire significant statutory powers to

---

[102] Ibid., p. 88.

[103] Walker, D. (2009). A Review of Corporate Governance in UK Banks and other Financial Industry Entities, 16 July 2009, London, HM Treasury. This report is available at: http://www.hm-treasury.gov.uk/walker_review_information.htm https://www.theqca.com/article_assets/articledir_38/19306/QCAResponse_WalkerReview_Oct09.pdf.

[104] Finch, J. (2009). Walker Report a 'Crashing Disappointment'. *The Guardian* (26 November), available at: https://www.theguardian.com/business/2009/nov/26/walker-report-banking-comment.

[105] UK Parliamentary Commission on Banking Standards. (2013). *Changing Banking for Good* (Vol. I), para. 181. The Stationery Office Limited, available at: https://publications.parliament.uk/pa/jt201314/jtselect/jtpcbs/27/27.pdf.

[106] Godwin, A., & Schmulow, A. (2021). *The Cambridge Handbook of Twin Peaks Financial Regulation.* Cambridge University Press.

[107] The Bank of England and the FSA, The Prudential Regulation Authority (2012); FSA. (2012) Journey to the FCA (Financial Services Authority).

licence and supervise banks until 1971.[108] It continued to maintain a non-interventionist approach to regulating the financial sector long after that.[109] The Central Bank and Financial Services Authority of Ireland Act of 2003 created the Irish Financial Services Regulatory Authority (the Financial Regulator) to focus on micro prudential and conduct issues, as a distinct entity within the Central Bank of Ireland, which would focus on macro-prudential issues (though it also shared this competence with the financial regulator, thereby potentially creating some ambiguity on the extent of their overlapping functions).[110] Much like the UK, Ireland regulated the financial services sector via a compliance-oriented, principles-based approach, underpinned by some specific technical rules. This approach "encourage[d] adherence to the spirit of sound regulatory standards, without being overly bureaucratic".[111] The principles required financial service providers to act in a transparent and accountable manner with prudence and integrity in the best interests of consumers, to have sufficient financial resources, sound corporate governance structures, risk management policies and oversight systems and internal controls. Additionally, they were required to obey the rules set down by the financial regulator and provide accurate information to him when requested to do so. In essence, financial service providers were allowed to make their own decisions on how to manage risk, provided they had effective systems and models for monitoring that risk. The "preferred approach to enforcement was to seek voluntary compliance with legislation, codes, and rules. ... To this extent, the underlying philosophy was oriented towards trusting a properly governed firm".[112] The rules-based approach, by contrast, was criticised by the CEO of the Financial Regulator as being "a very legalistic approach" which was costly, inflexible, and slow to react to changed circumstances.[113]

The preference for a compliance-orientated approach meant that the relationship between the Financial Regulator and credit institutions was largely

---

[108] Honohan, P. (1994). Currency Board or Central Bank? Lessons from the Irish Pound's Link with Sterling, 1928–79, 4–10, available at: https://www.researchgate.net/publication/4836435_Currency_B oard_or_Central_Bank_Lessons_from_the_Irish_Pound's_Link_with_Sterling_1928-79; Honohan, P. (2018). Three Quarter-Centuries of Central Banking in Ireland (No. 3/EL/18). Central Bank of Ireland. It existed previously as a Currency commission.

[109] Honohan, P. Three Quarter-Centuries of Central Banking in Ireland, available at: https://www.centralbank.ie/docs/default-source/publications/economic-letters/vol-2018-no.-3-three-quarter-centur ies-of-central-banking-in-ireland-(honohan).pdf?sfvrsn=4.

[110] Honohan P., Donovan, D., Gorecki, P., & Mottiar, R. (2010). *The Irish Banking Crisis: Regulatory and Financial Stability Policy*. Central Bank, 99.

[111] IFSRA. (2006). *Strategic Plan 2006*. Irish Financial Services Regulatory Authority, 12.

[112] Honohan, P. (2010). *The Irish Banking Crisis: Regulatory and Financial Stability Policy*. Central Bank, 43–44.

[113] O'Reilly, L. (2005). The Future of Financial Regulation: Principles or Rules Issues for the Irish Financial Services Sector. Finance Dublin Conference, Dublin Castle, 4–5.

collaborative. The Financial Regulator identified problems and concerns in credit institutions through audits, inspection reports or external reviews. The regulator and the regulated institution exchanged letters, arranged meetings, and discussed the problems with a view to resolving them. A solution would be negotiated and drawn up into an "action plan". The regulated institution would later assure the regulator that the plan had been implemented and these assurances would be accepted because the regulator trusted that "those running the banks and building societies were honourable persons striving to do their best to comply with the principles … [and] it was assumed that those in charge of institutions would, after careful consideration, do their best to comply".[114] In general, "threats of action by the [Financial Regulator] in the absence of compliance were not typically part of the process. … It was considered much better to resolve regulatory issues through voluntary compliance and discussion".[115]

Australia followed a regulatory trajectory that differed slightly from Ireland or the UK. Australia's light-touch regulatory approach emerged earlier, and was ameliorated in advance of the GFC, ensuring that Australia did not bail out any banks and escaped the worst of a recession, though some companies did fail.[116] Australia took steps towards deregulating the financial services industry in the late 1970s, but it wasn't until the 1980s that Australia embraced a system of light-touch regulation with the publication of the Campbell Report,[117] which welcomed globalisation and the transitioning of the economy away from manufacturing to a greater emphasis on financial services. Davis suggests that too much faith was placed in the markets' ability to govern themselves, resulting in a financial crisis in the late 1980s. He states that "[o]fficial regulation was not replaced by adequate market monitoring and capital market discipline, and management systems and governance practices within financial institutions were not adequate for the new competitive environment".[118] The 1990s, Davis notes, encompasses three periods of financial reform. Firstly, the excesses of deregulation were "mopped up" via the creation of new supervision powers and new regulatory agencies and oversight bodies, like the Australian Securities Commission

[114] Honohan, P. (2010). *The Irish Banking Crisis: Regulatory and Financial Stability Policy*. Central Bank, 55–56.

[115] Ibid., p. 55.

[116] Parliamentary Joint Committee on Corporations and Financial Services. (2009). Inquiry into Financial Products and Services in Australia. Senate Printing Unit, Parliament House.

[117] Campbell, K. (1980). *Australian Financial System—Interim Report*. Committee of Inquiry into the Australian Financial System.

[118] Davis, K. (2003). Financial Reform in Australia. In Hall, M. J. B. ed. *The International Handbook on Financial Reform*. Edward Elgar Publishing, 1–30.

(ASC) in 1991 (which would later become the Australian Securities & Investments Commission, ASIC in 1998) and the Council of Financial Supervisors in 1992. The second phase was designed to facilitate competition and protect consumers, as evidenced by the creation of the Australian Competition and Consumer Commission (ACCC), which was established in 1995. Thirdly, there was an emphasis on reforming company law and improving corporate governance standards. The 1997 Wallis Report warned that effective financial regulation required significant government oversight, providing an important point of reflection and caution that financial markets were changing and swept up in the tide of neoliberalism.[119]

Australia embraced a Twin Peaks model of financial regulation in 1998, replacing an architecture that was "complex, segmented and institutionally based" in which regulators had "overlapping functions, and ... increasingly blurred boundaries".[120] The Australian Prudential Regulation Authority (APRA) is responsible for prudential regulation whilst responsibility for conduct regulation and consumer protection is vested in ASIC. The Reserve Bank of Australia is the "third peak" with responsibility for monetary policy and economic prosperity. The Council of Financial Regulators coordinates these three bodies.[121] Curiously, the failure of HIH insurance in 2001, early in the tenure of the APRA, and the resulting Royal Commission Report,[122] is thought to have had a "profound and enduring effect on APRA's regulatory culture and style" prompting "a new regulatory framework, which was focused on close supervision, effective risk management, governance, and strong, well-enforced, capital adequacy rules".[123] In addition to evincing a more risk-based approach to supervision,[124] it created a cautious, conservative, and intense regulatory supervision approach which, it has been argued,

---

[119] Commonwealth of Australia. (1997). *Financial System Inquiry: Final Report* (Wallis Report).

[120] Hill, J. G. (2012). Why Did Australia Fare So Well in the Global Financial Crisis. In Ferran, E., Moloney, N., Hill, J. G., & Coffee Jr, J. C. eds., *The Regulatory Aftermath of the Global Financial Crisis*. Cambridge University Press, 203–300, 218.

[121] In 2021, the Australian parliament passes legislation to establish a new body, the Financial Regulator Assessment Authority (FRAA), to "to regularly review and report on the effectiveness and capability of the Australian Securities and Investments Commission (ASIC) and the Australian Prudential Regulation Authority (APRA)". See: The Hon Josh Frydenberg MP. (2021). Parliament Passes Legislation to Establish Financial Regulator Assessment Authority, available at: https://ministers.treasury. gov.au/ministers/josh-frydenberg-2018/media-releases/parliament-passes-legislation-establish-financial.

[122] Owen, N. J. (2003). *The Failure of HIH Insurance: Volume 1: A Corporate Collapse and Its Lessons.* HIH Royal Commission.

[123] Hill, J. G. (2012). Why Did Australia Fare So Well in the Global Financial Crisis. In Ferran, E., Moloney, N., Hill, J. G., & Coffee Jr, J. C. eds., *The Regulatory Aftermath of the Global Financial Crisis*. Cambridge University Press, 203–300, 287.

[124] Black, J. (2004). The Development of Risk-Based Regulation in Financial Services: Canada, the UK, and Australia. *ESRC Centre for the Analysis of Risk and Regulation Research Report*.

ultimately helped Australia fare the global crisis reasonably well.[125] As noted by an Australian Parliamentary Committee in 2009:

> The Australian Stock Exchange (ASX) fell and businesses exposed to the global economy or reliant on credit began to suffer. Job losses followed and consumer confidence began to wane, further impacting businesses and jobs. Australia, however, fared better than many—and continues to do so.[126]

Whilst Australian regulators were not severely criticised for administering a light-touch regulatory regime at the time of the GFC, critics have claimed that ASIC has been too deferential in its regulatory responses to the subsequent crises which unfolded. In accordance with the Australian Securities and Investments Commission Act 2001, which sets out ASIC's roles and responsibilities, it administers and enforces a variety of legislative frameworks, including those related to company law, financial services law, and consumer credit law.[127] It possesses a range of regulatory enforcement options when faced with non-compliance. In line with responsive regulation, which emphasises a progressive approach to enforcement using "little sticks" and "big sticks", it may negotiate an enforceable undertaking, take administrative action by imposing licensing conditions and seeking banning/disqualification orders, take civil proceedings, or pursue enforcement though the criminal courts.[128] The February 2019 Australian Royal Commission Final Report into misconduct in the banking, superannuation, and financial services industry (Hayne Report), however, emphasised that it was too ready to resolve wrongdoing with its softer powers, noting, in its interim report, "when deciding what to do in response to misconduct, ASIC's starting point appears to have been: How can this be resolved by agreement?"[129] In particular, ASIC was reluctant to escalate regulatory responses to financial wrongdoing in appropriate cases.

---

[125] Hill, J. G. (2012). Why Did Australia Fare So Well in the Global Financial Crisis. In Ferran, E., Moloney, N., Hill, J. G., & Coffee Jr, J. C. eds., *The Regulatory Aftermath of the Global Financial Crisis*. Cambridge University Press, 203–300.

[126] The Parliament of the Commonwealth of Australia. (2009). The Global Financial Crisis and regional Australia, para. 1.8, available at: https://www.aph.gov.au/binaries/house/committee/itrdlg/financialcrisis/report/gfc%20final%20report.pdf.

[127] Australian Securities Investment Commission (ASIC), Laws We Administer, available at: http://download.asic.gov.au/media/4058626/asic-annual-report-2015-2016-complete.pdf/.

[128] Nehme, D., Anderson, J., Dixon, O., & Kingsford-Smith, D. (2018). The General Deterrence Effects of Enforceable Undertakings on Financial Services and Credit Providers. ASIC, p. 6.

[129] Hayne, K. M. (2018). Interim Report of the Royal Commission into Misconduct in the Banking, Superannuation and Financial Services Industry, p. 277, available at: https://financialservices.royalcommission.gov.au/Documents/interim-report/interim-report-volume-1.pdf.

3.2   A More Stringent and Intrusive Approach Emerges

In the UK, the FSA adopted a more stringent and intrusive regulatory approach after the GFC. The FSA Chief Executive, Hector Sants, warned that "a principles-based approach does not work with individuals who have no principles".[130] In a move seen as a shift away from light-touch regulatory policies, he promised that people "should be very frightened of the FSA".[131] In particular, formal enforcement strategies would increasingly play a more important role in regulating the financial services sector as it more actively pursued a policy of "credible deterrence".[132] Credible deterrence is not specifically defined in FSA policy documents, but Margaret Cole, the Head of the Enforcement Division, explained that it makes "people realise that they can suffer meaningful consequences if they break the law and if they don't improve their standards of behaviour".[133] The FSA's business plan did elaborate, however, that it involved "robustly deploying our civil and criminal prosecution powers" to achieve its objectives,[134] though it did "little to illuminate how this philosophy actually works to achieve its objectives".[135] Nevertheless, whilst the FSA may have been reluctant to specifically define "credible deterrence", it was comfortable noting that it "was here to stay".[136]

The Central Bank of Ireland (CBI) has, since 2010, also evinced a more assertive attitude than that demonstrated prior to the GFC. Some have suggested the previous light-touch approach was partly cultural and stemmed from a close relationship between the regulator and the regulated in which they dined and played golf together.[137] On stepping down from his role in 2013, Matthew Elderfield, who was appointed Financial Regulator in 2010, remarked that he was able to enforce financial regulation, free of inhibiting cultural constraints not to enforce them, because he did not play golf with

---

[130] Sants, H. (2009) Delivering Intensive Supervision and Credible Deterrence, Speech on 12 March 2009 at Reuters Newsmakers Event.

[131] Ibid.

[132] Ibid.

[133] Cole, M. (2009). Delivering Credible Deterrence. FSA Annual Financial Crime Conference Speech (Vol. 27), available at: https://webarchive.nationalarchives.gov.uk/ukgwa/20130403125740/, http://www.fsa.gov.uk/library/communication/speeches/2009/0427_mc.shtml.

[134] FSA, 2012–2013, p. 8, available at: https://memofin-media.s3.eu-west-3.amazonaws.com/Books/0001/01/d0020c9ad9f7e95dedb3052c46ed0c37d002709d.pdf.

[135] Wilson, G., & Wilson, S. (2014). The FSA, "Credible Deterrence", and Criminal Enforcement-a "Haphazard Pursuit"? *Journal of Financial Crime*, 21(1), 4–28, 10.

[136] McDermott, T. (2012). Credible Deterrence: Here to Stay. FSA's Enforcement Conference Speech, 2 July, available at: https://webarchive.nationalarchives.gov.uk/ukgwa/20130201182559/, http://www.fsa.gov.uk/library/communication/speeches/2012/0702-tm.shtml.

[137] Ross, S. (2009). *The Bankers: How the Banks Brought Ireland to Its Knees*. Penguin.

bankers.[138] His comment emphasised a relational distance between enforcers and the regulated that supported and promoted enforcement, a hypothesis advanced much earlier in the literature by Black.[139] This hypothesis has found broad support from scholars who have tested it in the context of business regulation.[140] Scott explains that where

> parties have similar educational and professional backgrounds, perhaps high frequency of contact and shared sense of purpose then enforcement is likely to be less stringent than where that 'relational distance' is greater. In other words, membership of communities may sometimes trump hierarchy.[141]

The contemporary operational approach to regulation in Ireland is significantly different to the light-touch approach, premised on discussion and the absence of escalating enforcement up the pyramid, which had once been in vogue. In 2010, the CBI established its stand-alone Enforcement Directorate, separated from supervision functions, which was composed of multi-disciplinary teams. The CBI stated it was adopting a "new approach" to banking supervision which would adopt a "challenging, and where necessary, intrusive stance".[142] The CBI's Enforcement Strategy 2011–2012 also specified "a more vigorous application of Enforcement effort backed by sufficient resources to represent a credible threat of action".[143] Though the Directorate expressed a preference for administrative sanctions to discipline financial wrongdoing, stating that wrongdoing will only be channelled through the criminal courts in "exceptional circumstances", it stated that it was "currently scrutinising this policy to ensure that criminal prosecutions are pursued in all appropriate cases taking into account the seriousness, intent, and wilfulness of the contravention involved".[144] Previously, the Financial Regulator had stated that "In light of the limited penalties available pursuant to summary

---

[138] Smyth, J. (2013). Ireland's Financial Regulator Steps Down. *Financial Times*, available at: https://www.ft.com/content/d5218c0e-a116-11e2-bae1-00144feabdc0.

[139] Grabowsky, P., & Braithwaite, J. (1986). *Of Manners Gentle: Enforcement Strategies of Australian Business Regulators*. Oxford University Press; Hood, C., James, O., Scott, C., Jones, G. W., & Travers, T. (1999). *Regulation Inside Government: Waste Watchers, Quality Police, and Sleaze-Busters*. Oxford University Press.

[140] Black, D. (1976). *The Behaviour of Law*. Academic Press.

[141] Scott, C. (2008). Regulating Everything. Inaugural Lecture of the Chair in EU Regulation and Governance, UCD, p. 10, available at: https://www.researchgate.net/publication/23547141_Regulating_Everything.

[142] Central Bank of Ireland. (2010). *Banking Supervision: Our New Approach*. Central Bank of Ireland, 2.

[143] Central Bank of Ireland. (2010). *Annual Performance Statement 2011–2012*. Central Bank of Ireland, 5.

[144] Central Bank of Ireland. (2010). *Enforcement Strategy 2011–2012*. Central Bank of Ireland, 20.

criminal prosecutions, as a matter of general policy…[o]nly in exceptional circumstances will the Financial Regulator pursue a prescribed contravention via the criminal courts".[145] Much like in the UK and Australia, the CBI also continued to emphasise that its approach to supervision is "risk-based". In 2011, it introduced the Probability Risk and Impact SysteM (PRISM). This is both a supervisory tool and software application entailing "a system which encourages supervisors to focus on the issues which really count and to resolve them swiftly and efficiently".[146]

Since the GFC, the CBI has demonstrated a greater willingness to exercise its soft powers, albeit more intrusively. It has issued warnings and outlined its expectations of financial services providers via so-called "Dear CEO" letters and continues to implement risk mitigation programmes which detail specific remediation measures that must be undertaken by specified dates.[147] Moreover, however, it has also indicated that it has a clear escalation policy, which "makes it evident to the firm that the continuation of even minor breaches will lead to fines or other administrative sanctions".[148] In 2011, the CBI announced it would review the fitness and probity of individuals at all state-supported banks, and wrote to all 55 executive and non-executive directors of Ireland's six "covered" banks (those whose debts were covered by the State guarantee) seeking information as to whether they would remain in place after the 1 January 2012, prompting 26 bankers to confirm they would resign before that date or at the next AGM of the bank.[149]

More generally, the CBI is increasingly flexing its fitness and probity powers to critically review applicants for senior positions, who require prior CBI approval. Speaking in June 2021, for example, Derville Rowland (CBI Director General, Financial Conduct) stated that in 2020 alone, "some 20

---

[145] IFSRA. (2005). Outline of Administrative Sanctions Procedure. Irish Financial Services Regulatory Authority, para. 2.2.5.

[146] Central Bank of Ireland. (2016). PRISM Explained—How the Central Bank of Ireland Is Implementing Risk-Based Regulation, 2, available at: https://www.centralbank.ie/docs/default-source/regulation/how-we-regulate/supervision/prism/gns-4-1-2-2-5-prism-explained-feb-2016.pdf?sfvrsn=4.

[147] See: Central Bank of Ireland. Explainer—How Does the Central Bank Supervise Financial Services Providers?, available at: https://www.centralbank.ie/consumer-hub/explainers/how-does-the-central-bank-supervise-financial-services-providers; Central Bank of Ireland. (2020). Dear CEO—Letter to Schedule 2 firms on low level of compliance with Anti-Money Laundering and Counter Financing of Terrorism Obligations, available at: https://www.centralbank.ie/news/article/press-release-central-bank-publishes-dear-ceo-letter-to-schedule-2-firms-on-anti-money-laundering-and-counter-financing-of-terrorism-obligations-16-december-2020.

[148] Central Bank of Ireland. (2009). Annual Report. Central Bank of Ireland, p. 27, available at: https://www.centralbank.ie/docs/default-source/publications/corporate-reports/annual-reports/2009-cbfsai-annual-report.pdf?sfvrsn=10.

[149] Central Bank of Ireland. (2011). Annual Report. Central Bank of Ireland, p. 55, available at: https://www.centralbank.ie/docs/default-source/publications/corporate-reports/annual-reports/2011-central-bank-annual-report.pdf?sfvrsn=12.

applications were withdrawn by firms following referral to a specialist fitness and probity team based in our Enforcement Division".[150] In addition, the CBI has regularly employed its administrative sanctions procedure since the financial crash. By June 2021, the CBI had imposed 17 disqualifications and total fines of over €166m under its administrative sanctions procedure settlement process.[151] Also, the CBI has taken a number of cases through an inquiry process where a settlement has not been reached. In stark contrast to its earlier reputation for avoiding litigation and an unwillingness to test its powers, the CBI stated, "there is a very real and significant public interest in it defending the use of its statutory powers, which provide for an effective and credible enforcement regime. The Bank will continue to vigorously defend such cases when and if they arise".[152]

In Australia, ASIC has also emphasised that it will pursue an enforcement strategy not dissimilar to the credible deterrence approach adopted in Ireland and the UK, though some have criticised ASIC's continued "apparent reluctance to take on complex cases and investigate and take enforcement action against big businesses".[153] When critiquing ASIC's apparently deferential approach, suggesting that it was too quick to rely on its softer powers, the Interim Report of the Royal Commission into Misconduct in the Banking, Superannuation and Financial Services Industry (Interim Hayne Report) suggested that ASIC needs to ask if it was in the public interest to try to punish breaches of law, noting "Laws are to be obeyed. Penalties are prescribed for failure to obey the law because society expects and requires obedience to the law".[154] In its report to the Royal Commission, ASIC acknowledged that "for larger financial institutions it should deploy enforcement tools towards the apex of the enforcement pyramid more frequently" and that it must demonstrate "a clear willingness to employ severe sanctions

[150] Central Bank of Ireland. (2021). The Importance of Fitness, Probity, and Ensuring Responsibility, Director General Financial Conduct, Derville Rowland, available at: https://www.centralbank.ie/news/article/speech-importance-of-fitness-probity-and-ensuring-responsibility-derville-rowland-10-june-2021.

[151] Central Bank of Ireland. (2021). Public Statement Relating to Enforcement Action Against Gary McCollum, available at: http://www.centralbank.ie/docs/default-source/news-and-media/legal-notices/settlement-agreements/public-statement-relating-to-enforcement-action-against-gary-mccollum.pdf?sfvrsn=4.

[152] Central Bank of Ireland. (2015). Annual Report. Central Bank of Ireland, p. 34, available at: https://www.centralbank.ie/docs/default-source/publications/corporate-reports/annual-reports/2015-central-bank-annual-report.pdf?sfvrsn=16.

[153] Schmulow, A., Fairweather, K., & Tarrant, J. (2019). Restoring Confidence in Consumer Financial Protection Regulation in Australia: A Sisyphean Task? *Federal Law Review*, 47(1), 91–120, 97.

[154] Hayne, K. M. (2018). Royal Commission into Misconduct in the Banking, Superannuation and Financial Services Industry, Interim report, volume 1, 28 September, 277, available at: https://www.royalcommission.gov.au/banking/interim-report.

to punish those who commit serious or repeated violations".[155] In his final report, Hayne suggested that the breach of financial services laws should not be treated as less serious than breaches of other laws, and reiterated that the starting point for consideration is that the law must be obeyed and enforced.[156]

In 2018, ASIC announced its new enforcement approach: "why not litigate". As part of this approach, ASIC asks if enforcement is in the public interest, with ASIC Commissioner, Sean Hughes, suggesting that "the task we face is, I believe, akin to a prosecutorial office".[157] As part of this process, ASIC will consider whether civil or criminal enforcement is appropriate, and whether individuals or entities or both should be targeted. In line with the recommendations in the Hayne Report, it also established the Office of Enforcement to separate enforcement personnel from non-enforcement personnel. ASIC recognised that

> the deterrence value of our enforcement is also a function of how active we are seen to be across the regulatory pyramid. We continue to see an important role for all the regulatory tools, and often, using them in combination.[158]

The Australian government recently passed the Financial Regulator Assessment Authority Act 2021 to establish a new body, the Financial Regulator Assessment Authority (FRAA), to provide oversight of both ASIC and APRA.[159] This statutory intervention gives effect to the recommendations of the Hayne Report. In light of the Covid 19 pandemic, however, where there is now a greater emphasis on pro-business strategies to favour economic recovery, ASIC already appears to be favouring a less punitive and more cooperative approach to regulation. It advocates using a variety of less

---

[155] Hayne, K. M. (2018). Royal Commission into Misconduct in the Banking, Superannuation and Financial Services Industry, Submissions of the Australian Securities and Investments Commission Response to the Interim Report, para. 25, available at: https://financialservices.royalcommission.gov.au/Submissions/Documents/interim-report-submissions/POL.9100.0001.1060.pdf.

[156] Financial Services Royal Commission. (2019). *Final Report of the Royal Commission into Misconduct in the Banking, Superannuation and Financial Services Industry.* Financial Services Royal Commission, pp. 433–436.

[157] ASIC's approach to enforcement after the Royal Commission. A speech by ASIC Commissioner Sean Hughes at "Banking in the Spotlight": the 36th Annual Conference of the Banking and Financial Services Law Association, Gold Coast, Queensland, 30 August 2019, available at: https://asic.gov.au/about-asic/news-centre/speeches/asic-s-approach-to-enforcement-after-the-royal-commission/#_ftn4.

[158] Ibid.

[159] Financial Regulator Assessment Authority Bill 2021, available at: https://www.aph.gov.au/Parliamentary_Business/Bills_Legislation/Bills_Search_Results/Result?bId=r6701.

stringent regulatory tools in appropriate circumstances, but still reserves litigation for serious breaches of regulations that cause harm. The goal, it is suggested, is to "leave a lighter but more impactful regulatory footprint".[160]

3.3   Extending the Intrusive Regulatory Impulse: Individual Accountability Regimes (IARs) and Cultural Change

The above sections demonstrated that there has been a transition in all three jurisdictions, from a light-touch version of responsive regulation to a much more stringent and intrusive version of the same model. Whilst this more stringent, more deterrence-focused approach was adopted in the aftermath of the GFC, it was further precipitated by subsequent scandals involving the manipulation of the LIBOR and the mis-selling of PPI in the UK;[161] the tracker mortgages scandal in Ireland;[162] and the extensive catalogue of case-studies in financial wrongdoing documented by the Hayne Report in Australia.[163] The greater recourse to sanctioning approach bore some fruit; financial institutions paid seemingly large fines for misconduct over the last decade.[164]

Nevertheless, individual accountability for bankers often remained relatively elusive.[165] Very few individual bankers were successfully prosecuted for their roles in the financial crisis and civil sanctions were no panacea either. The "fit and proper" requirements, first proposed by the Basel Committee on

---

[160] Chester, K. (2021). Regulation for Recovery: When Pilots Become Enduring Practice. Available at: https://asic.gov.au/about-asic/news-centre/speeches/regulation-for-recovery-when-pilotsbecome-end uring-practice/. See also: ASIC. (2021). Corporate Plan 2021–25. Available at: https://asic.gov. au/media/qzcaljce/asic-corporate-plan-2021-25-focus-2021-22-published-26-august-2021.pdf; ASIC. (2021). Statement of Intent: Australian Securities and Investments Commission. Available at: https:// asic.gov.au/about-asic/what-we-do/how-we-operate/accountability-and-reporting/statements-of-expect ations-and-intent/statement-of-intentaustralian-securities-and-investments-commission-august-2021/.

[161] Parliamentary Commission on Banking Standards. (2013). Changing Banking for Good. Final Report. The Stationery Office Limited.

[162] Central Bank of Ireland. (2019). Tracker Mortgage Examination Final Report. Central Bank of Ireland, available at: https://www.centralbank.ie/consumer-hub/tracker-mortgage-examination.

[163] Financial Services Royal Commission. (2018). Interim Report of the Royal Commission into Misconduct in the Banking, Superannuation and Financial Services Industry; Financial Services Royal Commission. (2019). Final Report of the royal commission into misconduct in the banking, superannuation and financial services industry. Financial Services Royal Commission.

[164] MacNeil, I. (2015). Enforcement and Sanctioning. In Moloney, N., Ferran, E., & Payne, J. eds., *The Oxford Handbook of Financial Regulation*. Oxford University Press, 280–306.

[165] MacNeil, I. (2018). Regulating Instead of Punishing: The Senior Managers Regime in the UK. In Ligetti, K., & Tosza, S. eds., *White-Collar Crime: A Comparative Perspective*. Hart Publishing, 225–252.

banking Supervision in 1997, were arguably the key civil supervisory strategies which regulators in the UK, Ireland, and Australia had to ensure that individuals were qualified and competent to perform senior management roles in the financial services industry.[166] Though the detail and operation of the fit and proper requirements differ in each country, they did not adequately identify responsibilities within banks when things went wrong and regulators recognised that they had considerable difficulties enforcing the law against senior managers if they were able to close their eyes to wrongdoing, claim ignorance, or hide behind collective decision-making. In such circumstances, it was unlikely that senior managers could be held individually responsible.[167]

Recognising the limitations of sanctions, there have been significant international efforts to develop ethical cultures in the financial services industry. For example, the Financial Stability Board, the international body that makes recommendations on the global financial system, has produced a number of reports that are designed to help regulators to address misconduct risk and issues of culture within financial services firms.[168] National regulators have also demonstrated considerable commitment to instilling ethical cultures in firms in the financial services sector. In its supervision work, the FCA focuses on four key drivers of a firm's culture that can give rise to misconduct risk: purpose; leadership; approach to rewarding and managing people; and governance.[169] It does not, however, adopt a one-size-fits-all supervisory approach and it does not prescribe what any firm's culture should be.[170] Similarly, ASIC does not dictate a company's culture. Nevertheless, where it identifies elements of poor culture during its supervisory engagements, it brings these to the attention of the firm.[171] ASIC also indicated in its Corporate Plan for 2020–2024 that during 2020–2021 it aimed to carry out a targeted governance review of a select company to assess shortcomings in

---

[166] Basel Committee on Banking Supervision. (1997). Basel Core Principles for Effective Banking Supervision.

[167] Parliamentary Commission on Banking Standards. (2013). Changing Banking for Good. Final Report. The Stationery Office Limited.

[168] See, e.g., Strengthening Governance Frameworks to Mitigate Misconduct Risk: A Toolkit for Firms and Supervisors, Financial Stability Board, April 2018, available at: https://www.fsb.org/wp-content/uploads/P200418.pdf.

[169] See, generally, Culture and Governance, FCA, available at: https://www.fca.org.uk/firms/culture-and-governance.

[170] Ibid.

[171] Speech by ASIC Commissioner John Price, Reinforcing Culture in a Climate of Low Trust, 7 June 2018, available at: https://asic.gov.au/about-asic/news-centre/speeches/reinforcing-culture-in-a-climate-of-low-trust/.

culture, governance, and accountability frameworks.[172] Relatedly, APRA has also identified the transformation of culture in the financial services industry as a strategic focus area and has committed to "undertaking intensive reviews and prudential inquiries as appropriate"; requiring action of supervised firms where poor management of culture risks are identified; and "embedding a 'constructively tough' mindset" to the supervision of culture in regulated firms.[173] The Central Bank of Ireland also carried out a detailed review of the culture of the five retail banks in Ireland in 2018, relying on a methodology developed by the Dutch regulator, De Nederlandsche Bank.[174]

Emerging from this emphasis on generating cultural change, all three jurisdictions have implemented or are in the process of implementing new individual accountability regimes (IARs). The UK led the way with the introduction of the Senior Managers and Certification Regime (SMCR), which came into force in the UK in March of 2016.[175] Initially, the SMCR applied only to most PRA-authorised firms (including banks), but since December 2019, it applies to all firms authorised to provide financial services in the UK. It has also inspired the introduction of new IARs in Australia and Ireland (anticipated), as well as three jurisdictions outside the focus of this monograph—Hong Kong, Singapore, and Malaysia (anticipated).

Australia adopted a new Banking Executive Accountability Regime (BEAR) in February 2018.[176] It initially applied to the four largest authorised deposit-taking institutions (ADIs) in Australia and has been broadened to apply to all deposit-taking institutions as of July 2019. In January 2020, the Australian government issued a proposal paper to replace BEAR with FAR, the Financial Accountability Regime, extending the framework to a broader range of financial services providers and accountable persons therein.

---

[172] ASIC Corporate Plan 2020–2024, p. 21, available at: https://download.asic.gov.au/media/582 8033/corporate-plan-2020-24-published-31-august-2020-2.pdf.

[173] Corporate Plan 1919–1923, APRA, August 2019, p. 17, available at: https://www.apra.gov.au/ sites/default/files/APRA%20Corporate%20Plan%202019-23_0.pdf.

[174] Behaviour and Culture of the Irish Retail Banks. CBI, July 2018, available at: https://www.cen tralbank.ie/docs/default-source/publications/corporate-reports/behaviour-and-culture-of-the-irish-retail-banks.pdf?sfvrsn=2. The methodology developed by the De Nederlandsche Bank is set out in its monograph, Supervision of Behaviour and Culture: Foundations, Practice & Future Developments, available at: https://www.dnb.nl/media/1gmkp1vk/supervision-of-behaviour-and-culture_tcm46-380 398-1.pdf. For a review of this methodology, see e.g. Conley, J. M., Smeehuijzen, L., Williams, C. A., & Rupp, D. E. (2018). Can Soft Regulation Prevent Financial Crises: The Dutch Central Bank's Supervision of Behavior and Culture. *Cornell International Law Journal*, 51, 773–882.

[175] MacNeil, I. (2018). Regulating Instead of Punishing: The Senior Managers Regime in the UK. In Ligetti, K., & Tosza, S. eds., *White-Collar Crime: A Comparative Perspective*. Hart Publishing, 225–252.

[176] Manwaring, K., & Hanrahan, P. F. (2019). BEARing Responsibility for Cyber Security in Australian Financial Institutions: The Rising Tide of Directors' Personal Liability. *Journal of Banking and Finance Law and Practice*, 30(1), 20–42.

In Ireland, in July 2021, the government published the General Scheme of a Central Bank (Individual Accountability Framework) Bill 2021, which would give effect to a new framework including a Senior Executive Accountability Regime (SEAR), similar to the SMCR in the UK.[177] This initiative results from the publication by the CBI of a culture review of the retail banks in Ireland in 2018.[178] This review stated that the CBI's existing powers were not sufficient and that the law specifying the individual accountability of senior bankers needed to be strengthened.

Though each of these individual accountability regimes differ somewhat in various respects, they all aim to address a lack of personal responsibility in the financial services sector and the problem of wilful blindness at senior levels in complex organisations. Crucially, they also move the enforcement discourse beyond compliance and sanctioning models of financial regulation; ultimately these frameworks aim to generate positive cultural change in financial services organisations. In broad outline, these IARs require certain types of larger financial services providers to map key responsibilities across the organisation to named senior managers and then make those maps available to the relevant financial regulator. This makes it clear to specific managers that they are responsible for particular business areas and activities, forcing them to own and oversee the activities performed by their more junior staff. The failure to do so effectively can result in sanctions for that individual executive. IARs are designed to ensure that senior managers are fully engaged in the execution of their duties. If unethical misconduct is executed at a lower level, this now happens in their names. It is anticipated that the IARs should change the tone at the top to influence behaviour at the bottom of the organisation. It is hoped that this in turn will result in clearer, more active corporate governance protocols and generate better and more consumer centred behaviours. Over time, the ultimate goal is that financial services providers will internalise good governance norms and ethical values, in line with responsive regulatory theory. The IARs are analysed in more detail in Chapter 5 of this monograph.

IARs reflect an important and welcome enhancement to the second side of the regulatory pyramid, which requires financial services entities to take more ownership of their own activities in order to curtail wrongdoing and irresponsibility. IARs require financial organisations to define and map their responsibilities, which, in turn, require them to ensure that they devote

---

[177] The General Scheme of the Central Bank (Individual Accountability Framework) Bill 2021, available at: https://www.gov.ie/en/publication/d28d9-general-scheme-central-bank-individual-accountability-framework-bill/.

[178] Central Bank of Ireland. (2018). Behaviour and Culture of the Irish Retail Banks. Central Bank of Ireland, available at: https://www.centralbank.ie/docs/default-source/publications/corporate-reports/behaviour-and-culture-of-the-irish-retail-banks.pdf?sfvrsn=2.

enough time and resources so that ethical behaviour is routinised, expected, and lived. This enables the State to have less of a direct responsibility for compliance and enforcement. Failure to curtail wrongdoing, however, effectively re-engages the first face of the regulatory pyramid, resulting in state-led or regulator-led powers and sanctions in appropriate cases, using the civil jurisdiction of law to discipline individuals. This reflects adherence to the core contribution of "enforced self-regulation" or meta-regulation theory because the State requires and oversees that regulated entities have internal checks and systems to ensure regulatory goals and objectives are met. The State is requiring firms to exercise some self-regulation, and those privately written rules which specify internal accountability are then publicly enforced, when necessary.

Ayres and Braithwaite noted that enforced self-regulation was not without weaknesses, but they emphasised that the strengths were significant. In particular, they noted that enforced self-regulation: allows businesses to tailor systems to their own particular organisational arrangements, making them simpler and more specific, and that these systems could be adjusted much faster than legislative rules to changing business practices; offers the potential for regulatory innovation by tapping into firms' top-level "managerial genius"; allows for internal rules that are more comprehensive in coverage; and offers fewer opportunities for dissonance between corporate rulebooks and government legislation. They also asserted that businesses would bear more of the costs for their own regulation, and that more wrongdoing would be detected internally and sanctioned with greater ease without the problems of diffused accountability.[179] Ultimately, they argued that it could result in the internalisation of governance norms, where companies preferred to resolve matters internally without the adverse publicity arising from formal external enforcement; it was in their interests to prevent wrongdoing so that "compliance would become the path of least corporate resistance".[180] By harnessing corporate identity and culture to generate responsibility, companies themselves would recognise that "the most responsible way is the company way".[181] The question which remains is whether IARs will be successful in generating meaningful, lasting cultural change.

---

[179] Ayres, I., & Braithwaite, J. (1992). *Responsive Regulation: Transcending the Deregulation Debate.* Oxford University Press, 110–130.

[180] Ibid., p. 115.

[181] Ibid., p. 130.

4 Conclusion: Atrophy or the Potential to Flex a New Muscle?

This chapter analysed how the financial services sector is regulated in theory and practice. It critically described the important contributions of responsive regulation, which argued that regulators work best when they use a combination of compliance and deterrence-oriented approaches, using both persuasion and punishment, to act as "benign big guns" who "speak softly" and "carry a big stick". This theory was developed and enhanced in different ways by scholars researching risk-based regulation, smart regulation, meta-regulation, and governmentality theory. These theorists further elaborated the need to target limited resources to achieve outcomes, to harness third parties in enforcement, and to ensure that self-regulatory processes operate with government oversight. Such developments, it was noted, resonate with governmentality theory, which argues that power is increasingly exercised by non-state actors using instrumental solutions to avoid politically charged discourse relating to the appropriate role of government over market controls.

The chapter also showed that aspects of the responsive model were adopted in practice, with a shift from a non-interventionist, principles-based responsive model to a more intrusive, stringent responsive model, and a greater willingness to utilise measures across the enforcement pyramid. More recently, as part of this more stringent approach, there have been legislative interventions to define and map the individual responsibilities of senior managers in financial services organisations. These measures require senior managers to take more ownership of the business areas they oversee. Whilst these frameworks will make it easier to hold senior managers responsible for wrongdoing within their spheres of influence, the ultimate goal of such initiatives is less about sanctions and more about generating positive cultural change in organisations so that ethical behaviours are routinised and embedded.

Individual accountability regimes raise significant questions about the proper role of the state in regulatory supervision and enforcement. Ayres and Braithwaite originally saw the State as having a central, but not exclusive, role in regulatory processes. The government's ability to achieve its objectives is naturally limited by information asymmetries and epistemic dependence.[182] Some have since argued, however, that the State's role in regulation has been weakened, that State power is applied indirectly, and devolved through smart

---

[182] Hardwig, J. (1985). Epistemic Dependence. *The Journal of Philosophy*, 82(7), 335–349.

and meta-regulation.[183] As Grabosky notes, "Governments have begun to 'steer' rather than to 'row', structuring the marketplace so that naturally occurring private activity may assist in furthering public policy objectives".[184] Private certification regimes, as mandated though IARs, are an example of this form of indirect regulation. Grabosky notes the increased withdrawal of the State from direct regulatory activity as non-governmental agencies increasingly fill the vacuum left behind.[185] Others have noted that such withdrawals reflect a "post-regulatory world" in which regulation is increasingly fragmented and disaggregated.[186] Regulation is increasingly pluralistic, as the regulatory pyramid is reconceived as a three-sided tetrahedron: encompassing state regulation, self-regulation, and third party involvement.[187] Reflecting on the merits and dangers of the increasing reliance on non-state actors in regulatory enforcement, Grabosky notes that such involvement may "have a capacity building effect, raising local awareness, higher standards, and inspiring states to develop more rigorous regulatory institutions". He also cautions, however, that further reliance on these third parties may cause the State "to withdraw to the side-lines, and existing institutions to become atrophied".[188]

Nevertheless, it is submitted that IARs do not evince atrophy; instead, a new muscle is being flexed. IARs require financial services firms themselves to improve their own internal governance systems, to drive their own cultural change, to devise their own systems to deal with risk, albeit that this is overseen by regulators. IARs reflect an application of meta-regulation in practice and reflect what some governmentality theorists call "governance at

---

[183] Grabosky, P. (2017). Meta-Regulation. In Drahos, P. ed., *Regulatory Theory: Foundations and Applications*. ANU Press, 149–162, 153; Scott, C. (2004). Regulation in the Age of Governance: The Rise of the Post-regulatory State. In Jordana, J. & Levi-Faur, D. eds, *The Politics of Regulation: Institutions and Regulatory Reforms for the Age of Governance*. Edward Elgar, 145–174, 148.

[184] Grabosky, P. (2017). Meta-Regulation. In Drahos, P. ed., *Regulatory Theory: Foundations and Applications*. ANU Press, 149–162, 153.

[185] Grabosky, P. (2013). Beyond Responsive Regulation: The Expanding Role of Non-state Actors in the Regulatory Process. *Regulation & Governance*, 7(1), 114–123.

[186] Scott, C. (2004). Regulation in the Age of Governance: The Rise of the Post-regulatory State. In *The Politics of Regulation: Institutions and Regulatory Reforms for the Age of Governance*, 145; Vaughan, B., & Kilcommins, S. (2013). *Terrorism, Rights and the Rule of Law*. Routledge.

[187] Grabosky, P. N. (1997). Discussion Paper: Inside the Pyramid: Towards a Conceptual Framework for the Analysis of Regulatory Systems. *International Journal of the Sociology of Law*, 25(3), 195–201; Gunningham, N., Grabosky, P., & Sinclair, D. (1998). Smart Regulation. *Regulatory Theory*, 133.

[188] Grabosky, P. (2013). Beyond Responsive Regulation: The Expanding Role of Non-state Actors in the Regulatory Process. *Regulation & Governance*, 7(1), 114–123, 121.

a distance".[189] Contrary to the views of certain scholars, however, IARs do not reflect a State apparatus in retreat. The State is not being divested of its power, or "hollowed out" in some way through meta-regulation. Instead, the State amasses more enforcers to do its bidding, has more instruments of control, exercised through new sites of power. The State is being "rolled out" rather than "rolled back".[190] Whilst IARs represent forms of regulation in which government responsibility is defined indirectly, and where greater direct responsibilities for compliance are allocated to private interests, these patterns of laying blame and allocating responsibility are valuable in reflecting States' increasing tendency to adopt potentially preventative techniques that "manage" wrongdoing rather than simply punish it after the fact.

---

[189] Rose, N., & Miller, P. (2010). Political Power Beyond the State: Problematics of Government. *The British Journal of Sociology*, 61, 271–303.

[190] McGrath, J. (2019). Regulating White-Collar Crime in Ireland: An Analysis Using the Lens of Governmentality. *Crime, Law, and Social Change*, 72(4), 445–465.

3

The Systemic Problem of Unethical Behaviours in Financial Services

1   Introduction

This chapter critically analyses the nature, extent, and causes of misconduct in the financial services industry in the UK, Australia, and Ireland, with a particular focus on the banking sector.

Black explains that conduct is

> shaped by the complex interplay of factors at the individual level (incentive structures and interests of key individuals); the level of internal organisational systems, processes and cultures; and at the macro-level: not only the organisation's immediate field but also the deeper normative and cognitive environment.[1]

Using this analytical framework, this chapter critically explores the causes of misconduct in the financial services sectors along three lines: individual motivations to engage in wrongdoing; organisational cultures in firms that generate or facilitate misconduct; and the wider market structure factors that influence them. Individual motivations for misconduct are evaluated by reference to scholarship in psychology, criminology, and the behavioural sciences.

---

[1] Black, J. (2012). "New Governance" Techniques and the Financial Crisis. *Modern Law Review*, 75, 1037–1063, 1058. See also, McGrath, J. (2020). Why Do Good People Do Bad Things: A Multi-level Analysis of Individual, Organizational, and Structural Causes of White-Collar Crime. *Seattle University Law Review*, 43, 525–553.

© The Author(s), under exclusive license to Springer Nature Switzerland AG 2022
J. McGrath and C. Walker, *New Accountability in Financial Services*,
Palgrave Socio-Legal Studies,
https://doi.org/10.1007/978-3-030-88715-5_3

It is demonstrated that, whilst incentives/pressures to engage in misconduct (e.g. bonus structures; sales targets) and opportunities to do so are important factors, individuals are unlikely to engage in misconduct unless they can rationalise and neutralise their misconduct to themselves in such a way that allows them to maintain their view of themselves as an ethical person.[2]

It is also argued that organisational culture is a significant causal factor that can encourage or facilitate wrongdoing. In particular, firm cultures are shaped to an important extent by profit maximisation and shareholder primacy norms which can generate unethical conduct. It is argued that these norms can "crowd out" ethical considerations and "narrow the cognitive map" for bankers in organisations where there is a particular emphasis on shorter-term profit-maximising. There are various structural factors giving rise to misconduct in financial services, which are inter-related with individual motivations and firms' culture. Apart from the shareholder primacy norm and the "morals of the market place", this chapter highlights a structural factor inherent to the nature of financial services: the management of financial risk. By its nature, a core feature of the financial services industry is that it is focused on managing financial risks (e.g. insurance, investments); both the inherent uncertainty of future risk events and the likely information asymmetry between firms and their customers can create opportunities for firms to take advantage of less-informed customers.

This chapter is structured in two parts and further subdivided under various headings for the ease of the reader. Part one argues that misconduct in the financial services sector is systemic in nature, and not merely the result of the actions of a few "bad apples". It demonstrates this point by critically describing the scale and nature of high-profile financial scandals in the UK, Australia, and Ireland. Part two analyses the generative conditions for financial misconduct. It demonstrates that there are individual, organisational, and structural explanations for wrongdoing. This chapter is necessary and important because it demonstrates that the causes of financial misconduct are complex and that legal strategies which attempt to address only individual and organisational factors are incomplete. The broader structural environment that informs individual actions and organisational cultures must also be addressed. This analysis provides the foundation for subsequent chapters which argue that new individual accountability regimes (IARs) do not sufficiently address structural causes of wrongdoing.

---

[2] See, e.g. Shalvi, S., Gino, F., Barkan, R., & Ayal, S. (2015). Self-Serving Justifications: Doing Wrong and Feeling Moral. *Current Directions in Psychological Science*, 24(2), 125–130; Gino, F., & Ariely, D. (2016). Dishonesty Explained: What Leads Moral People to Act Immorally. In *The Social Psychology of Good and Evil*, 322–344; Mazar, N., Amir, O., & Ariely, D. (2008). The Dishonesty of Honest People: A Theory of Self-Concept Maintenance. *Journal of Marketing Research*, 45(6), 633–644.

2 The Scale of Unethical Behaviours in the Financial Services Sector

Corporate misconduct is not limited to the financial services sector. Quite apart from the various high-profile corporate scandals in the financial services industry, such as LIBOR in the UK and Wells Fargo in the United States, there have been many well-publicised corporate scandals in other industries across the globe in recent decades. The collapse of Enron and Worldcom, together with the more recent Volkswagen emissions issue, are a few very well-known examples. More generally, there are indications that these major scandals are symptomatic of a much broader and increasing problem of unethical behaviours in corporations across industries. Recent surveys, for example, point to a significant increase in the incidence of corporate fraud across the globe.[3] The regularity and scale of unethical behaviours by corporations has led some to suggest that corporations are facing a "crisis of trust" which has, inter alia, potentially legitimised populist and reactionary sentiment against "elites" and "big business".[4] As stated in the 2013 UK Parliamentary Commission on Banking Standards Report (PCBS Report), "to some degree, the loss of trust in banking has taken place alongside erosion of trust in other sectors".[5]

Nevertheless, widespread misconduct and the resulting loss of trust is a particular challenge for the banking sector. In 2016, then Deputy Director of the Bank of England, Minouche Shafik, described an "ethical drift" in the financial services industry internationally. She stated that, whilst misconduct in financial services has always been a feature for as long as commerce has existed, "[n]ever before has misconduct occurred so systematically, in such a large scale and across multiple jurisdictions. Clearly it was not a case of a few bad apples, but something was rotten in the entire barrel".[6] The then Governor of the Bank of England, Mark Carney, noted that misconduct

---

[3] See, e.g. PwC's 2020 Global Economic Crime and Fraud Survey, available at: https://www.pwc.com/gx/en/forensics/gecs-2020/pdf/global-economic-crime-and-fraud-survey-2020.pdf. As Soltes has noted, in the multi-national companies he has looked into for his research, "a bribe, a fraudulent accounting entry, or an inappropriate use of company data is not a once in a year event but rather something that I discovered happening multiple times a week at each company"; Soltes, E. (2016). *Why They Do It: Inside the Mind of the White-Collar Criminal*. PublicAffairs, x.

[4] See, e.g. Kirby, N., Kirton, A., & Crean, A. (2018). Do Corporations Have a Duty to Be Trustworthy? *Journal of the British Academy*, 75–129, 77.

[5] Changing Banking for Good, UK Parliamentary Commission on Banking Standards. The Stationery Office Limited, Vol. II, Annex 2, p. 528.

[6] Shafik, M. (2016). From Ethical Drift' to Ethical Lift': Reversing the Tide of Misconduct in Global Financial Markets, speech, 20 October, available at: https://www.bankofengland.co.uk/-/media/boe/files/speech/2016/from-ethical-drift-to-ethical-lift-reversing-the-tide-of.pdf?la=en&hash=C120FF0FF7E00FB7DE07858D2CD7DE95CC1BA695.

in the financial services sector had the potential to create systemic risks by undermining trust in both financial institutions and markets.[7] The size of fines imposed on financial services firms is one useful indicator of the extent of the problem. A 2019 European Central Bank (ECB) report estimated that the total costs for 26 global banks for their misconduct over the previous decade, in terms of damages, fines, settlements, and litigation, amounted to over $350 billion.[8] Similarly, a 2020 study by the CASS Business School indicates that, for the period 2008–2018, twenty of the largest global banks paid over £377 billion in various costs (including fines) for misconduct.[9]

The paragraphs below examine the scale and systemic nature of the wrongdoing in the financial services in the UK, Australia, and Ireland, the jurisdictions that are the focus of this book. Needless to state, evidence of serious and systemic misconduct by financial services firms is readily available from a number of other jurisdictions. In the United States, for example, the 2011 National Commission Financial Crisis Inquiry Report concluded that one of the factors that caused the 2007–2008 financial crisis was a systemic breakdown in ethics in the financial services industry.[10] More recently, in Europe, Danske Bank has been embroiled in what has been described as one of the largest money-laundering scandals ever seen.[11]

2.1   UK

The PCBS Report was scathing in its criticism of widespread misconduct in the banking industry. It noted that the UK banking sector's ability to perform its crucial role in support of the real economy and to maintain international pre-eminence "has been eroded by a profound loss of trust born of profound lapses in banking standards".[12] More generally, the PCBS Report stated:

---

[7] Letter from Mark Carney, Chairman Financial Stability Board to G20 Leaders, 30 August 2016, available at: https://www.fsb.org/wp-content/uploads/P20160831.pdf.

[8] Implications of Bank Misconduct Costs for Bank Equity Returns and Valuations, ECB, 19 November 2019, available at: https://www.ecb.europa.eu/pub/financial-stability/fsr/focus/2019/html/ecb.fsrbox201911_03~511ae02cc5.en.html.

[9] "The CBR Conduct Costs Project, CASS Business School, 2020, available at: https://www.cass.city.ac.uk/__data/assets/pdf_file/0005/558284/CBR-Conduct-Costs-Project-report-September2020.pdf.

[10] Financial Crisis Inquiry Commission. (2011). The Financial Crisis Inquiry Report: Final Report of the National Commission on the Causes of the Financial and Economic Crisis in the United States. US Government Printing Office.

[11] Prosecutors Charge ex-Danske Bank Chief in Money-Laundering Probe, *Financial Times*, 7 May 2019, available at: https://www.ft.com/content/a78b04ba-70d5-11e9-bf5c-6eeb837566c5.

[12] Changing Banking for Good, UK Parliamentary Commission on Banking Standards. The Stationery Office Limited, Vol. I, p. 8, available at: https://publications.parliament.uk/pa/jt201314/jtselect/jtpcbs/27/27.pdf.

It has been more than 25 years since Tom Wolfe used the term 'master of the universe', to describe a New York bond trader, but it has never been more apt as a description of bankers than as in the last decade. Bankers prioritised short term personal gain over their customers and shareholders and recklessly failed to prevent wrongdoing. It was a culture, in places, suffused with corruption.[13]

The LIBOR scandal, which was a significant factor giving rise to the setting up of the UK Parliamentary Commission on Banking Standards, epitomised the problem. The London Interbank Offered Rate (LIBOR) refers to a series of daily interest rates that is calculated across a number of currencies and borrowing periods. At the relevant time, the British Bankers' Association (BBA) administered and calculated the rates on the basis of daily submissions made to the BBA by a number of major banks.[14] The banks would typically submit the actual interest rates they were paying, or would expect to pay, for borrowing from other banks. It is a key benchmark rate (which is being replaced, as a result of the scandal relating to it), as it is used as the reference rate for the calculation of interest on many financial products, from home and student loans to hundreds of trillions of dollars in derivatives trading.

The scandal arose when it was discovered that a number of banks had been submitting false rates, so as to profit from trades or to give the impression that they were more creditworthy than they were. This was done largely through collusion between the banks. The nature and extent of collusion between banks to manipulate this rate for short-term gain gave rise to particular public opprobrium,[15] due to the pervasive and open nature of the misconduct. In particular, there was plentiful evidence, including from recorded conversations between the traders directly involved in the misconduct, of "casual corruption set against a luxurious lifestyle"[16] which "seemed to confirm a pervasive, much-caricatured, unethical, greedy, and selfish behaviour on the

---

[13] PCBS Report, Vol. II, para. 48.

[14] See, The Wheatley Review of LIBOR: Final Report, para. 1.1, available at: https://assets.pub lishing.service.gov.uk/government/uploads/system/uploads/attachment_data/file/191762/wheatley_rev iew_libor_finalreport_280912.pdf.

[15] Andrew Tyrie, Chairman of the UK Parliament Treasury Select Committee, stated, on the publi-cation of a report by the Treasury Select Committee into the Libor scandal, in August 2012, "The sustained rigging of a crucial benchmark rate has done great damage to the UK's reputation. Public trust in banks is at an all-time low" (see https://www.itv.com/news/update/2012-08-18/libor-scandal-did-great-damage-to-uks-reputation/).

[16] PCBS Report, Vol. II, para. 41.

trading floors of investment banks".[17] The LIBOR scandal resulted in fines in excess of $9 billion being imposed on the banks involved.[18]

The PCBS Report also detailed the payment protection insurance (PPI) mis-selling scandal. PPI policies are intended to provide insurance cover to individuals for loan repayments, where they become unable to repay the loans as a result of a specified event (such as loss of employment or an illness). A 2005 Citizens Advice report described the PPI business in the UK (with its estimated 20 million policies in force and annual gross premiums for the retail banks in excess of £5 billion at the time) as a "protection racket".[19] The PPI policies, which were enormously profitable for retail banks, were often mis-sold to customers who did not properly understand them or for whom they were not appropriate. A remediation scheme was set up for affected customers and, as of May 2020, over £38 billion in refunds and compensation has been paid to affected customers.[20]

2.2   Australia

The 2019 Australian Royal Commission Final Report into misconduct in the banking, superannuation and financial services industry (Hayne Report) describes in great detail widespread misconduct in the financial services industry in Australia.[21] It looked at case studies across a number of financial services sectors and, as part of its work, received over 10,000 complaints about financial services entities from members of the public.[22] Also, the Interim Report of the Royal Commission into Misconduct in the Banking, Superannuation and Financial Services Industry (Interim Hayne Report) found that much of the widespread problem of misconduct arose from "greed—the pursuit of short-term profit at the expense of basic standards

---

[17] Salz Review: An Independent Review of Barclays' Business Practices, April 2013, para. 3.21, cited in the PCBS Report, Vol. II, para. 41.

[18] A useful brief overview of the LIBOR scandal and repercussions for the banks and individuals involved can be found at: https://www.cfr.org/backgrounder/understanding-libor-scandal.

[19] Tutton, P. (2005). Protection Racket: CAB Evidence on the Cost and effectiveness of Payment Protection Insurance, Citizens Advice Bureau, available at: https://www.citizensadvice.org.uk/Global/Migrated_Documents/corporate/protection-racket-final.pdf.

[20] Monthly PPI Refunds and Compensation, FCA, May 2020, available at: https://www.fca.org.uk/data/monthly-ppi-refunds-and-compensation. See, generally, in relation to the PPI scandal, Walker, C. (2019). The Role of the Board of Financial Services Firms in Improving Their Firm's Culture. *Seattle University Law Review*, 43, 723–764, 740–742.

[21] Royal Commission Report into Misconduct in the Banking, Superannuation and Financial Services Industry, February 2019, available at: https://www.royalcommission.gov.au/system/files/2020-09/fsrc-volume-1-final-report.pdf.

[22] Ibid., p. xxxv.

of honesty. How else is charging continuing advice fees to the dead to be explained?".[23]

The Hayne Report, together with the Interim Hayne Report, catalogued a wide range of misconduct by a range of financial services providers, such as: charging of unwarranted commission payments, on-going charging of fees without providing services, knowingly accepting falsified documentation when processing home loans and knowingly providing financial products and services that were inappropriate for customers and which led to poor customer outcomes but generated commissions for the financial services providers. For example, during the period 2010–2018, financial services firms paid approximately AUS $250 million to almost 540,000 customers as a result of misconduct (reliance on fraudulent documentation, processing or administration errors or breaches of responsible lending obligations) relating to the provision of home loans.[24] Approximately 65,000 customers who bought credit card insurance, which provided benefits in circumstances where they suffered temporary or permanent disability or involuntary unemployment, were not eligible to benefit from the insurance because they were unemployed when they bought the policy.[25] There were also instances of banks charging fees for advice to deceased account holders.[26]

The various specific cases of misconduct described in the Hayne Report and Interim Hayne Report reflected a broader corporate culture in the financial services industry which was insufficiently consumer-centred. In particular, these reports demonstrated that individual financial incentives drove unethical behaviours, which occurred within a broader corporate culture in which profit maximisation was championed to the neglect of other considerations, where financial service providers were slow or reluctant to remediate wrongdoing, and evasive and less than frank in reporting problems to regulators. The public reaction to the findings was overwhelmingly negative, with some noting that "greed ... leads Australian banks to steal from dead people".[27]

---

[23] Interim report of the Australian Royal Commission into Misconduct in the Banking, Superannuation and Financial Services Industry, September 2018; Vol. 1, p. xix, available at: https://financialser vices.royalcommission.gov.au/Documents/interim-report/interim-report-volume-1.pdf.

[24] Ibid., pp. 35–36.

[25] Ibid., pp. 48–49.

[26] Hayne Report, pp. 147–148.

[27] Denniss, R. (2008). It Is Greed That Has Led Australian Banks to Steal from Dead People. *The Guardian* (3 October), available at: https://www.theguardian.com/commentisfree/2018/oct/03/it-is-greed-that-has-led-australian-banks-to-steal-from-dead-people. See also, e.g. Ferguson, A. (2019). *Banking Bad: Whistle-Blowers, Corporate Cover-Ups, One Journalist's Fight for the Truth.* ABC Books.

2.3   Ireland

Arguably the most significant instance of financial wrongdoing in Ireland, after the GFC, was the tracker mortgages scandal. Tracker mortgages are so called because the interest rate charged under these mortgages directly "tracked" the ECB interest rate by a margin. They were offered to Irish customers in a period of intense competition amongst banks, in particular between 2003 and 2008. During the period 2006–2008, when interest rates rose, many customers chose to switch their mortgage from their tracker rate to a fixed rate of interest for a period (and were encouraged to do so by the banks). Once the interest rates subsequently decreased, however, the banks (which had stopped offering tracker mortgages from 2008 as they had become too costly for them), often chose not to enable their customers to revert to the lower tracker rate or otherwise benefit from a tracker rate. This was despite the terms of the relevant mortgage contracts, which appeared to permit customers to benefit from a tracker rate. This resulted in significant overcharging of customers. In response, in 2015 the Central Bank of Ireland (CBI) launched "the largest, most complex, and significant consumer protection review" in its history.[28] The CBI found that the scandal affected over 40,000 customers, 99 of whom lost their homes as a result of over-charging.[29] The wrongdoing cost the lenders €683 million, as at May 2019, in redress and compensation to affected customers.[30] The CBI also imposed fines on a number of the lenders involved, including a fine of €37.7 million on one of the lenders, the highest single fine the CBI has imposed to date under its administrative sanctions procedure.[31]

The tracker mortgage scandal generated considerable public disquiet in relation to the banking industry in Ireland. The behaviour of the Irish banks was described by the Irish Minister of Finance in a press statement as "disgraceful" and "the legalistic approach taken by some banks to avoid doing the

---

[28] The Tracker Mortgage Examination: Final Report, Central Bank of Ireland, July 2019, p. 4, available at: https://www.centralbank.ie/docs/default-source/consumer-hub-library/tracker-issues/update-on-tracker-mortgage-examination---july-2019.pdf?sfvrsn=6.

[29] Ibid., p. 6.

[30] Ibid. Some reports indicate that the overall cost of the scandal to the banks has been around €1.5 billion; see e.g.: https://www.rte.ie/news/business/2021/0326/1206353-ulster-bank-tracker-mortgage-fine/.

[31] CBI announcement of fine imposed on Ulster Bank Ireland DAC, 25 March 2021; information on this is available at: https://www.centralbank.ie/docs/default-source/news-and-media/legal-notices/settlement-agreements/public-statement-relating-to-settlement-agreement-between-the-central-bank-of-ireland-and-ulster-bank-ireland-dac.pdf?sfvrsn=6.

right thing is simply unacceptable".[32] He argued that "it is now time that all banks seek to regain the trust of the Irish people by actions, not words".[33] This sentiment was echoed by the CBI, which stated that the actions of the banks had "damaged the already fragile public trust in financial institutions—many of which had been bailed out at enormous public cost during the financial crash".[34]

Concerns regarding the general behaviours of the banks in Ireland had also emerged some time prior to the tracker mortgage scandal. In 2005, for example, an Oireachtas (Irish Parliament) Committee report into the behaviours of the banks concluded that "the banking and finance sector in Ireland is not sufficiently competitive. As a result, consumers are paying too much for credit and money payment services".[35] The Committee report also stated that it was "concerned at the number of incidents in recent years in which banks have failed to comply with acceptable standards of behaviour with respect to prudential, consumer and fiscal obligations".[36] Also, post-GFC reports into the financial collapse and its causes in Ireland found that "the major responsibility lies with the directors and senior managements of the banks that got into trouble".[37] In particular, there was evidence of "a comprehensive failure of bank management and direction to maintain safe and sound banking practices, instead incurring huge external liabilities in order to support a credit-fuelled property market and construction frenzy".[38]

In summary, scandals in the UK, Australia, and Ireland demonstrated that widespread misconduct in the financial services industry was not merely the

---

[32] Statement by Minister Paschal Donohoe, 25 October 2017, available at: https://merrionstreet.ie/en/news-room/releases/statement_by_the_minister_for_finance_paschal_donohoe_on_the_tracker_mortgage_examination.html.

[33] Ibid.

[34] Speech by the CBI's Derville Rowland, 22 February 2019, available at: https://www.centralbank.ie/news/article/why-culture-matters-insights-from-the-central-bank-of-ireland-review-of-behaviour-and-culture-in-the-irish-banking-sector---director-general-derville-rowland.

[35] Joint Committee on Finance and the Public Service. (2005). Interim Report on the Policy of Commercial Banks Concerning Customer Charges and Interest Rates, p. 9, available at: https://opac.oireachtas.ie/knowvation/app/consolidatedSearch/#search/v=grid,c=1,q=qs%3D%5BInterim%20Report%20%5D%2Ccreator%3D%5B%22Joint%20Committee%20on%20Finance%20and%20the%20Public%20Service%22%5D%2Ctitle%3D%5B%22Interim%20Report%22%5D%2CqueryType%3D%5B16%5D,sm=s,sb=0%3Atitle%3AASC,l=library3_lib,a=t.

[36] Ibid., p. 9.

[37] Honohan, P., Donovan, D., Gorecki, P., & Mottiar, R. (2010). The Irish Banking Crisis: Regulatory and Financial Stability Policy 2003–2008, May, para. 1.6, available at: https://www.socialjustice.ie/sites/default/files/attach/policy-issue-article/3077/2010-06-08-the honohanreport-theirishbankingcrisisregulatoryandfinancialstabilitypolicy2003-2008.pdf. See also, 2016 Oireachtas Joint Committee Report into the Banking Crisis, available at: https://inquiries.oireachtas.ie/banking/wp-content/uploads/2016/01/02106-HOI-BE-Report-Volume1.pdf.

[38] Ibid., para. 1.30.

result of the actions of a few bad apples. Misconduct was often widespread and systemic across organisations and the industry more generally. Moreover, the pursuit of profit motivated the misconduct. Consumer interests were neglected and marginalised. The next section of this chapter explores the factors which generate misconduct in the financial services sector.

3   Causal Factors

The previous section briefly outlined the extent of misconduct in financial services in the UK, Australia, and Ireland. This section critically explores causal factors giving rise to this systemic level of misconduct. As noted above, behaviour is shaped by a complex interplay of factors at the individual level, the organisational level, and the wider macro-structural level.[39] This section is structured accordingly along these three inter-related lines of inquiry.

3.1   Individual Motivations for Unethical Conduct

There is considerable scholarship in psychology, criminology, other behavioural sciences and law exploring why individuals engage in unethical conduct.[40] A comprehensive examination of this literature is beyond the scope of this monograph. This section confines itself to a brief examination of a number of causal factors.

The relevant scholarship highlights the importance to an individual of maintaining a self-image as ethical, even whilst engaging in unethical acts. As stated by Ariely, "I believe that all of us continuously try to identify the line where we can benefit from dishonesty without damaging our own self-image".[41] He has identified a "fudge factor" that individuals rely on to

---

[39] Black, J. (2012). "New Governance" Techniques and the Financial Crisis. *Modern Law Review*, 75, 1037–1063, 1058. See also, McGrath, J. (2020). Why Do Good People Do Bad Things: A Multilevel Analysis of Individual, Organizational, and Structural Causes of White-Collar Crime. *Seattle University Law Review*, 43, 525–553.

[40] See, e.g. Soltes, E. (2016). *Why They Do It: Inside the Mind of the White-Collar Criminal*. PublicAffairs; Shalvi, S., Gino, F., Barkan, R., & Ayal, S. (2015). Self-Serving Justifications: Doing Wrong and Feeling Moral. *Current Directions in Psychological Science*, 24(2), 125–130; Mazar, N., Amir, O., & Ariely, D. (2008). The Dishonesty of Honest People. *Journal of Marketing Research*, 45, 633–644; Gino, F., & Ariely, D. (2016). Dishonesty Explained: What Leads Moral People to Act Immorally. In *The Social Psychology of Good and Evil*, 322–344; Ariely, D. (2012). *The (Honest) Truth About Dishonesty*. Harper Collins Publishers; Heffernan, M. (2011). *Wilful Blindness: Why We Ignore the Obvious*. Simon and Schuster; Bazerman, M. H., & Tenbrunsel, A. E. (2011). *Blind Spots*. Princeton University Press.

[41] Ariely, D. (2012). *The (Honest) Truth About Dishonesty*. Harper Collins Publishers, 28.

rationalise cheating a little whilst maintaining a self-image as ethical.[42] Similarly, referencing relevant scholarship in this area, the UK Financial Conduct Authority has stated: "People like to think of themselves as moral, and their actions determine the extent to which they can maintain such a view. This means that people will break rules when they can rationalise the benefits of rule breaking as being consistent with their status as a good, virtuous person".[43]

A long line of research supports the idea that individuals think of themselves as ethical whilst engaging in unethical conduct. Cressey's research in the 1950s, for example, examined the factors that caused convicted embezzlers to engage in this type of fraud. He concluded that there were three factors that caused them to do so: a non-shareable pressure (generally financial); a perceived opportunity to embezzle; and rationalisation of the planned violation.[44] Significantly, Cressey noted that rationalisation was the crucial step that determined whether or not the individual engaged in illicit behaviour. Cressey believed that individuals devised rationalisations prior to perpetrating their illicit acts. "If he cannot do this", Cressey wrote, "he does not become an embezzler".[45] Evolving from the work of Cressey, various organisations have adopted a "fraud triangle" model to analyse the circumstances in which individuals might engage in fraud.[46] The fraud triangle sets out three factors that are considered to be the key factors in considering whether individuals might engage in fraud: incentives or pressure; opportunity, and rationalisation. More recently, the fraud triangle has been updated to include a fourth factor, capability, and reconstituted as the "fraud diamond".[47] It has also been the subject of much discussion, and some criticism and subsequent suggested

---

[42] Ibid., p. 27.

[43] FCA Occasional paper 24, Behaviour and compliance in Organisations, December 2016, p. 6, available at: https://www.fca.org.uk/publication/occasional-papers/op16-24.pdf.

[44] Cressey, D. R. (1953). *Other People's Money; A Study of the Social Psychology of Embezzlement*. Free Press.

[45] Cressey refers to "neutralizing verbalizations" individuals use to justify to themselves their illegal actions. These "neutralizing verbalizations" "make up the most important element in the process which gets a trusted person in trouble, or keeps the person out of trouble. If a man sees a possibility for embezzlement, it is because he has defined the relationship between an unshareable problem and an illegal solution in language that lets him look on trust violation as something other than trust violation. If he cannot do this, he does not become an embezzler. If he can do so, trust violation is inevitable" (Cressey, D. [1986]. Why Managers Commit Fraud. *Australian and New Zealand Journal of Criminology*, 195–209, 200).

[46] E.g. the Association of Certified Fraud Examiners ("ACFE"), American Institute of Certified Public Accountants ("AICPA") and the International Auditing and Assurance Standards Board ("IAASB"); see, ISA 240, available at: https://www.ifac.org/system/files/downloads/a012-2010-iaasb-handbook-isa-240.pdf.

[47] Wolfe, D. T., & Hermanson, D. R. (2004). The Fraud Diamond: Considering the Four Elements of Fraud. *The CPA Journal*, 74(12), 38–42.

modifications.[48] Behavioural science research in this area has demonstrated that individuals in financial services have significant incentives/pressures, together with opportunities and capabilities, to engage in unethical conduct. Furthermore, there are numerous means by which individuals, particularly at the most senior levels, can maintain a self-image as ethical, whilst engaging in or tolerating unethical conduct.

Various official reports into misconduct in financial services have identified the enormous incentives and pressures for individuals in the industry to engage in short-term profit-maximising conduct at the expense of ethical considerations. The PCBS Report, for example, highlighted the very high remuneration paid to investment bankers and noted that they were financially incentivised to focus on highly leveraged short-term growth at the expense of sustainability and good conduct.[49] Retail staff were incentivised to generate high volumes of sales. Staff who did not meet ambitious sales targets faced possible performance management and dismissal, thereby effectively encouraging mis-selling.[50] In Ireland, reports into the financial crisis in 2007–2008 also noted that "there was a culture of excessive executive remuneration in the banks",[51] which also contributed to irresponsible risk taking.[52]

Similarly, the Interim Hayne Report found that the misconduct it identified was driven by the remuneration practices of the financial institutions: the "pursuit of profit has trumped consideration of *how* the profit is made".[53] The Interim Hayne Report concluded, "the culture and conduct of the banks was driven by, and was reflected in, their remuneration practices and policies".[54] It determined that the "central tenet" of the remuneration policies of the banks:

---

[48] See, generally, e.g. Vousinas, G. L. (2019). Advancing Theory of Fraud: The Score Model. *Journal of Financial Crime*, 26(1) 372–381; Carson, D., & Robinson, B. (2019). Corporate Investigations. In McGrath, J. ed., *White-Collar Crime in Ireland: Law and Policy*. Clarus Press, 49–73.

[49] PCBS Report, Vol. II, para. 116.

[50] PCBS Report, Vol. II, para. 119.

[51] Joint Committee of Inquiry into the Banking Crisis. (2016). Report of the Joint Committee of Inquiry into the Banking Crisis, Houses of the Oireachtas, p. 7, available at: https://inquiries.oireachtas.ie/banking/wp-content/uploads/2016/01/02106-HOI-BE-Report-Volume1.pdf. See also, Nyberg, P. (2011). "Misjudging Risk: Causes of the Systemic Banking Crisis in Ireland". Government Publications Office (the "Nyberg Report"): "Financial incentives, whilst not the major cause of the crisis, likely contributed to the rapid expansion of bank lending since the incentives did not sufficiently stress modifiers for risk" (para. 5.2.6), available at: https://www.nuigalway.ie/media/housinglawrightsandpolicy/nationalpolicy/Nyberg-Report-Mis juding-Risk---Causes-of-the-Systemic-Banking-Crisis-in-Ireland.pdf.

[52] McGrath, J. (2020). 'Walk Softly and Carry No Stick': Culture, Opportunity, and Irresponsible Risk-Taking in the Irish Banking Sector. *European Journal of Criminology*, 17(1) 86–105.

[53] Interim Hayne Report, p. 269.

[54] Ibid., p. 340.

has been to reward what the organisation treats as important: sales and profit. If there were exceptions to this approach, they were immaterial. The conduct identified and criticised in this report was driven by the pursuit of profit – the entity's revenue and profit and the individual actor's profit. Employees of banks learned to treat sales, or revenue and profit, as the measure of their success.[55]

Individuals in the industry also had a wide range of opportunities to engage in unethical and illegal conduct. The Interim Hayne Report determined that financial institutions engaged in unethical and illegal conduct "because they can" and "because they profit from the misconduct".[56] In addition, the banking sector tolerated conflicts of interest. The Hayne Report, for example, noted that it had often been the case that consumers dealt with financial institutions via intermediaries and it was assumed that the intermediary was acting in their interests, even though in many cases the intermediary was being paid by, and acting in the interests of, the financial institution.[57]

Opportunities for unethical or illegal conduct have also arisen because of inadequacies of internal controls.[58] The PCBS Report found that the three lines model for controlling risk "appears to have promoted a wholly misplaced sense of security", whereby "responsibilities [were] blurred, accountability diluted, and officers in risk, compliance [both second line functions] and internal audit [third line function] have lacked the status to challenge front-line staff [first line] effectively" and much of the system was "box-ticking".[59] Moreover, the PCBS Report found that, with regard to the serious misconduct that had occurred, including payment protection insurance and LIBOR, "one of the most striking features...has been the absence of whistle-blowing".[60] Accordingly, individuals who engaged in misconduct often did not run a high risk of their misconduct being "called out" by colleagues or otherwise being reported on internally. In addition, the expertise and position

---

[55] Ibid., pp. 301–302.

[56] Interim Hayne Report, p. 269.

[57] Hayne Report, p. 2.

[58] The 2011 US Senate report describes in detail the high-risk sub-prime mortgage lending practices of Washington Mutual Bank, which led to its collapse in 2008. It found that Washington Mutual's practices were profitable for a time because they sold on the mortgages by securitising them. This, however, involved senior management of Washington Mutual doing little or nothing when informed of extensive loan fraud (loans that were provided on the basis of fraudulent information). US Senate Report. (2011). Wall Street and the Financial Crisis: Anatomy of a Financial Collapse; see, pp. 95–103 of the report, available at: https://www.hsgac.senate.gov/imo/media/doc/PSI%20R EPORT%20-%20Wall%20Street%20&%20the%20Financial%20Crisis-Anatomy%20of%20a%20F inancial%20Collapse%20(FINAL%205-10-11).pdf.

[59] PCBS Report, p. 141, para. 143.

[60] PCBS Report, p. 137, para. 132.

of authority of many senior managers in financial services firms would have provided them with the capabilities to engage in or tolerate misconduct.[61]

Furthermore, the relative lack of market competition in many financial services markets, that would otherwise constrain financial services firms from unfairly taking advantage of customers, provides opportunities for unethical behaviours. The Hayne Report, for example, noted that there was a "marked imbalance of power and knowledge" between financial services firms and customers.[62] It concluded that "competition within the banking industry is weak".[63] Similarly, the PCBS Report found that there was insufficient market discipline on banks to reduce prices and improve service.[64] In Ireland, the first of the list of recommendations of the 2016 Oireachtas (Parliament) Joint Committee Report into the 2007–2008 banking crisis was that Ireland's competition authority "should conduct an immediate review of the impact on consumers, due to the perceived lack of competition in banking in Ireland".[65] This recommendation has not, to date, been implemented.[66] Although increased competition does not always produce positive consumer outcomes, especially where there is an information asymmetry between the parties,[67] the official inquiries identified limited competition in the retailing banking sector as a significant cause of misconduct.

Even if there are incentives/pressures to engage in unethical conduct, and opportunities, together with capabilities, to do so, there is then the key factor of whether an individual can maintain a self-image as ethical whilst engaging in unethical conduct. As outlined below, there have been various means by which individuals, particularly senior individuals, in the financial services industry could justify to themselves their unethical conduct whilst maintaining a self-image as ethical.

---

[61] With regard to the capability aspect of the fraud diamond, see generally e.g. Ruankaew, T. (2016). Beyond the Fraud Diamond. *International Journal of Business Management and Economic Research (IJBMER)*, 7(1), 474–476.

[62] Hayne Report, p. 2.

[63] Interim Hayne Report, p. 268.

[64] PCBS Report, Vol. II, para. 167.

[65] Report of the Joint Committee of Inquiry into the Banking Crisis, 2016, Oireachtas, p. 8, available at: https://inquiries.oireachtas.ie/banking/.

[66] In November 2021, however, the Minister for Finance published the Terms of Reference for a Retail Banking Review, to be conducted by the Department of Finance, which will include a review of retail competition. See, Department of Finance Press Release, 23 November 2021; available at: https://www.gov.ie/en/press-release/d9ba7-minister-donohoe-publishes-term-of-reference-for-retail-banking-review/.

[67] Akerlof, G. A. (1970). The Market for "Lemons": Quality Uncertainty and the Market Mechanism. *Quarterly Journal of Economics*, 84(3), 488–500.

Senior individuals in financial services may justify to themselves unethical actions, on the basis that the actions are legal and are in the interests of shareholder value. As stated in the Hayne Report, profit had become the defining measure of success of Australian banks and this was "justified as being in the interests of shareholders and, because superannuation funds hold bank shares, as being in the interests of all Australians".[68] Similarly, with regard to the PPI scandal in the UK, described above, an independent review (hereinafter the Salz Review) of Barclays bank business practices noted that the board of Barclays was aware of the very high profits it was getting from PPI and "the high profitability of PPI should have raised questions as to whether this was consistent with Barclays' obligations to customers"[69]—but it clearly did not.

Individuals may also be strongly influenced by the normalisation of poor behaviours in the industry and a "common is moral" heuristic.[70] In particular, individuals may be strongly guided by the "morals of the marketplace", in which it is broadly expected and legitimate that the individual's firm pursue profits on the basis of freely negotiated and, importantly, self-interested, exchange.[71] Significantly, individuals who seek to go against the tide of the "morals of the marketplace" will face difficulties. As Akerlof pointed out in his famous 1970 article on the impact of information asymmetry and the "market for lemons",[72] where there is information asymmetry between buyers and sellers and where buyers cannot adequately distinguish between higher-quality goods and lower-quality goods ("lemons"), this information asymmetry is likely to drive down the quality of goods on the market. Ethical firms will struggle to compete with their less ethical competitors, who mislead customers as to the quality of their products or services in situations where customers are not in a position effectively to compare the respective products or services of the various competitors. Over time, this may lead to overall levels of ethical conduct in the market deteriorating. As Akerlof and Shiller argue, competitive pressures mean that "even firms guided by those with real moral integrity will usually have to [exploit buyers' psychological weaknesses

---

[68] Interim Hayne Report, p. 269.

[69] Salz Review: An Independent Review of Barclays' Business Practices, p. 58, available at: https://online.wsj.com/public/resources/documents/SalzReview04032013.pdf. See, generally, Heffernan, M. (2011). *Wilful Blindness: Why We Ignore the Obvious*. Simon and Schuster.

[70] Lindström, B., Jangard, S., Selbing, I., & Olsson, A. (2018). The Role of a "Common Is Moral" Heuristic in the Stability and Change of Moral Norms. *Journal of Experimental Psychology: General*, 147(2), 228–242.

[71] Omarova, S. T. (2017). Ethical Finance as a Systemic Challenge: Risk, Culture, and Structure. *Cornell Journal of Law & Public Policy*, 27, 797–839, 810.

[72] Akerlof, G. A. (1970). The Market for "Lemons": Quality Uncertainty and the Market Mechanism. *Quarterly Journal of Economics*, 84(3), 488–500.

and ignorance] in order to compete and survive".[73] Information asymmetry as between firms and their customers is a particular issue in financial services, notably in retail markets. In retail markets, many customers may not be sufficiently financially literate to appreciate the implications for them of the products they are being offered. There is a real problem of low levels of financial literacy, so retail customers risk being "bamboozled" by financial jargon, even where regulators require firms to present the required information in a customer-friendly format. As noted by the Governor of the Central Bank of Ireland, "[a] vast empirical literature shows that consumers tend to make poor financial choices, taking on too much debt, misunderstanding investment risk and choosing financial products that do not match their needs".[74]

More generally, there is the "slippery slope" problem, whereby ethical considerations fade over time as misbehaviours become more habitual; this slippery slope may make it easier for individuals to maintain a self-image as ethical whilst engaging in increasingly unethical acts. The slippery slope problem is interesting, particularly in light of recent research by neuroscientists.[75] Langevoort notes that this research indicates that:

> Using magnetic imaging of the brain during ethics-related laboratory experiments, they have found that the amygdala is normally strongly activated by ethical stress (pressures to misbehave). That emotions-driving portion of the brain plays a big role in doing what's right. But if there is a small step toward cheating, the level of activation goes down slightly in the next opportunity. This goes on and on, down the slippery slope. Gradually, the amygdala's electrical energy dims to indifference.[76]

More generally, given the multiple decisions that senior executives face in their busy and pressurised daily working lives, it may well be that "blind spots"[77] can develop in relation to ethical considerations. Short-term pressures can also lead to a "narrowing of the cognitive map", whereby the ethical

---

[73] Akerlof, G. A., & Shiller, R. J. (2015). *Phishing for Phools: The Economics of Manipulation and Deception*. Princeton University Press, xii.

[74] Speech by Philip Lane, 23 February 2017, available at: https://www.centralbank.ie/news/article/financial-regulation-protecting-consumers-governor-lane.

[75] E.g. Garrett, N., Lazzaro, S. C., Ariely, D., & Sharot, T. (2016). The Brain Adapts to Dishonesty. *Nature Neuroscience*, 19(12), 1727–1732; Engelmann, J. B., & Fehr, E. (2016). The Slippery Slope of Dishonesty. *Nature Neuroscience*, 19(12), 1543–1544, cited by Langevoort in, Langevoort, D. C. (2019). Gatekeepers, Cultural Captives, or Knaves?: Corporate Lawyers Through Different Lenses. *Fordham Law Review*, 88, 1683–1698, 1690.

[76] Langevoort, D. ibid., pp. 1690–1691.

[77] See, Bazerman, M. H., & Tenbrunsel, A. E. (2011). *Blind Spots*. Princeton University Press.

implications of actions are not consciously recognised.[78] This can also arise, for example, from the remoteness of the decision-making industry executive from the harmful consequences for consumers or other customers of his or her decisions.[79] Many senior executives in financial services typically make business decisions on the basis of analyses of data and other impersonal factors rather than personal contact with affected customers. Recent research has indicated that the part of the brain associated with emotional engagement and compassion (the ventromedial pre-frontal cortex) is more likely to be engaged where an individual is confronted with the impact of their decisions on specific nearby individuals, as opposed to more distant groupings of people.[80] Soltes notes that this research explains why, in many cases, business executives are not sufficiently discomforted when engaging in business malfeasance:

> With the harm neither present nor visible, the affective system [of the brain] does not whirl into gear to promote avoidance of harmful action. There isn't an internal signal that warns 'Stop!' and prompts the executive to choose a different course of action.[81]

A significant further key factor that has enabled individuals to engage in, or tolerate unethical conduct, whilst maintaining an ethical self-image, has been a relative lack of individual accountability. The PCBS Report emphasised, as a key factor in the misconduct in financial services, the "striking limitation on the sense of personal responsibility and accountability of the leaders within the industry for the widespread failings and abuses over which they presided".[82] The relative lack of individual accountability (which is being addressed by the new individual accountability regimes) has made it easier for senior individuals to turn a "blind eye" to misconduct, whilst maintaining a self-image as ethical or has facilitated a "narrowing of the cognitive map" of senior individuals, resulting in ethical considerations being "crowded-out".

---

[78] For the famous Princeton Theological Seminary experiment that explores this, see, Darley, J. M., & Batson, C. D. (1973). "From Jerusalem to Jericho": A Study of Situational and Dispositional Variables in Helping Behaviour. *Journal of Personality and Social Psychology*, 27(1), 100–108.

[79] See, e.g. FCA Occasional Paper 24, Behaviour and Compliance in Organisations, December 2016, pp. 22–23, available at: https://www.fca.org.uk/publication/occasional-papers/op16-24.pdf.

[80] See, e.g. Greene, J. D., Nystrom, L. E., Engell, A. D., Darley, J. M., & Cohen, J. D. (2004). The Neural Bases of Cognitive Conflict and Control in Moral Judgement. *Neuron*, 44(2), 389–400. See also, Greene, J. D. (2013). *Moral Tribes*. Penguin Press.

[81] Soltes, E. (2016). *Why They Do It: Inside the Mind of the White-Collar Criminal*. PublicAffairs, 124.

[82] PCBS Report, Vol. I, para. 14.

In summary, in order for regulators and other interested parties to influence and improve behaviours in the financial services industry, it will be important for them to understand that it is not simply a matter of dealing with "bad apples"; it will also be a matter of influencing the behaviours of individuals who perceive themselves as "good" but who do not recognise the negative ethical implications of their actions.[83] A key element will involve making it more difficult for individuals to maintain a self-image as an ethical person whilst engaging in, or tolerating, unethical or illegal acts.

3.2 Firms' Culture: The Influence of the Shareholder Primacy Norm

An individual's motivations for engaging in unethical conduct, discussed in the previous section, will be strongly influenced by the culture of the firm in which the individual operates, which is considered in this section. In this very brief discussion of this issue, the focus is on the implications of the shareholder value norm on individual behaviours. Whilst the shareholder value norm is an industry-wide factor influencing individual behaviours, the influence of this norm may differ from firm to firm, hence it is considered in this section rather than the following section which addresses wider structural factors.

Research suggests that individuals learn and adopt values, attitudes, and behaviours of their organisations that can lead them to engage in misconduct that they can justify to themselves.[84] Individuals want to fit in, or identify with, the prevailing organisational culture, to "act banker".[85] In this regard, some scholars note that organisational wrongdoing is "socially organized and systematically produced by social structures … embedded in the banality of organizational life".[86] As stated by the FCA, individuals will change their beliefs and behaviours to fit in with their organisational culture:

---

[83] See, e.g. Feldman, Y. (2018). *The Law of Good People: Challenging States' Ability to Regulate Human Behavior*. Cambridge University Press; Bazerman, M. H., & Tenbrunsel, A. E. (2011). *Blind Spots*. Princeton University Press.

[84] Cressey, D. R. (1986). Why Managers Commit Fraud. *Australian & New Zealand Journal of Criminology*, 19(4), 195–209, 195–196. See, also e.g. McGrath, J. (2019). Why Do Good People Do Bad Things: A Multi-level Analysis of Individual, Organizational, and Structural Causes of White-Collar Crime. *Seattle University Law Review*, 43, 525–554.

[85] A. Haldane, Bank of England, Worthy of Trust? Law, Ethics and Culture in Banking, UK Banking Standards Board Blog Series, p. 18, available at: https://financialservicescultureboard.org.uk/wp-content/uploads/2017/12/Worthy-of-trust-Nov17.pdf.

[86] Vaughan, D. (1996). *The Challenger Launch Decision: Risky Technology, Culture, and Deviance at NASA*. University of Chicago Press, xiv.

There is strong evidence of the effect of organisational culture and social norms on the likelihood of rule breaking, with factors such as the extent of disapproval among peers being a strong predictor of the likelihood of rule breaking. Experimental evidence suggests that rule breaking is contagious, becoming more widespread when people from one's own group are seen breaking rules, whereas seeing 'outsiders' cheat can actually reduce such infringements.[87]

What do we mean by a firm's culture and how can this be analysed? The organisational psychologist Edgar Schein has developed a very influential framework for identifying and assessing organisational culture. According to Schein, culture exists simultaneously on three different levels: on the surface are "visible and feelable" artefacts; under the surface are espoused values and beliefs; at the core is the key level of taken-for-granted underlying basic assumptions. These are assumptions about behaviour, where members of a group holding these assumptions may find behaviour based on any other premise "inconceivable".[88] The Dutch regulator, De Nederlandsche Bank, has described this third layer as the "mindset".[89] Schein has stated that, "where there is a culture in an organisation involving widespread discrepancies between desired behaviors and observed behaviors, leaders seeking to achieve cultural change will need to "locate the cultural DNA and change some of that".[90] An important element of the mind-set within financial services firms is likely to involve assumptions in relation to the purpose of the firm and the influence of the shareholder primacy norm. This may include assumptions about the (ir)relevance of ethical considerations when considering a course of action that may be within the letter of the law and may be profit-maximising for shareholders, at least in the short term, but detrimental for customers.

The on-going debates around shareholder primacy go back at least to the famous Berle and Means/Dodd debates on these issues in the 1930s in the United States.[91] These debates have evolved over time, taking account of the particular political, social, and economic context. From the early 1960s, the

---

[87] Behaviour and Compliance in Organisations. (2016). FCA, p. 28, available at: https://www.fca.org.uk/publications/occasional-papers/no-24-behaviour-compliance-organisations.

[88] Schein, E., & Schein, P. (2017). *Organisational Culture and Leadership*. 5th ed. Wiley, 21–22.

[89] Supervision of Behaviour and Culture: Foundations, Practice & Future Developments, DNB, p. 51.

[90] Schein, E., & Schein, P. (2017). *Organisational Culture and Leadership*. 5th ed. Wiley, 27.

[91] An excellent analysis of the history of these debates can be found in Bratton, W. W., & Wachter, M. L. (2008). Shareholder Primacy's Corporatist Origins: Adolf Berle and the Modern Corporation. *Journal of Corporation Law*, 34, 99–152. See also, O'Kelley, C. R. (2013). The Evolution of the Modern Corporation: Corporate Governance Reform in Context. *University of Illinois Law Review*, 1001–1050.

debate significantly shifted, in light of the increasing influence of neoclassical economic and libertarian thinking. In particular, Friedman advanced the theory of shareholder primacy, arguing that as agents of the firm's owners (the shareholders) the duty of the managers of a firm was to maximise profits for shareholders, so long as they stayed within the rules.[92] He asserted that for an executive to spend other people's (i.e. the shareholders') money on "social responsibility" or any purposes other than profit-maximisation for shareholders would be "intolerable", as the executive would in effect be making use of shareholder funds to address issues that should more properly be addressed by politicians or civil servants.[93]

The shareholder primacy norm does not assume that the directors and executives will disregard stakeholders other than shareholders. Indeed, it is unlikely that the interests of shareholders (particularly their longer-term interests) would be served if the company's directors and executives chose to ignore the concerns of its employees, customers, and other stakeholders. In reality, however, it is a short step for many company executives to conflate the shareholder primacy norm with a norm that requires them to focus solely or mainly on short-term profit-maximisation for shareholders, and essentially ignore ethical norms not embodied in legal requirements, particularly when pressurised by shareholders (or their representatives, such as hedge funds) with short-term shareholding interests.[94]

Indeed, a shareholder value norm evolved from the shareholder primacy norm. The shareholder value norm became influential as a concept in business, in particular, from the early 1980s.[95] Its early influence is ascribed by some to Jack Welch, the then CEO of General Electric in 1981,[96] though he later rejected it as "the dumbest idea in the world".[97] This norm prioritises the maximisation of shareholder returns in the shorter term, particularly by

---

[92] Friedman, M. (1962). *Capital and Freedom.* Chicago University Press.

[93] Friedman, M. (1970). The Social Responsibility of Business Is to Increase Its Profits. *New York Times Magazine* (13 September), available at: http://www.umich.edu/~thecore/doc/Friedman.pdf.

[94] The psychologist Dan Ariely, for example, has stated that "I suspect that companies that adapt the ideology of maximising shareholder value above all else can use this motto to justify a broad range of misbehaviours, from financial to legal to environmental cheating. The fact that the compensation of the executives is linked to the stock price probably only increases their commitment to 'shareholder value'" (Ariely, D. [2012]. *The (Honest) Truth About Dishonesty.* Harper Collins Publishers, 208.

[95] For a history of the development of the norm see e.g. Heilbron, J., Verheul, J., & Quak, S. (2014). The Origins and Early Diffusion of "Shareholder Value" in the United States. *Theory and Society,* 43(1), 1–22.

[96] Kay J. (2016). *Other People's Money: Masters of the Universe or Servants of the People?* Profile Books, 46.

[97] See e.g. Denning, S. (2011). The Dumbest Idea in the World: Maximising Shareholder Value. *Forbes* (28 November), available at: https://www.forbes.com/sites/stevedenning/2011/11/28/maximi zing-shareholder-value-the-dumbest-idea-in-the-world/#468b818d2287.

reference to share price valuations. The norm has been heavily criticised for its negative impacts on society.[98] It "has especially been held to have been a root cause of the global financial crisis".[99]

Proponents of the shareholder primacy norm claim that it enhances the welfare of society by encouraging economic efficiency and that any social costs of its activities are limited because of restrictions imposed by law and regulation.[100] This argument has been sharply criticised, on the basis that firms are more likely to "game" the legal and regulatory requirements they face than comply with the letter and spirit of the requirements.[101] Firms may be more likely to adopt an "is it legal?" approach and not consider themselves to be constrained in their activities by ethical considerations that are not reflected in the clear letter of law and regulation.[102]

There is very considerable on-going academic and public debate in relation to the role of the corporation in society, the shareholder value norm, and the extent to which corporations should take into account the interests of other stakeholders,[103] with some suggesting that "[a] battle rages between the partisans of shareholder and stakeholder capitalism; the very heart and soul of corporate governance is at stake".[104] In this context, the recent US Business Roundtable's revised "Statement on the purpose of the corporation"

---

[98] See, e.g. Stout, L. A. (2012). *The Shareholder Value Myth: How Putting Shareholders First Harms Investors, Corporations, and the Public*. Berrett-Koehler Publishers.

[99] Hodges, C. (2015). *Law and Corporate Behaviour: Integrating Theories of Regulation, Enforcement, Compliance, and Ethics*. Bloomsbury, 675.

[100] See, e.g. Armour J., & Gordon J. (2014). Systemic Harms and the Limits of Shareholder Value. In Morris, N., & Vines, D. eds., *Capital Failure: Rebuilding Trust in Financial Services*. Oxford University Press, 234–251.

[101] Ibid.

[102] See, e.g. Speech by Ed Sibley, Deputy Governor of the CBI, 14 November 2017, in which he sharply criticised the "is it legal?" approach of financial institutions: "Decisions were made in the short-term interest of the shareholder (or at least management's interpretation of it), and whether decisions were legal, with too little consideration of whether they were ethical or in the interests of the customer. Ironically, this behaviour has been massively destructive for long-term shareholder value, as well as customers, and financial stability"; https://centralbank.ie/news/article/is-it-legal-a-que stion-of-culture---deputy-governor-ed-sibley.

[103] See e.g. Stout, L. A. (2012). *The Shareholder Value Myth: How Putting Shareholders First Harms Investors, Corporations, and the Public*. Berrett-Koehler Publishers; Hsieh, N. H., Meyer, M., Rodin, D., & van't Klooster, J. (2018). The Social Purpose of Corporations. *Journal of the British Academy*, 49–73; Kershaw, D., & Schuster, E. P. (2019). The Purposive Transformation of Corporate Law. LSE Legal Studies Working Paper No. 4/2019. Available at: https://papers.ssrn.com/sol3/papers.cfm?abs tract_id=3363267; Bebchuk, L., & Tallarita, R. (2020). The Illusory Promise of Stakeholder Governance. *Cornell Law Review*, 106, 91–177; Hopt K. (2020). Corporate Governance of Banks and Financial Institutions: Economic Theory, Supervisory Practice, Evidence, and Policy. European Corporate Governance Institute working paper 507/2020. Available at: https://papers.ssrn.com/sol3/papers. cfm?abstract_id=3553780.

[104] Rogge, M. (2020). Bringing Corporate Governance Down to Earth: From *Culmination* Outcomes to *Comprehensive* Outcomes in shareholder and Stakeholder Capitalism, April Working Paper No. 72, Harvard Kennedy School, p. 1. Available at: https://doi.org/10.2139/ssrn.3572765. See, also, the

is an interesting development.[105] The accompanying press release stated that this revised Statement moved the debate away from shareholder primacy and included a fundamental commitment to all stakeholders, including customers and employees.[106] The new statement was signed by 181 CEOs of many of the largest companies in the United States and a number of global financial institutions.

This revised US Business Roundtable Statement has been roundly criticised by some as being a mere public relations exercise with little or no impact on the approach adopted by corporations to its stakeholders and aiming to progress a "managerialist" agenda to reduce the accountability of managers to shareholders for their actions.[107] Nevertheless, despite this concern about "managerialism", Larry Fink, the CEO of BlackRock, the largest asset management firm in the world, issued a letter to CEOs stating that "the importance of serving stakeholders and embracing purpose is becoming increasingly central to the way that companies understand their role in society… a company cannot achieve long-term profits without embracing purpose and considering the needs of a broad range of stakeholders".[108]

The foregoing demonstrates the history of short-term profit-maximisation and shareholder primacy norms in corporations. The centrality of these norms to corporate life is important because they have a significant impact on organisational cultures and, therefore, individual decision-making.

3.3   Structural Issues: The Nature of the Financial Services Industry

Whilst individual decision-making will be very significantly influenced at the levels of individual motivations and the culture of the firm in which individuals operate, as discussed in the previous sections, a further, inter-related, level of influence affecting individual decision-making is the structure and norms of the wider industry (and stakeholders, such as regulators). These

---

series of essays in 2020 10(3) *Accounting, Economics and Law: A Convivium*, "The Corporate Issue: A Tribute to Lynn Stout".

[105] Statement on the Purpose of a Corporation, August 2019, available at: https://opportunity.busine ssroundtable.org/ourcommitment/.

[106] US Business Roundtable, Press Release. (2019). Available at: https://www.businessroundtable. org/business-roundtable-redefines-the-purpose-of-a-corporation-to-promote-an-economy-that-serves-all-americans.

[107] See, in particular, Bebchuk, L., & Tallarita, R. (2020). The Illusory Promise of Stakeholder Governance. *Cornell Law Review*, 106, 91–177.

[108] Fink, L. (2020). A Fundamental Reshaping of Finance, available at: https://www.freshlawblog. com/wp-content/uploads/sites/15/2020/05/Larry-Finks-2020-Letter-to-CEOs-BlackRock.pdf.

levels are inter-related, so some of the factors at the level of industry structure and norms (such as the shareholder value norm, the impact of market competition, the "morals of the marketplace", and the industry-wide normalisation of poor behaviours) have already been discussed in the previous sections.

Of the very wide range of industry and societal structural factors and norms influencing behaviours at the level of firms and individuals, this section very briefly discusses one that relates to the inherent nature of the financial services industry: the role of the financial services industry in the management of risk.

A core feature of the financial services industry is its focus on managing risk.[109] Firms and individuals typically rely on the financial services industry to ensure that their finances (mortgages, investments, insurance etc.) are managed to take account of the risks of future events that may have a material positive or negative impact on their finances. The risks that need to be managed can materialise from some combination of a change in individual circumstances (e.g. loss of job; damage or loss of property; business reduction or failure) or external financial circumstances (e.g. rises or falls in interest rates, global trade flows, stock market performance). Uncertain future events are not necessarily negative; they can include favourable investment outcomes.[110] They are, however, typically very hard or impossible to predict by their nature. This inherent uncertainty in financial risk management has led regulators to require financial services firms to provide appropriate warnings to consumers about this inherent uncertainty.[111] The required warnings to consumers may be along the lines of "the value of your investment may go down as well as up". This inherent uncertainty does not exist to an equivalent extent in most other industries (in which firms are very unlikely to be required to inform their customers that their products or services might, or might not, work).

This points to the critical importance of trust for the proper functioning of the financial services industry, to an extent that is greater than in many other industries. As stated by the Dutch regulator, De Nederlandsche Bank

---

[109] See, e.g. Shiller, R. J. (2009). *The New Financial Order: Risk in the 21st Century*. Princeton University Press.

[110] See, e.g. Buckle, M., & Thompson, J. (2020). Financial Intermediation and Recent Developments in the UK Financial System. In Buckle, M & Thompson, J. *The UK Financial System: Theory and Practice*. Manchester University Press.

[111] For a discussion of the types of warnings that regulators may require, see, e.g. Awrey, D., Blair, W., & Kershaw, D. (2013). Between Law and Markets: Is There a Role for Culture and Ethics in Financial Regulation. *Delaware Journal of Corporate Law*, 38, 191–246, 200–202.

(DNB), "trust is the foundation on which our financial system is built".[112] If the financial services industry is not trusted, customers may choose to engage less by investing less in their pension, saving less, or purchasing fewer financial services products. This, in turn, "will damage both the industry and the economy, by reducing the availability of capital for productive purposes".[113] A difficulty with developing trust in the financial services industry, however, is that historically the industry has been subject to frequent "boom and bust" cycles.[114] This can lead to investors and consumers making financial decisions (and being encouraged to do so by the financial services industry), particularly during the "boom" part of the cycle that eventually turn out badly for the investors and consumers, leading to increased distrust in the financial services industry.[115] As stated in the PCBS Report, the "'irrational exuberance' of the build-up to the [2007–8] financial crisis reads as a lesson in failing to learn the lessons of history".[116]

Furthermore, the financial services sector is typically characterised by information asymmetry as between the financial services firms and their customers, particularly retail customers. Financial services firms will usually be in a far better position than their customers to assess the financial risks of the products being offered, and may use this position to take advantage of customers. This is a particular concern, as outlined above, in retail markets, where there is a real problem of low levels of financial literacy amongst customers. Indeed, even in competitive markets which should give rise to better customer outcomes, Akerlof and Shiller have argued that sellers (including in financial services markets) systematically exploit, for their profit, our psychological weaknesses and our ignorance through manipulation and deception.[117]

---

[112] Raaijmakers, M., et al. (2015). Supervision of Behaviour and Culture: Foundations, Practice & Future Developments. DNB, p. 30. Available at: https://www.dnb.nl/media/1gmkp1vk/supervision-of-behaviour-and-culture_tcm46-380398-1.pdf.

[113] Jaffer, S., Morris, N., & Vines, D. (2014). Why Trustworthiness Is Important. In *Capital Failure: Rebuilding Trust in Financial Services*. Oxford University Press, 8.

[114] For a general discussion of this issue, see, e.g. Quinn, W., & Turner, J. D. (2020). *Boom and Bust: A Global History of Financial Bubbles*. Cambridge University Press.

[115] As stated by then US Treasury Secretary, Tim Geithner, in a written submission to the US Congress in 2009, "A long period of home price appreciation encouraged borrowers, lenders, and investors to make choices that could only succeed if home prices continued to appreciate. We had a system under which firms encouraged people to take unwise risks on complicated products, with ruinous results for them and for our financial system". Available at: https://www.treasury.gov/press-center/press-releases/Pages/tg71.aspx.

[116] PCBS Report, Vol. II, para. 58.

[117] Akerlof, G. A., & Shiller, R. J. (2015). *Phishing for Phools: The Economics of Manipulation and Deception*. Princeton University Press, xii.

In summary, the inherent uncertainty in the management of financial risks, together with the typical information asymmetry between financial services firms and their customers can create industry-wide opportunities for unethical behaviours and the taking advantage of customers.

4   Conclusion

The problem of unethical conduct in the financial services industry is systemic in the sense that it is clearly a regular occurrence and very widespread internationally. It is also not confined to an identifiable and limited number of firms or individuals. To some extent, this is a reflection of an increase in unethical conduct across industries more generally. This chapter analysed a number of factors that give rise to this systemic problem, focusing separately on individual-specific, organisational and wider structural factors. At the individual level, it is clear that individuals in the financial services industry can be incentivised and pressured to engage in misconduct. There are also opportunities for misconduct that are particular to the financial services industry. Since the GFC, regulators internationally have made significant efforts to tackle the incentives (such as remuneration) and opportunities (such as ineffective internal controls) that give rise to misconduct in the industry. They have also increased their focus on going beyond the symptoms of misconduct to assess and supervise cultural factors in firms that can give rise to it. Regulators will also benefit from the considerable on-going research in the behavioural sciences that is providing increasingly valuable insights into why people who have a strong self-image as being ethical engage in unethical conduct. Addressing this is a key element for improving behaviours in the financial services industry.

At the organisational level, one of the factors that can give rise to the prioritisation of short-term profitability over ethical considerations, which is not specific to the financial services industry, is the influence of the shareholder value norm. The shareholder value norm tends to focus the minds of executives of firms on the interests of shareholders (particularly their shorter-term interests), sometimes to the detriment of the interests of other stakeholders, such as customers, unless these other interests are protected by specific legal requirements on firms. This can lead to a "narrowing of the cognitive map" and a lack of adequate consideration of ethical aspects in business decision-making, thereby facilitating misconduct. In order to improve the culture of financial services firms, the firms and their regulators need to engage more fully in the wider academic and policy debate on the shareholder value norm and the purpose of a company.

Furthermore, the role of financial services, in terms of managing financial risks for customers, combined with information asymmetry between firms and their customers is one of the wider structural factors that gives rise to the potential for misconduct.

4

Generating Cultures of Compliance: The Limits of the "Big Stick"

1   Introduction

Many jurisdictions are increasingly concerned with crime in financial services and are responding in increasingly stringent ways to this form of wrong-doing.[1] These responses are emerging because of a greater recognition that financial crimes can be as harmful as so-called ordinary crimes and because of the increased demand for corporate accountability.[2] It is also recognised that under-enforcement can threaten the State's reputation as an attractive place in which to do business and that legitimate market players must be protected from the fraudulent activities of others.[3] Similarly, over-enforcement can threaten the State's desirability as a location to do business, but for different reasons.

Enforcement and sanctioning practices, however, can be more compli-cated than laws, public attitudes, or political rhetoric which demand tougher

---

[1] Rorie, M. L. (2019). *The Handbook of White-Collar Crime*. Wiley; van Erp, J., Huisman, W., & Walle, G. V. (Eds.). (2015). *The Routledge Handbook of White-Collar and Corporate Crime in Europe*. Routledge.

[2] Cullen, F. T., Hartman, J. L., & Lero Jonson, C. (2009). Bad Guys: Why the Public Supports Punishing White-Collar Offenders. *Crime, Law, and Social Change*, 51, 31–44.

[3] McGrath, J. (2015). *Corporate and White-Collar Crime in Ireland: A New Architecture of Regulatory Enforcement*. Manchester University Press.

© The Author(s), under exclusive license to Springer Nature
Switzerland AG 2022
J. McGrath and C. Walker, *New Accountability in Financial Services*,
Palgrave Socio-Legal Studies,
https://doi.org/10.1007/978-3-030-88715-5_4

punishments for "bad guys" who engage in misconduct.[4] More punitive laws do not always manifest in harsher punishments and understanding enforcement practices requires more than an understanding of laws. Fewer prosecutions, for example, do not necessarily mean less enforcement, especially when limited resources are targeted at more serious frauds and when enforcement is channelled into the civil enforcement.[5] Countries with bigger economies, which are home to large international businesses, are not necessarily tougher than less significant economic players when enforcing regulations. Some small countries, like Ireland in the late twentieth century, had advertised themselves as "flexible" places in which to do business, perhaps to attract international investment inwards.[6] Other small countries, like Iceland, can suddenly garner a more significant reputation for successfully prosecuting bankers compared with larger countries,[7] like the United States, which has long been considered to be a "role model" or "world leader" for its apparently harsh approach to tackling white-collar crime.[8]

This chapter examines the approach to sanctioning crime in financial services in the UK, Australia, and Ireland since the GFC. It demonstrates that there are new, more punitive, ways of thinking about regulating the financial services sectors in these jurisdictions. This has manifested in new laws and new enforcement practices. In particular, new laws have been introduced to criminalise more forms of wrongdoing and to make it easier to detect, investigate, and harshly punish financial misconduct. Law has been weaponised as politicians and regulators seek to "act out" for public approval. Nevertheless, difficulties remain with enforcement in practice because law alone is a limited instrument in changing behaviour. Sanctions alone may not always generate accountability, do not prevent misconduct, and may not generate meaningful, lasting, cultural change. As observed by the Financial Conduct Authority (FCA) in the UK, "The evidence that we have suggests that there

---

[4] Garland, D. (2018). Theoretical Advances and Problems in the Sociology of Punishment. *Punishment and Society*, 20(1), 8–33; Newburn, T., Jones, T., & Blaustein, J. (2018). Policy Mobilities and Comparative Penalty. *Theoretical Criminology*, 22(4), 563–581.

[5] Healy, D., & McGrath, J. (2019). Simple Rhetoric and Complex Punitiveness: Federal Criminal Justice Responses to White-Collar Criminality. *Justice Quarterly*, 36(7), 1258–1283; McGrath, J., & Healy, D. (2021). Theorising the Drop in White-Collar Crime Prosecutions: An Ecological Model. *Punishment & Society*, 23(2), 164–189.

[6] McGrath, J. (2015). The Prosecution of White-Collar Crime in a Developing Economy: A Case Study of Ireland in the twentieth Century. In van Erp, J., et al. eds., *Handbook on White-Collar Crime in Europe*. Routledge, 399–417.

[7] Will, S. (2015). The Icelandic Approach to the 2008 Banking Crisis. In van Erp, J., et al. eds., *The Routledge Handbook of White-Collar and Corporate Crime in Europe*. Routledge, 276–291.

[8] Francis, A., & Ryder, N. (2019). Preventing and Intervening in White-Collar Crimes: The Role of Regulatory Agencies. In Rorie, M. L. ed., *The Handbook of White-Collar Crime*. Wiley, 262–278.

are limitations on the extent to which greater compliance can be achieved by increasing fines and the probability of detection".[9]

Chapter 2 noted that regulatory tripartism emphasises that State led-enforcement is merely one aspect of an effective regulatory regime; industry may play a self-regulatory role and the capacities of third parties as regulators can also be harnessed in the public interest.[10] This chapter focuses on the State-led aspect of the regulatory pyramid, in which the "big stick" is often a last resort strategy.[11] In particular, this chapter demonstrates considerable practical difficulties with successfully relying on criminal law as a tool to regulate the financial services industry. Whilst there have been quite a number of criminal cases (and civil actions too), this has not led to significant, meaningful, and sustained cultural change. Documenting new ways of thinking, new legislative developments, and changed sanctioning practices requires mapping a significant landscape of enforcement. Doing so in detail would easily exceed the scope of this monograph, let alone this chapter. Accordingly, this chapter seeks to capture the character and movement of enforcement practices after the GFC, rather than comprehensively detail and document them. In taking an analytical rather than an archival approach, this chapter critically describes a truncated version of these developments but which are considered to be representative of the architecture of enforcement more generally.

2   Politicisation: Bankers as Thieves, Crooks, and Terrorists

This section demonstrates that wrongdoing in the financial services sector was politicised after the GFC, as politicians competed to be tough on white-collar crime. This analysis is important because subsequent sections detail how new laws and enforcement practices were introduced in order to act out for public approval, despite doing little to address the underlying organisational cultures and systemic influences generating wrongdoing. In the wake of the GFC in the UK, for example, spurred on further by subsequent scandals, wrongdoing in the financial services sector was intensely politicised.

---

[9] Iscenko, Z., Pickard, C., Smart, L., & Vasas, Z. (2016). Behaviour and Compliance in Organisations. FCA Occasional Paper 24, p. 15.

[10] Ayres, I., & Braithwaite, J. (1992). *Responsive Regulation: Transcending the Deregulation Debate*. Oxford University Press.

[11] Hawkins, K. (2002). *Law as Last Resort: Prosecution Decision-Making in a Regulatory Agency*. Oxford University Press.

In part, public anger was fuelled by reports of enormous bankers' bonuses, as it emerged that "rewards have been paid for failure".[12] The then Prime Minister, Gordon Brown stated: "I'm angry at irresponsible behaviour. And where there is excessive and irresponsible risk-taking, that is going to be punished".[13] David Cameron, the leader of the Conservative Party, promised a "day of reckoning" for bankers in the City.[14] When Cameron became Prime Minister, the Coalition Agreement reached by the Conservative Party and the Liberal Democrats in 2010 pledged to "take white-collar crime as seriously as other crime".[15] The then Chancellor of the Exchequer and Conservative Party member, George Osborne, also promised, "to deal with abuses".[16] In 2015, he stated that bankers were responsible for "the biggest single crash of our lifetimes", explicitly equating traders with common thieves:

> If you go and shoplift at the local WH Smiths you go to prison. But if you're the market trader on the trading floor of a big investment bank, and you rip off people to the tune of millions of pounds, there are no criminal offences to deal with you.[17]

The then Mayor of London, Boris Johnson, agreed that white-collar crime should be "rooted out and punished".[18] Condemnation even seemed to cross heaven and earth when the Archbishop of Canterbury, Justin Welby, weighed in with fire and brimstone, arguing that British banks should clean up the industry, operating with a "fear of hell and the hope of heaven".[19]

---

[12] PCBS, Vol. II, Para. 111.

[13] Brogan, B. (2008). Fat Cats Hit by a Left and a Right: Cameron and Brown Talk Tough on City Bonuses. *Daily Mail* (10 October), available at: https://www.dailymail.co.uk/news/article-1073831/Fat-cats-hit-Left-Right-Cameron-Brown-talk-tough-City-bonuses.html.

[14] Cameron, D. (2008). Conservative Party Conference, available at: https://www.theguardian.com/politics/2008/oct/01/davidcameron.toryconference1.

[15] HM Treasury. (2010). Speech by the Chancellor of the Exchequer, Rt Hon George Osborne MP, at Mansion House, June 16, available at: https://www.gov.uk/government/speeches/speech-by-the-chancellor-of-the-exchequer-rt-hon-george-osborne-mp-at-mansion-house.

[16] Osborne Pledges Criminal Action Against Banks and Traders, 11 June 2014, available at: https://www.bbc.com/news/business-27805419.

[17] Spense, P., & Wallace, T. (2015). Bad Bankers Are Like Shoplifters, Says George Osborne. *The Telegraph* (11 November), available at: https://www.telegraph.co.uk/finance/financial-crime/11988110/Bad-bankers-are-like-shoplifters-says-George-Osborne.html.

[18] Kuchler, H., & Jenkins, P. (2013). David Cameron Backs Criminal Sanctions for 'Reckless' Bankers. *Financial Times* (19 June), available at: https://www.ft.com/content/3a711c1c-d8b4-11e2-a6cf-00144feab7de.

[19] Salmon, J. (2013). Jail Rogue Bankers in the Future, Say MPs. *Daily Mail* (14 June), available at: http://www.dailymail.co.uk/news/article-2341363/Jail-rogue-bankers-future-say-MPs-Long-awaited-report-criminal-sanctions-involved-banking-scandals.html.

Channelling public sentiments, the Parliamentary Commission on Banking Standards Report (PCBS Report) stated in 2013:

> The public have the sense that advantage has been taken of them, that bankers have received huge rewards, that some of those rewards have not been properly earned, and in some cases have been obtained through dishonesty, and that these huge rewards are excessive, bearing little or no relationship to the value of the work done. The public are angry that senior executives have managed to evade responsibility. They want those at the highest levels of the banks held accountable for the mis-selling and poor practice.[20]

White-collar crime was similarly politicised in Ireland and Australia in the same period. In Ireland, extensive wrongdoing in the financial services sector was revealed, precipitated by light-touch regulation and ineffective enforcement.[21] Ireland experienced a severe economic crisis in which the national economy declined and the rate of unemployment soared from 4.8% in 2007 to 15% by 2012.[22] These events were the tipping point that crystallised sentiments that had been growing for some time.[23] The then Taoiseach (Prime Minister), Brian Cowen acknowledged the "inadequacy of financial regulatory controls" and the "failure to implement more intensive compliance regulation".[24] The then Minister for Justice in 2009, Dermot Ahern, emphasised that the law would "bring to justice those who may have played hard and fast with the financial security of this country [and] that, whether you have a balaclava, a sawn-off shotgun or a white-collar and designer suit, the same rules apply".[25] Minister for Transport, Noel Dempsey, opined that bankers

---

[20] Changing Banking for Good, UK Parliamentary Commission on Banking Standards. The Stationery Office Limited. Vol. I, p. 15, para. 8, available at: https://publications.parliament.uk/pa/jt201314/jtselect/jtpcbs/27/27.pdf; Vol. II, available at: https://www.parliament.uk/globalassets/documents/banking-commission/Banking-final-report-vol-ii.pdf.

[21] Honohan, P. (2010). *The Irish Banking Crisis Regulatory and Financial Stability Policy 2003–2008.* Dublin. Central Bank; Regling, K., & Watson, M. (2010). *A Preliminary Report on the Sources of Ireland's Banking Crisis.* Dublin: Stationery Office.

[22] Central Statistics Office. Measuring Ireland's Progress 2013, available at: https://www.cso.ie/en/releasesandpublications/ep/p-mip/measuringirelandsprogress2013/economy/economy-employmentunemployment/.

[23] McGrath, J. (2015). *Corporate and White-Collar Crime in Ireland: A New Architecture of Regulatory Enforcement.* Manchester University Press.

[24] Cowen, B. (2010). Speech by An Taoiseach, Mr. Brian Cowen TD, North Dublin Chamber of Commerce, Dublin City University—'The Irish Banking Crisis'—'The Mistakes, the Responses, and the Lessons'—13 May, Dublin: Department of the Taoiseach.

[25] Gardaí Raid Offices of Anglo Irish Bank in Dublin, *Irish Times*, 25 February 2009, 1, available at: https://www.irishtimes.com/news/garda%C3%AD-raid-offices-of-anglo-irish-bank-in-dublin-1.836618.

were guilty of "economic treason".[26] Not to be outdone, then opposition spokesman and subsequent Taoiseach, Leo Varadkar, stated that bankers did more damage than the Irish Republican Army (IRA) to the State and should be treated like subversives.[27] Similarly, in Australia, Prime Minister, Kevin Rudd, announced that "the great neo-liberal experiment of the past 30 years has failed" and blamed the GFC on "free-market fundamentalism, extreme capitalism, and excessive greed which became the economic orthodoxy of our time".[28] He continued, "we are still cleaning up the mess of the twenty-first-century children of Gordon Gekko",[29] referencing the infamous movie character who once claimed that "greed is good".[30] Much like other politicians in Ireland and the UK, Rudd complained that bankers had claimed enormous bonuses in the years before the GFC, as they "literally laughed all the way to the bank".[31] Other Australian politicians also "slammed" and "roasted" bankers, calling them "white-collar crooks" who act in a "predatory" manner.[32]

The GFC was not the only stimulus for change in these jurisdictions. Various inquiries and investigations revealed significant wrongdoing in the financial sector in the UK. As discussed in Chapter 3, banks had fraudulently rigged the London Inter-Bank Offered Rate (LIBOR) and other benchmarks, like the Euro Interbank Offered Rate (EURIBOR).[33] Transcripts of conversations between the traders demonstrated a willingness to vary interest rates with regularity, as reflected by a trader saying he was "like a whore's drawers" in his eagerness to move rates up and down, promising a steak dinner and Bollinger champagne as a token of gratitude for rate changes. The PCBS Report noted such conversations demonstrated "casual corruption set against

---

[26] McGee, H. (2009). Dempsey Accuses Wrongdoers at Anglo of Economic Treason. *Irish Times* (24 February), 1.

[27] Burke-Kennedy, E. (2010). Bankers Did More Economic Damage Than IRA. *Irish Times* (29 October), 10.

[28] Rudd, K. (2009). The Global Financial Crisis. *The Monthly* (February), 20, available at: https://www.themonthly.com.au/issue/2009/february/1319602475/kevin-rudd/global-financial-crisis#mtr.

[29] Rudd, K. (2008). The Children of Gordon Gekko. *The Australian* (6 October), 8.

[30] This is loosely based on the statement made by Ivan Boesky who was convicted of insider trading. For an accessible and engaging account of this individuals exploits, as located in the broader cultural and market context, see: Stewart, J. (1992). *Den of Thieves*. Simon & Schuster.

[31] Rudd, K. (2008). The Children of Gordon Gekko. *The Australian* (6 October), 8.

[32] Coorey, P. (2016). Malcolm Turnbull Slams Banks, Saying They Have 'Not Always Treated Customers Right'. *Financial Review* (6 April), available at: https://www.afr.com/politics/malcolm-turnbull-slams-banks-saying-they-have-not-always-treated-customers-right-20160406-gnzcm3.

[33] Wheatley, M. (2012). The Wheatley Review of Libor. *Final Report*. Available at: https://assets.publishing.service.gov.uk/government/uploads/system/uploads/attachment_data/file/191762/wheatley_review_libor_finalreport_280912.pdf.

a luxurious lifestyle".[34] Similarly, the Salz Review into Barclays' activities noted that conversations "seemed to confirm a pervasive, much-caricatured, unethical, greedy, and selfish behaviour on the trading floors of investment banks".[35] Public confidence in the banking sector was further damaged, as Ed Balls MP acknowledged the "massive public anger that has erupted".[36] In addition, as previously discussed, it also emerged that banks had mis-sold Payment Protection Insurance (PPI) to customers, generating massive profits whilst rarely making payments on those policies to customers.[37] These scandals suggested the banks were characterised by a culture of routine corporate irresponsibility which was insufficiently customer-oriented. As other allegations of serious financial wrongdoing emerged, the PCBS noted that this was a period of "scandal after scandal" in the banking sector. Moreover, there was a growing dissonance between rising public anger and a more casual attitude from senior representatives from the banking community that sought to minimise the significance of this misconduct. For instance, when a trader in JP Morgan misled regulators and lost over £2 billion, the CEO, Jamie Dimon, called the incident a "tempest in a teapot". In a pithy comment, the PCBS Report noted, "the penny has still not dropped for some at the top of the industry".[38]

Arguably, the most significant instance of financial wrongdoing in Ireland, post-GFC, was the tracker mortgages scandal, described in more detail above in Chapter 3, which resulted in a gross overcharging of customers, and prompted an extensive consumer protection review.[39] The CBI concluded: "These failures have damaged the already fragile public trust in financial institutions—many of which had been bailed out at enormous public cost during the financial crash".[40] Members of the Irish media suggested that this trust would not be restored until banking executives are made accountable for their actions.[41]

---

[34] PCBS Report, Vol. II, para. 41.

[35] Salz Review: An Independent Review of Barclays' Business Practices, April 2013, para. 3.21.

[36] HC Deb 5 July 2012, Col. 1112.

[37] R v FCA [2011] EWHC 999.

[38] PCBS Report, Vol. II, para. 46.

[39] Central Bank of Ireland. (2019). Tracker Mortgage Examination Final Report. Available at: https://www.centralbank.ie/docs/default-source/consumer-hub-library/tracker-issues/update-on-tracker-mortgage-examination---july-2019.pdf?sfvrsn=6.

[40] Ibid., p. 37.

[41] Curran, R. (2020). Trust Won't Return to Banking Until Executives Are Held to Account. *Irish Independent* (27 October), available at: https://www.independent.ie/business/irish/trust-wont-return-to-banking-until-executives-are-held-to-account-39563243.html.

More recently, the CBI fined J&E Davy, Ireland's largest stockbroker, €4.1 million for breaches of regulatory requirements arising out of profitable trading carried out by senior individuals in the firm, including the then CEO, in their personal capacities in bonds the firm acquired from a client. The CBI stated that "[i]n permitting a group of employees to pursue a personal investment opportunity, conflicts of interest were not properly considered, the rules in place in relation to personal account dealing were easily sidestepped and Davy's compliance function was kept in the dark". Once information about the transaction entered the public domain and Davy engaged with the CBI about it, "Davy provided vague and misleading details and wilfully withheld information that would have disclosed the full extent of the wrongdoing as was known to Davy at the time".[42] To date, no individuals have been sanctioned in relation to these matters. Appearing on behalf of the CBI before a parliamentary committee following the fining of the firm, during which she was questioned about individual accountability in the context of this matter, Derville Rowland again called for the introduction of the Senior Executive Accountability Regime (SEAR) to generate greater individual accountability.[43] Deputy Mick Barry agreed that "The long arm of the law needs to feel a few white-collars here".[44]

There have been numerous Australian financial scandals since the GFC. As described above, the Interim Hayne Report catalogued inappropriate actions and misconduct by a range of financial services providers, conducted over many years since the GFC. It catalogued a variety of wrongs including overcharging customers, undisclosed conflicts of interests, failing to exercise due skill and care, irresponsible lending practices, and the inappropriate misselling of products. The case studies presented in the Interim Report brought home the impact of financial misconduct on ordinary members of the public. They were considered to reflect a broader corporate culture in the financial services industry which was: insufficiently consumer-centred; in which individual financial incentives drove unethical behaviours; occurring within a broader corporate culture in which profit maximisation was championed

---

[42] Public Statement, Enforcement Action: Central Bank of Ireland and J&E Davy, March 2021, available at: https://www.centralbank.ie/docs/default-source/news-and-media/legal-notices/settlement-agreements/public-statement-relating-to-settlement-agreement-between-the-central-bank-of-ireland-and-j-e-davy.pdf?sfvrsn=7. See also, Statement of Derville Rowland, available at: https://www.oireachtas.ie/en/oireachtas-tv/video-archive/committees/.

[43] Statement of Derville Rowland, Director General, Financial Conduct, 9 Mar 2021 *Committee on Finance, Public Expenditure and Reform, and Taoiseach*, Engagement with Central Bank of Ireland, available at: https://www.oireachtas.ie/en/oireachtas-tv/video-archive/committees/.

[44] Lord, M. (2021). Miriam Lord: Central Bank Recommends a Shot of Vitamin D for the Davy Gang. *Irish Times* (9 March), available at: https://www.irishtimes.com/news/politics/miriam-lord-central-bank-recommends-a-shot-of-vitamin-d-for-the-davy-gang-1.4505831.

to the neglect of other considerations; where financial service providers were slow or reluctant to remediate wrongdoing; and less than frank in reporting problems to regulators. The Interim Hayne Report also detailed how banks were charging fees for advice to deceased account holders.

Gathering these developments together, politicians sharply criticised financial misconduct in the wake of the GFC and subsequent scandals. Politicians in all three countries condemned bankers using zero-tolerance rhetoric which equated bankers with ordinary criminals. Such rhetoric may merely evidence a politically expedient rationality in which politicians seek to advance themselves by "acting out" for public approval. However, it may also be a strategy to advance new solutions which may not otherwise be realisable. As noted by Miller and Rose, political discourse is "a kind of intellectual machinery or apparatus for rendering reality thinkable in such a way that it is amenable to political deliberations… to codify and contest the nature and limits of political power".[45] As such, this kind of "tough on crime" rhetoric can sometimes be used to justify the fortification of laws to enhance executive power in the fight against white-collar crime in the financial services sector. These developments are discussed below.

3   Weaponising the Law

The previous section showed that financial wrongdoing became politicised in the wake of GFC and other subsequent scandals. Politicians compared bankers to thieves and terrorists. This rhetoric was adopted to give voice to the public's concern with wrongdoing in financial markets and allowed politicians to "act out" for public approval. This section examines how zero-tolerance rhetoric was translated into legal responses to financial misconduct. These responses take the form of new laws and the increased imposition of sanctions in practice. In the first instance, the section demonstrates that the UK, Australia, and Ireland enhanced their respective mechanisms for the detection, investigation, and sanctioning of financial crime. In particular, they criminalised more forms of wrongdoing and bolstered existing sanctions, whilst also proposing and creating alternative sanctioning pathways to addressing financial misconduct. These alternative pathways have taken the form of civil and administrative sanctions and negotiated settlements, amongst others. Moreover, there is a greater willingness to sanction financial

---

[45] Rose, N., & Miller, P. (2010). Political Power Beyond the State: Problematics of Government. *The British Journal of Sociology*, 61, 271–303, 277.

misconduct in practice, both through criminal prosecution and the imposition of civil and administrative sanctions. These issues are teased out in the paragraphs below. In particular, it shows that a number of senior bankers in the UK and Ireland were prosecuted for criminality that occurred during the GFC or which was associated with it. Australia, having already adopted an intrusive approach to financial regulation before the GFC, and which had suffered relatively less damage by international comparisons, did not actively prosecute misconduct arising from the crash in the same way as some other jurisdictions. Much like the UK and Ireland, however, it did actively scrutinise the powers and performance of its regulators. Ultimately, it also "tooled up" its arsenal by enhancing the investigative tools and resources available to enforcers and by ratcheting up punishments for financial wrongdoing.

3.1   UK

Public enforcement of corporate obligations is an important feature of corporate governance in the UK.[46] Before the GFC, the FSA (subsequently the FCA) already possessed a variety of little and big sticks in its arsenal. These tools included public censure,[47] unlimited civil financial penalties for market abuse (insider trading and market manipulation),[48] prohibition orders which prevented persons from conducting investment business,[49] restitution orders which compensated victims,[50] and criminal prosecutions.[51] It operated a responsive model in which it preferred not to take formal enforcement action for transgressions, provided the respondent was cooperative and remediated the breach.[52] After the GFC, however, following intense

---

[46] Armour, J. (2008). Enforcement Strategies in UK Corporate Governance: A Roadmap and Empirical Assessment. In *The Law and Economics of Corporate Governance: Changing Perspectives*.

[47] FSMA 2000 ss 66, 87M, 89, 89K. Whilst a censure may appear on the lower tier of the regulatory pyramid, recent research suggests that this form of reputational sanction is more severe because "their stock price impact is on average nine times larger than the financial penalties imposed by the FSA". See: Armour, J., Mayer, C., & Polo, A. (2017). Regulatory Sanctions and Reputational Damage in Financial Markets. *Journal of Financial and Quantitative Analysis*, 52(4), 1429–1448. Such findings can suggests that the implementation of the responsive model is complicated in practice where softer measures have punitive impacts.

[48] Financial Services and Markets Act 2000, ss. 118, 123.

[49] Financial Services and Markets Act 2000, ss. 56, 63.

[50] Financial Services and Markets Act 2000, ss. 380–384.

[51] Financial Services and Markets Act 2000, ss. 401–402. For an overview of these powers and sanctions, see MacNeil, I. (2007). The Evolution of Regulatory Enforcement Action in the UK Capital Markets: A Case of "Less Is More"? *Capital Markets Law Journal*, 2(4), 345–369.

[52] Financial Services Authority. (2009). *The Enforcement Guide*. London, 12.

criticism of principles-based regulation,[53] new criminal offences were created to address wrongdoing in the financial services sector. Section VII of the Financial Services Act 2012 criminalised various types of financial misconduct, including the making of misleading statements which might induce or inhibit a party from entering into a transaction,[54] and creating a misleading impression as to the value or price of an investment resulting in a gain for himself or a loss for another.[55] Following on from LIBOR manipulations,[56] the statute also criminalised the manipulations of "benchmark" rates used to value or price financial instruments and underlying assets.[57] The Financial Services (Banking Reform) Act 2013 also criminalised the causing of a financial institution to fail.[58] Only a senior manager of a relevant financial institution may commit the offence, which is punishable by up to 7 years imprisonment and an unlimited fine. There were also parallel developments, in the form of the Crime and Courts Act 2013, under which the State is empowered to seek to resolve criminal wrongdoing by negotiating out of the criminal justice process through deferred prosecution agreements.[59]

The UK also actively prosecuted a range of serious financial crimes related to the manipulation of LIBOR, EURIBOR, and illegal capital-raising activities. These crimes are considered to be those most associated with the GFC in the UK because they helped banks to project financial soundness and made trading appear more profitable.[60] The Serious Fraud Office (SFO) prosecuted 13 traders with the offence of conspiracy to defraud for manipulating LIBOR. Eight were acquitted.[61] Five were convicted,[62] one of whom pleaded

---

[53] McNeil, I. (2010). The Trajectory of Regulatory Reform in the UK in the Wake of the Financial Crisis. *European Business Organization Law Review*, 11, 483–526.

[54] Financial Services Act 2012, s. 89.

[55] Financial Services Act 2012, s. 90.

[56] See: Jordanoska, A., & Lord, N. (2020). Scripting the Mechanics of the Benchmark Manipulation Corporate Scandals: The "Guardian" Paradox. *European Journal of Criminology*, 17(1), 9–30.

[57] Financial Services Act 2012, s. 91.

[58] Financial Services (Banking Reform) Act 2013, s. 36.

[59] King, C., & Lord, N. (2018). *Negotiated Justice and Corporate Crime: The Legitimacy of Civil Recovery Orders and Deferred Prosecution Agreements.* Palgrave.

[60] Francis, A., & Ryder, N. (2020). Preventing and Intervening in White-Collar Crimes: The Role of Regulatory Agencies. In Rorie, M. L. (2019), *The Handbook of White-Collar Crime.* Wiley, 262–278.

[61] Five Cleared Over Libor Rate Rigging, 7 May 2018, available at: https://www.bbc.com/news/business-35422866; Sixth Ex-Broker Cleared in London Libor Trial, 28 January 2016, available at: https://www.nytimes.com/2016/01/29/business/dealbook/sixth-ex-broker-cleared-in-london-libor-trial.html; Former Barclays Traders Acquitted in UK's Fourth Libor Trial. Reuters, 6 April 2017, available at: https://www.reuters.com/article/us-court-libor-barclays-idUSKBN178126.

[62] Convicted LIBOR Manipulators Sentenced, Serious Fraud Office. 7 July 2016, available at: https://www.sfo.gov.uk/2016/07/07/text-temporarily-removed-for-legal-reasons/; Lee, G. (2017). FactCheck: How Many Bankers Were Jailed for Their Part in the Financial Crisis? Channel 4 News

guilty.[63] One convicted trader, Tom Hayes, had argued that his actions were common practice, considered legitimate, and encouraged by the banking industry. He received an 11-year prison sentence, reduced on appeal from 14 years, though it was emphasised that serious financial crime merited long custodial sentences.[64] Most of the other cases were unsuccessful. The cases ran for approximately seven years and cost £60 million,[65] where "more have been acquitted than convicted".[66] The conviction of Tom Hayes, is being reviewed by the Criminal Cases Review Commission to determine if the case was a miscarriage of justice.[67]

Following on from the LIBOR investigations, the SFO announced in 2015 it had commenced criminal proceedings against individuals from Deutsche Bank and Barclays Bank for allegedly manipulating EURIBOR.[68] The SFO ultimately issued proceedings against 11 people in these two banks.[69] Some of the defendants noted that there was no formal training on EURIBOR, that they learned on the job, and that the practice of seeking to influence the rate was a routine one, "openly discussed and conducted without subterfuge".[70] In doing so, the evidence reflected that for those prosecuted for LIBOR manipulation, such wrongdoing was common, routine, and expected. These prosecutions also bore mixed results. Some individuals were successfully prosecuted and received jail time. Others fled to jurisdictions that had no equivalent offences, frustrating the SFO's applications for extradition orders.[71] In the end, just seven individuals were tried. Four were convicted

---

(20 November), available at: https://www.channel4.com/news/factcheck/factcheck-how-many-bankers-were-jailed-for-their-part-in-the-financial-crisis.

[63] SFO. (2016). Convicted LIBOR Manipulators Sentenced, available at: https://www.sfo.gov.uk/2016/07/07/text-temporarily-removed-for-legal-reasons/.

[64] R v Hayes [2015] EWCA Crim 1944, para. 109.

[65] King, I. (2019) The Libor Investigation May Be Over but We Haven't Heard the Last of It, 18 October, available at: https://news.sky.com/story/the-libor-investigation-may-be-over-but-we-havent-heard-the-last-of-it-11838780.

[66] Verity, A. (2021). They Wanted to Jail a Banker—I Was That Banker, 22 February, available at: https://www.bbc.com/news/business-56088419.

[67] Godfrey, H. (2021). Tom Hayes Libor Conviction Being Examined for Miscarriage of Justice, 22 February, available at: https://www.cityam.com/tom-hayes-libor-conviction-being-examined-for-miscarriage-of-justice/.

[68] SFO. (2015). SFO Charges First Individuals with EURIBOR Manipulation, available at: https://www.sfo.gov.uk/2015/11/13/sfo-charges-first-individuals-with-euribor-manipulation/.

[69] SFO. (2015). EURIBOR, available at: https://www.sfo.gov.uk/cases/euribor/.

[70] Bermingham & Anor v R. [2020] EWCA Crim 1662.

[71] Ridley, K. (2020). French Court Rejects UK Extradition Request for Convicted Ex Barclays Trader, November 4, available at: https://www.reuters.com/article/france-euribor-extradition-idUSL1N2HQ2UQ; Beioley, K. (2020). UK's SFO Closes Euribor Probe After Extradition Requests Refused, available at: https://www.ft.com/content/e7eb3b07-4efe-42b3-8fee-e56e043da1b9.

(with one absconding) and three were acquitted.[72] The SFO concluded its eight-year investigation of EURIBOR manipulation in 2020. The media noted the results were "mixed" and "messy".[73]

The SFO also attempted to prosecute Barclays Bank and four senior executives for engaging in illegal capital-raising activities. To avoid being bailed out by the British government, Barclays had sought injections of capital in the amount of approximately £4 billion from Qatari entities to improve its balance sheet. A difficulty arose as to whether the fees and payments associated with the capital-raising activities, as recorded in the prospectus and subscription agreements, were false or misleading. On reviewing the evidence, which was considered "of fabulous complexity and intricacy", the Crown Court dismissed all charges against Barclays.[74] It was determined that the executives directly involved in the capital-raising activities could not be considered "the directing mind and will" of the company. In addition, it would not fashion special rules of attribution to fix the intention of these individuals to the bank.[75] Davis LJ, effectively hearing the case on appeal, refused to allow Barclays to be tried on indictment. Barclays was the only bank to be prosecuted for activities related to the financial crisis and all charges were dismissed. As regards the four individuals prosecuted by the SFO, all were acquitted.[76] The SFO also appealed this decision. The Court of Appeal refused the appeal in the case of John Varley, the first CEO of a major bank to be prosecuted for misconduct associated with the GFC.[77] The three others were retried and acquitted by the jury.[78]

---

[72] Ridley, K. (2020). Britain Closes Euribor Enquiry, Withdraws Arrest Warrants, available at: https://www.reuters.com/article/us-britain-euribor-investigation/britain-closes-euribor-enquiry-withdraws-arrest-warrants-idUKKBN23I2SH?edition-redirect=uk.

[73] UK's SFO Closes Euribor Probe After Extradition Requests Refused, available at: https://www.ft.com/content/e7eb3b07-4efe-42b3-8fee-e56e043da1b9.

[74] R v Barclays PLC and Barclays Bank PLC [2018] (Southwark Crown Court).

[75] For an overview, see: Law Commission. (2021). Corporate Criminal Liability, A discussion paper, paras. 2.48–2.60, available at: https://s3-eu-west-2.amazonaws.com/lawcom-prod-storage-11jsxou24 uy7q/uploads/2021/06/Corporate-Criminal-Liability-Discussion-Paper.pdf. It is now presumed that the identification doctrine applies in such cases and that it will only be displaced by other rules of attribution when the application of the identification doctrine would defeat the intention of the legislature and the aims of the statute.

[76] SFO. (2020). Former Barclays Executives Acquitted of Conspiracy to Commit Fraud, available at: https://www.sfo.gov.uk/2020/02/28/former-barclays-executives-acquitted-of-conspiracy-to-commit-fraud/; Regina v John Varley, Roger Jenkins, Thomas Kalaris, Richard Boath [2019] EWCA Crim 1074.

[77] R v John Varley, Roger Jenkins, Thomas Kalaris, Richard Boath [2019] EWCA Crim 1074.

[78] SFO. (2020). Former Barclays Executives Acquitted of Conspiracy to Commit Fraud, available at: https://www.sfo.gov.uk/2020/02/28/former-barclays-executives-acquitted-of-conspiracy-to-commit-fraud/.

Other forms of financial crimes, not associated with the GFC, were also prosecuted, even those that had not traditionally been the subject of enforcement. For example, although insider trading has been a criminal offence in the UK since 1980, it was not prosecuted until 2009, resulting in the conviction of two individuals.[79] There was a significant uptick in enforcement activity thereafter. The FSA (later the FCA) secured 23 convictions for insider trading between 2009 and 2013.[80] There appears, however, to have been a small decline in such prosecutions thereafter. The FCA prosecuted just eight cases and secured just 12 convictions for insider trading between 2013 and 2018.[81] The FCA also commenced criminal proceedings against NatWest for alleged breaches of the Money Laundering Regulations 2007, the first such prosecution under these regulations. In October 2021, Natwest entered pleas of guilty to the charges.[82]

A very small number of cases concerning corporate wrongdoing have been dealt with through negotiated settlements or deferred prosecution agreements (DPAs). DPAs are agreements to suspend and ultimately forgo a prosecution provided the company does not reoffend within a period of time, usually paired with a fine and a commitment to overhaul the company's internal corporate governance arrangements. Although only a small number of DPAs have been concluded, prosecutors in the UK in 2015 entered the first DPA with a financial institution, Standard Bank, for the offence of failing to prevent bribery.[83] Though not yet a significant feature of the regulatory landscape, and though they have yet to be used for offences specified in the Financial Services and Markets Act 2000, some have noted that DPAs represent a hybrid form of regulation, which addresses criminal wrongs

[79] Bromberg, L., Gilligan, G., & Ramsay, I. (2017). The Extent and Intensity of Insider Trading Enforcement—An International Comparison. *Journal of Corporate Law Studies*, 17(1), 73–110, 82.

[80] FCA. (2014). Why Has the FCA's Market Cleanliness Statistic for Takeover Announcements Decreased Since 2009, p. 20, available at: https://www.fca.org.uk/publication/occasional-papers/op-4-market-cleanliness.pdf.

[81] Chapman, B. (2018). FCA: City Watchdog Secures Just 12 Insider Trading Convictions in Five Years. *Independent*, available at: www.independent.co.uk/news/business/news/fca-citylondon-insider-trading-convictions-five-years-financial-conduct-authority-a8167486.html.

[82] FCA. (2021). FCA Starts Criminal Proceedings Against NatWest Plc, available at: https://www.fca.org.uk/news/press-releases/fca-starts-criminal-proceedings-against-natwest-plc; NatWest Plc pleads guilty in criminal proceeding, available at: https://www.fca.org.uk/news/press-releases/natwest-plc-pleads-guilty-criminal-proceedings.

[83] Contrary to Section 7 of the Bribery Act 2010. See further: SFO v Standard Bank plc, 30 November 2015, available at: https://www.judiciary.uk/wp-content/uploads/2015/11/sfo-v-standard-bank_Final_1.pdf.

with civil settlements, with greater potential to emphasise prevention over punishment.[84]

On the face of it, civil sanctions, by contrast, proved to be quite effective in addressing wrongdoing like LIBOR and EURIBOR manipulations, and subsequent misconduct like the mis-selling of PPI. The FSA imposed enormous fines on various banks for these failings.[85] The costs are even higher once corporate governance improvements and class action settlements are included. Citing research by the Conduct Costs Project,[86] MacNeil notes that the total costs imposed on the five big banks in the UK for misconduct in the period of 2011–2015 amounted to £66 billion, much more than the £12 billion which had been imposed in 2008–2012, and was equal to "around three years of pre-tax profits for the banks and therefore represent a major financial burden for the shareholders of those organisations".[87] However, the impact of the fines was limited and did not deter similar misconduct.[88] The FCA fined more banks for the subsequent manipulation of their foreign exchange business (FX).[89] Enormous fines were also imposed for the mis-selling of PPI but they were considered "a tiny proportion of the revenue they

---

[84] Bronitt, S. (2017). Regulatory Bargaining in the Shows of Preventive Justice: Deferred Prosecution Agreements. In Tulich, T., Ananian-Welsh, R., Bronitt, S., & Murray, S. eds., *Regulating Preventive Justice: Principle, Policy, and Paradox*. Routledge, 211–227. See also: Campbell, L. (2019). Trying Corporations: Why Not Prosecute? *Current Issues in Criminal Justice*, 31(2), 269–291.

[85] Financial Services Authority. (2012). UBS Fined £160 Million for Significant Failings in Relation to LIBOR and EURIBOR, available at: https://www.fca.org.uk/news/press-releases/ubs-fined-£160-million-significant-failings-relation-libor-and-euribor; Financial Services Authority. (2013). RBS Fined £87.5 Million for Significant Failings in Relation to LIBOR, available at: https://www.fca.org.uk/news/press-releases/rbs-fined-£875-million-significant-failings-relation-libor; Financial Conduct Authority. (2013). The FCA Fines Rabobank £105 Million for Serious LIBOR-Related Misconduct, available at: https://www.fca.org.uk/news/press-releases/fca-fines-rabobank-£105-million-serious-libor-related-misconduct; Financial Conduct Authority. (2014). Lloyds Banking Group Fined £105m for Serious LIBOR and Other Benchmark Failings, available at: https://www.fca.org.uk/news/press-releases/lloyds-banking-group-fined-£105m-serious-libor-and-other-benchmark-failings; Financial Conduct Authority. (2014). Martin Brokers (UK) Limited Fined £630,000 for Significant Failings in Relation to LIBOR, available at: https://www.fca.org.uk/news/press-releases/martin-brokers-uk-limited-fined-£630000-significant-failings-relation-libor.

[86] CCP Research Foundation. (2015). Conduct Costs Project Report 2015, available at: https://ccpresearchfoundation.com.

[87] MacNeil, I. (2019). Regulating Instead of Punishing: The Senior Managers Regime in the UK. In Ligeti, K., & Tosza, S. eds. (2018), *White-Collar Crime: A Comparative Perspective*. Bloomsbury Publishing, 225–252, 227.

[88] Francis, A., & Ryder, N. (2019). Preventing and Intervening in White-Collar Crimes: The Role of Regulatory Agencies. In Rorie, M. L., *The Handbook of White-Collar Crime*. Wiley, 262–278.

[89] Financial Conduct Authority. (2014). FCA Fines Five Banks £1.1 Billion for FX Failings and Announces Industry—Wide Remediation Programme, available at: https://www.fca.org.uk/news/press-releases/fca-fines-five-banks-£1.1-billion-fx-failings-and-announces-industry-wide-remediation-programme; Financial Conduct Authority. (2015). FCA Fines Barclays £284,432,000 for Forex Failings, available at: https://www.fca.org.uk/news/press-releases/fca-fines-barclays-£284432000-forex-failings.

gained from selling this highly profitable product", suggesting that the fine was merely seen as the cost of doing business.[90] Similarly, when reviewing the fines imposed for LIBOR and EURIBOR manipulation, the PCBS Report noted that "The fines enforced by the FSA on Barclays, UBS, and RBS are by some distance the largest in their history. However, such punishments are unlikely to have any impact on individuals, who have little or no loyalty to the firm and are primarily motivated by short-term revenue generation".[91]

Several conclusions may be discerned from these cases. In the first instance, the UK sought to persevere with difficult, complex, criminal cases that required significant resources to prosecute various forms of financial crimes. These cases were painstakingly built over many years at great cost. The EURIBOR investigations, for example, dating from the time of the GFC, did not conclude until 2020. In the second instance, it is clear that such wrongdoing was not considered by those involved, even those convicted, to be dishonest or criminal. Instead, their activities were routine and expected in the financial services environments in which they operated. They were not "bad apples" acting independently and covertly, they were operating in a "corrupting barrel" where such behaviour was promoted and presumed.[92] These cases demonstrate how cultural contexts can be important facilitators for the commission of crimes. In the third instance, the results of the cases have been mixed. Some cases were successful but most did not result in convictions, which must cast some doubt on the utility of criminal sanctions not only to punish financial misconduct but also to deter it. Often, there were additional struggles in which highly mobile and well-resourced individuals skipped trial and resisted extradition. Nevertheless, when juries did convict, judges imposed substantial prison sentences on offenders. The Law Commission is now undertaking a review of corporate criminal liability with a view to addressing the issues raised by the *Barclays* case and others.[93] Civil sanctions, by contrast, appeared to be quite successful because they generated seemingly enormous fines. In reality, however, they did not deter misconduct and the fines were small compared to the profits of the organisation, furthering the

---

[90] Parliamentary Commission on Banking Standards, Changing Banking for Good. London: The Stationery Office Limited, para. 201. https://publications.parliament.uk/pa/jt201314/jtselect/jtpcbs/27/27ii05.htm.

[91] PCBS Report, Vol. II, para. 202.

[92] Scholten, W., & Ellemers, N. (2016). Bad Apples or Corrupting Barrels? Preventing Traders' Misconduct. *Journal of Financial Regulation and Compliance*, 24(4), 366–382.

[93] See: Law Commission. (2021). Corporate Criminal Liability. A discussion paper, available at: https://s3-eu-west-2.amazonaws.com/lawcom-prod-storage-11jsxou24uy7q/uploads/2021/06/Corporate-Criminal-Liability-Discussion-Paper.pdf. The most likely outcome may be the introduction of a "failure to prevent economic crime" offence, similar to that provided by Section 7 of the Bribery Act 2010.

idea that fines are sometimes seen as the cost of doing business. This suggests that fines do not significantly impact organisations to generate meaningful cultural change.

3.2   Australia

The Australian Prudential Regulation Authority (APRA) and the Australian Securities & Investments Commission (ASIC) play investigative roles in addressing financial crime in Australia. ASIC, in particular, has an important investigative role and although enforcement is merely one of its many statutory functions,[94] it identifies as "a law enforcement agency. We devote around 70% of our regulatory resources to surveillance and enforcement".[95] ASIC may even prosecute some minor regulatory offences.[96] In circumstances where more serious criminality is suspected, however, it refers cases to the Commonwealth Director of Public Prosecutions (CDPP) which prosecutes financial crimes.[97]

Civil and administrative powers and sanctions are also an important part of the regulatory arsenal. ASIC has the power to seek court-imposed civil fines and seek court ordered injunctions.[98] ASIC may also pursue remedies to protect investors and consumers. These include disqualifications from managing a corporation and bans on providing financial services or engaging in credit activities; revoking, suspending, and varying the conditions of a licence; and public warning notices. They are administrative actions that do not require court involvement but ASIC may seek a court-order to disqualify

---

[94] Australian Securities and Investments Commission Act 2001, s.1(2). See Dixon, O., & Hill, J. G. (2018). Australia. The Protection of Investors and the Compensation for their Losses. In Conac, P. H., & Gelter, M. (Eds.). (2019). Global Securities Litigation and Enforcement. Cambridge University Press.

[95] Australian Securities and Investments Commission. (2016). Annual Report 2014–2015 (ASIC), p. 4, available at: https://asic.gov.au/media/3437945/asic-annual-report-2014-15-full.pdf.

[96] Australian Securities and Investments Commission. (2014). Report 387: Penalties for Corporate Wrongdoing (ASIC), pp. 9–10.

[97] A variety of other regulatory and investigative agencies may also refer cases to the CDPP. These include the Australian Federal Police (AFP), the Australian Competition and Consumer Commission (ACCC), Australian Criminal Intelligence Commission, the Australian Taxation Office (ATO), Australian Financial Security Authority (AFSA) and the Department of Human Services. The Attorney-General's Department also works with these agencies to provide legal and policy advice on white-collar crime. In addition, the Serious Financial Crime Taskforce (SFCT), established in 2015, is a multi-agency body designed to bring together knowledge and experience together to fight financial crime.

[98] ASIC, Information Sheet 151, available at: https://download.asic.gov.au/media/1339118/INFO_151_ASIC_approach_to_enforcement_20130916.pdf.

as part of an enforcement action.[99] These civil penalties are considered to be of crucial importance to regulators because they provide "an additional component of the 'pyramid of enforcement', whereby serious misconduct (such as director negligence) could be met with substantial penalties, but without the moral opprobrium of a criminal conviction or a custodial sentence".[100] In order of decreasing severity, the available enforcement methods can be broadly categorised as follows: criminal; civil; administrative; enforceable undertakings/negotiated outcomes; and public warnings.[101] At the base of the pyramid, ASIC possesses informal regulatory tools, including "engagement with industry and stakeholders, surveillance, guidance, education, and policy advice".[102] These act as alternatives to formal enforcement action.

Given that Australia had a stricter approach to regulation before the GFC, and suffered relatively little harm compared to other jurisdictions, it is perhaps understandable that there were fewer prosecutions for wrongdoing associated with the GFC. Nevertheless, some commentators point out that a number of high-profile companies collapsed due to significant corporate wrongdoing in the wake of the GFC, and that still no prosecutions were forthcoming.

For example, in a close analysis of the case of Storm Financial, Haines noted that it encouraged homeowners to re-mortgage their homes and take out loans to invest in an index fund that tracked the prices of shares in leading Australian companies. Whilst generating huge fees, Storm Financial provided misleading reassurances to investors that their homes were safe. Nevertheless, many investors ultimately lost their savings and their homes during the GFC, whilst paying off additional bank loans and increased mortgages. Haines notes that no individuals were prosecuted, although ASIC did pursue civil cases against the directors of Storm Financial, Emmanuel and

---

[99] ASIC, Information Sheet 151, available at: https://download.asic.gov.au/media/1339118/INFO_151_ASIC_approach_to_enforcement_20130916.pdf. See also: Australian Law Reform Commission. (2002). Principled Regulation: Federal Civil and Administrative Penalties in Australia (ALRC), available at: http://www.alrc.gov.au/sites/default/files/pdfs/publications/ALRC95.pdf.

[100] Australian Securities and Investments Commission, *Submission 49*, p. 17. Cited in: Senate Economic References Committee. (2017). "Lifting the Fear and Suppressing the Greed": Penalties for White-Collar Crime and Corporate and Financial Misconduct in Australia, para. 3.8, available at: https://www.aph.gov.au/Parliamentary_Business/Committees/Senate/Economics/WhiteCollarCrime45th/Report.

[101] Ramsay, I., & Webster, M. (2017). ASIC Enforcement Outcomes: Trends and Analysis. *Company and Securities Law Journal*, 35(5), 289–321.

[102] Australian Securities & Investments Commission. (2013). Information Sheet 151, ASIC's Approach to Enforcement, p. 1, available at: http://download.asic.gov.au/media/1339118/INFO_151_ASIC_approach_to_enforcement_20130916.pdf.

Julie Cassimatis.[103] In failing to provide reasonable and appropriate advice to investors, the Federal Court of Australia determined that they breached their duties of care as directors.[104] Although the proceedings cost ASIC some $56 million,[105] the defendants were each fined just $70,000 and received a seven-year disqualification order.[106] On appeal, the Full Court of the Federal Court of Australia upheld the finding that they had breached their duties in 2020, approximately a decade after ASIC first initiated proceedings. The High Court subsequently dismissed the Cassimatises' application for leave to appeal on the 5th of August 2020.[107]

The case is not an isolated one; observers have generally noted that senior company officers are rarely prosecuted for financial crimes despite the existence of evidence of wrongdoing, even in the aftermath of the GFC in Australia.[108] Others have noted that even when ASIC takes enforcement action, it targets the low-hanging fruit and is reluctant to prosecute complex cases or take action against large market players.[109]

Following the recommendations of the Cooney Committee,[110] the Corporate Law Reform Act 1992 prioritised civil sanctions over criminal sanctions for the enforcement of director's duties, mapping enforcement practices onto regulatory theory.[111] The civil enforcement of directors' duties, when sought, has generally proven more successful. Welsh noted that of the 33 known finalised cases for civil penalties for breaches of director's duties taken between

[103] Haines, F. (2017). Corporate and White-Collar Crime. In *The Palgrave Handbook of Australian and New Zealand Criminology, Crime and Justice*. Palgrave Macmillan, 237–249.

[104] Corporations Act 2001, s. 180(1). See: Hanrahan, P. (2018). Directors' Counsel: Not-SD-Perfect Storm. *Company Director*, 34(6), 40.

[105] Walsh, L. (2020). ASIC's Massive Storm Financial Bill Revealed, available at: https://www.afr.com/companies/financial-services/asic-s-massive-storm-financial-bill-revealed-20200519-p54ubf.

[106] Hargovan, A. (2018). Corporate Law: Storm Without Power: Low Civil Penalties for Directors of Storm Financial. *Governance Directions*, 70(4), 197–201.

[107] Vickovich, A. (2020). Storm Financial Directors Found Negligent, a Decade On, available at: https://www.afr.com/companies/financial-services/storm-financial-directors-found-negligent-a-decade-on-20200329-p54eyw. See also: ASIC. (2020). 20-074MR Federal Court confirms Storm Financial directors breached duties. Available at: https://asic.gov.au/about-asic/news-centre/find-a-media-release/2020-releases/20-074mr-federal-court-confirms-storm-financial-directors-breached-duties/.

[108] Walsh, L. (2019). Gone Bust but Not Busted. *The Courier Mail*, 64.

[109] Schmulow, A., Fairweather, K., & Tarrant, J. (2019). Restoring confidence in Consumer Financial Protection Regulation in Australia: A Sisyphean Task? *Federal Law Review*, 47(1), 91–120, 97.

[110] Senate Standing Committee on Legal and Constitutional Affairs. (1989). Company Directors' Duties: Report on the Social and Fiduciary Duties and Obligations of Company Directors.

[111] Gilligan, G., Bird, H., & Ramsay, I. (1999). Civil Penalties and the Enforcement Of Directors' Duties. *University of New South Wales Law Journal*, 22, 417–461.

1993 and 2013, 29 resulted in a declaration of contravention and the imposition of a fine on at least one named respondent.[112] Hedges et al. note
that the banning order (a form of disqualification) has become the dominant
form of corporate enforcement in Australia.[113] In the decade from 2005–
2006 to 2014–2015, they note that there were more banning orders than
all other types of major enforcement actions combined, including criminal
prosecutions by the CDPP and other civil proceedings brought by ASIC.
Such actions are useful for regulators, they note, because they are mostly the
result of administrative decisions taken by ASIC, occurring in the absence
of a court hearing, and do not require adherence to the laws of evidence
that govern criminal prosecutions. Other actions which do not require litigation in court are also popular. For example, in a study of enforcement
actions against liquidators and auditors between 2011 and 2019, Ramsay
and Webster note that ASIC preferred negotiated outcomes and administrative actions over more formal court-based actions. Of the 129 enforcement
actions, just eight were civil outcomes and four were criminal outcomes.[114]
Hedges et al. note, however, that summary prosecutions taken by ASIC for
minor regulatory offences are very frequent but mostly result in small fines.[115]
They estimate that ASIC prosecuted 6,742 cases on a summary basis between
1997 and 2015.[116] In a study of summary offences prosecuted between 2006
and 2010, Kenan determined that 80% of successful prosecutions were for
insolvency-related crimes where individuals failed to assist liquidators,[117] that
96% of all summary prosecutions resulted in fines and that the average fine
was $917.85.[118]

This would suggest that such prosecutions relate to a very constrained
field of wrongdoing, where fines are relatively small, and custodial sentences
are rare. Indeed, just two of the 4,429 contraventions prosecuted by ASIC
resulted in imprisonment.[119] Moreover, whilst the high cumulative numbers

---

[112] Welsh, M. (2014). Realising the Public Potential of Corporate Law: Twenty Years of Civil Penalty
Enforcement in Australia. *Federal Law Review*, 42(1), 1–22.

[113] Hedges, J., Gilligan, G., & Ramsay, I. (2017). Banning Orders: An Empirical Analysis of the
Dominant Mode of Corporate Law Enforcement in Australia. *Sydney Law Review*, 39, 501–537.

[114] Ramsay, I., & Webster, M. (2021). An Analysis of ASIC Enforcement Against Auditors and
Liquidators. *Company and Securities Law Journal*, 38(2), 112–137.

[115] See further: Australian Securities & Investments Commission. (2021). Summary Prosecutions of
Companies and Directors, para. 16, available at: http://asic.gov.au/online-services/search-asicsregisters/
additional-searches/summary-prosecutions-of-companies-and-directors/.

[116] Hedges, J., Gilligan, G., & Ramsay, I. (2017). Banning Orders: An Empirical Analysis of the
Dominant Mode of Corporate Law Enforcement in Australia. *Sydney Law Review*, 39, 501–537.

[117] Contrary to Section 475 and 530A of the Corporations Act 2001.

[118] Keenan, P., Australian Institute of Criminology, & Australia. (2013). Convictions for Summary
Insolvency Offences Committed by Company Directors. Research in Practice, pp. 1–8.

[119] Ibid., p. 5.

of prosecutions may be surprising in a responsive model, Welsh noted there is some gap between this theory and ASICs practices because ASIC often only pursues civil sanctions after it has ruled out a criminal prosecution.[120] This may reflect the political pressure on ASIC to generate prosecutions and evince tough approaches to financial misconduct.

Offering a nuanced view of ASICs activities, Ramsay and Webster note, in an empirical analysis of enforcement from 2011 to 2016, that its choice of enforcement actions and the frequency of their use depends on the area of regulatory responsibility.[121] They determined that most enforcement outcomes are in the areas of small business compliance and deterrence (70% of all of ASICs enforcement activity), then financial services, followed by corporate governance and then market integrity. ASIC is most likely to resort to administrative sanctions in the field of financial services but most likely to resort to criminal sanctions in the field of market integrity, which includes insider trading.

Much like the UK, Australia has demonstrated an increased appetite for prosecuting insider trading. As is the case in Ireland and the UK, insider trading is both a criminal offence and, since 2001, a civil wrong in Australia. Since the GFC, ASIC has demonstrated a preference for criminally prosecuting this misconduct, though it reserves its civil powers for circumstances where "there is either insufficient evidence to criminally prosecute, the conduct falls short of criminality or criminal proceedings are otherwise not available".[122] In an empirical analysis on the enforcement of insider trading laws between 1973 and 2013, Lei and Ramsay show that Australia has increasingly prosecuted insider trading, particularly since the financial crash.[123] Similarly, in an empirical study of insider trading enforcement between 2009 and 2015, comparing enforcement approaches in the UK and Australia, Bromberg et al. determined that Australia took twice as many enforcement actions as the UK, once each jurisdiction was adjusted for market share.[124] In addition, the authors noted that the number of insider dealers being sentenced in Australia exceeded those receiving administrative

---

[120] Welsh, M. (2009). Civil Penalties and Responsive Regulation: The Gap Between Theory and Practice. *Melbourne University Law Review*, 33, 908–933.

[121] Ramsay, I., & Webster, M. (2017). ASIC Enforcement Outcomes: Trends and Analysis. *Company and Securities Law Journal*, 35(5), 289–321.

[122] See Australian and Securities and Investment Commission. (2014). Report 421: ASIC Enforcement Outcomes: July to December 2014.

[123] Lei, V., & Ramsay, I. (2014). Insider Trading Enforcement in Australia. *Law and Financial Markets Review*, 8(3), 214–226.

[124] Bromberg, L., Gilligan, G., & Ramsay, I. (2017). The Extent and Intensity of insider Trading Enforcement—An International Comparison. *Journal of Corporate Law Studies*, 17(1), 73–110, 89.

bans and civil fines. Australian regulators took 30 enforcement actions for 21 insider trading events. In 19 of the 30 cases, jail time was imposed, though approximately half of these sentences were suspended.

Nevertheless, despite the absence of criminal prosecutions for serious financial crimes in the years after the GFC, allowing for insider trading as an exception to that general rule, there was a growing public and political demand for a tougher approach to wrongdoing. This was not stimulated by the GFC but by subsequent scandals, as previously noted. The apparent relative impunity for those committing financial crimes in Australia was such that the Chairman of ASIC, Greg Medcraft, stated in 2014 that the country was a "paradise for white-collar crime".[125] He called for increased civil penalties and more jail time to "lift the fear and suppress the greed" of white-collar criminals. The Australian Senate subsequently instructed the Economics Reference Committee to review the law addressing white-collar crime. Ultimately, it recommended, amongst other things, that the civil penalties for breaching the Corporations Act should be increased, noting that criminal punishments were already broadly in line with international norms.[126] Separately, the Financial System Inquiry (FSI) also recommended that ASIC should intensify its efforts at industry supervision and recommended taking various measures to help it to weed out misconduct. It concluded that ASIC needed greater resources, enhanced regulatory tools, stronger licensing powers, and that wrongdoing should be met with increased criminal and civil penalties.[127]

After that report, the Minister for Revenue and Financial Services, Kelly O'Dwyer, commissioned a task force to review ASIC's enforcement regime. The task force recommended, amongst other things, enhancing the self-reporting requirements for contraventions by financial services and credit licensees, the enhancement of search warrant powers to expand the scope of material subject to search and seizure, providing the ability to intercept phone calls to investigate serious offences, strengthening the requirements relating to licensing powers, broadening the criteria for granting banning orders, and increasing civil and criminal penalties for wrongdoing. In short, the review sought to significantly expand the tools available to the regulator

---

[125] Mitchell, S. (2014). Australia "Paradise" for White-Collar Criminals, Says ASIC Chairman Greg Medcraft. *Sydney Morning Herald*, available at: https://www.smh.com.au/business/australia-paradise-for-whitecollar-criminals-says-asic-chairman-greg-medcraft-20141021-119d99.html.

[126] Senate Economic References Committee. (2017). "Lifting the Fear and Suppressing the Greed": Penalties for White-Collar Crime and Corporate and Financial Misconduct in Australia, available at: https://www.aph.gov.au/Parliamentary_Business/Committees/Senate/Economics/WhiteCollarCrime45th/Report.

[127] The Treasury, Australian Government. (2015). Fit for the Future: A Capability Review of the Australian Securities and Investments Commission, available at: https://treasury.gov.au/publication/fit-for-the-future-a-capability-review-of-the-australian-securities-and-investments-commission.

to more effectively detect, investigate, and punish financial misconduct.[128] The Government responded to the taskforce review by broadly accepting all of its recommendations.[129]

The subsequent Hayne Report, as previously discussed, also investigated misconduct in the financial services industry. As noted by Gilligan, the Royal Commission (resulting in the Hayne Report) was the product of years of "sustained exasperation, anger, and resentment", not only on the part of the public but on the part of:

> many parliamentarians from all the major political parties at not only what seemed to be entrenched systemic misconduct within the Australian financial sector, but also perceived disdain amongst many of the major players within the sector about the prevalence of such misconduct and its harmful impacts.[130]

It represented a tipping point, capturing the public imagination and a desire for change, making the inquiry "regularly front-page news in many newspapers and first feature in national television and radio news broadcasts".[131] This report also generated a push for more criminal prosecutions of white-collar crime following revelations that banks were charging advice fees to deceased account holders.[132] Hayne seemed perplexed that ASIC had not considered whether this misconduct might be liable to prosecution until he prompted ASIC's representative to do so.[133] He noted that punishment should flow from misconduct that was harmful to society and that financial misconduct was harmful to the economy which harmed society in general.[134] Although not directly related to the cases before the Royal Commission, ASIC did seem more willing to prosecute in appropriate cases thereafter when it subsequently successfully prosecuted the Commonwealth Bank for

---

[128] The Treasury, Australian Government. (2017). ASIC Enforcement Review Taskforce 2017, available at: https://treasury.gov.au/sites/default/files/2019-03/ASIC-Enforcement-Review-Report.pdf.

[129] The Treasury, Australian Government. (2018). Australian Government Response to the ASIC Enforcement Review Taskforce Report, available at: https://treasury.gov.au/publication/p2018-282438.

[130] Gilligan, G. (2019). The Hayne Royal Commission—Just Another Piece of Official Discourse? Law and Financial Markets Review, 13(2–3), 114–123, 115.

[131] Ibid., p. 116.

[132] Hayne, K. M., Cosgrove, P., Orr, R., Hodge, M., Dinelli, A., Dias, E., & Costello, M. (2019). Royal Commission into Misconduct in the Banking, Superannuation and Financial Services Industry. Commonwealth of Australia.

[133] Ibid., p. 138.

[134] Ibid., p. 426.

87 counts of charges relating to the sale of life insurance through unsolicited phone calls.[135]

The Treasury Laws Amendment (Strengthening Corporate and Financial Sector Penalties) Act 2019 was enacted to underpin existing corporate obligations with new civil sanctions, to increase maximum periods of imprisonment to 15 years on conviction in certain criminal cases, and increase civil penalties for individuals and companies respectively, and to allow for disgorgement orders. The Government subsequently took action to implement the Hayne Report's proposals and committed to providing ASIC with increased powers in line with the recommendations of ASIC Enforcement Review Taskforce. These measures are set out in the Financial Sector Reform (Hayne Royal Commission Response—Stronger Regulators (2019 Measures)) Act 2020.[136] In parallel with these developments, there were also inquiries to consider the introduction of settlement agreements to enhance the prosecutorial toolkit. In 2016, the Attorney General's Department published its consultation paper seeking views on the introduction of a DPA regime in Australia.[137] The Crimes Legislation Amendment (Combatting Corporate Crime) Bill 2017 was subsequently published. If it had been enacted, it would have empowered the CDPP to enter a DPA with companies for a range of offences, including offences under the Corporations Acts.[138] It lapsed, however, in 2019.[139] A similar bill, the Crimes Legislation Amendment (Combatting Corporate Crime) Bill 2019, if enacted, will introduce DPAs.[140]

Gathering these threads together, there were few prosecutions for serious financial misconduct associated with the GFC and wrongdoing was more likely to be addressed as a breach of directors' duties. Sometimes these cases could be expensive and prolonged. Civil cases seem to have met with

---

[135] Letts, S. (2019). CBA Pleads Guilty to Criminal Breaches over Hawking Life Insurance Policies, 19 November, available at: https://www.abc.net.au/news/2019-11-19/cba-pleads-guilty-to-criminal-bre achs-in-hawking-life-insurance/11717630.

[136] Available at: https://www.legislation.gov.au/Details/C2020A00003. See also: The Treasury, Australian Government. (2020). Implementation of ASIC Enforcement Review Taskforce—Directions Power, available at: https://treasury.gov.au/consultation/c2020-48919h.

[137] AG's Department, Australian Government. (2016). Improving Enforcement Options for Serious Corporate Crime: Consideration of a Deferred Prosecution Agreements Scheme in Australia, available at: https://www.ag.gov.au/sites/default/files/2020-03/A-proposed-model-for-a-deferred-prosec ution-agreement-scheme-in-australia.pdf.

[138] See further: Campbell, L. (2019). Trying Corporations: Why Not Prosecute? *Current Issues in Criminal Justice*, 31(2), 269–291.

[139] Crimes Legislation Amendment (Combatting Corporate Crime) Bill 2017, available at: https://www.aph.gov.au/Parliamentary_Business/Bills_Legislation/Bills_Search_Results/Result?bId=s1108.

[140] Crimes Legislation Amendment (Combatting Corporate Crime) Bill 2019. See also: Campbell, L. (2021). Revisiting and Resituating Deferred Prosecution Agreements in Australia: Lessons from England and Wales. *Sydney Law Review*, 43(2), 187.

more success. Administrative orders were also regularly employed to address wrongdoing and the banning order was the empirically dominant form of corporate enforcement in Australia. ASIC also frequently prosecuted minor criminal cases on a summary basis though these cases often resulted in small fines. In general, the form and frequency of enforcement strategies varied by the enforcement team administering them in particular regulated fields and sectors. ASIC favoured administrative sanctions when addressing financial services contraventions and favoured criminal sanctions for breaches of market integrity rules.

There was, however, a growing public and political demand for a tougher approach to corporate enforcement. Dissatisfaction with an apparently insufficient architecture of enforcement generated a sustained period of catalytic inquiry and scrutiny of both financial misconduct and the regulatory responses to that misconduct. The increased demand for regulatory intervention and corporate accountability gave these inquiries power, revealed systemic abusive activities and inadequate enforcement practices, and set the agenda for new policies. They generated new laws that gave ASIC more powers and ratcheted up both civil and criminal penalties for wrongdoing. Law was valorised and enhanced in the hope it would act as an agent of behavioural change in the financial services sector.

3.3 Ireland

In Ireland, the State also sought to enhance its legislative framework to facilitate the detection, investigation, and punishment of financial crime following the GFC. The Criminal Justice Act 2011 was enacted to enhance the investigative powers of regulators and to reduce delays in the investigation and prosecution of white-collar crimes. It empowered Gardaí to break up and extend detention periods, to draw adverse inferences from refusals to explain suspicious circumstances involving the accused, to require people with relevant information to answer questions, made it easier to determine if the information is legally privileged, and criminalised the failure to report information to the Gardaí about corporate or financial crime.[141]

The Central Bank (Supervision and Enforcement) Act 2013 further increased the investigative and sanctioning powers of the CBI by specifying new information-gathering powers, specifying rules to make it easier to identify and separate non-privileged from privileged information, protecting

---

[141] See McGrath, J. (2015). *Corporate and White-Collar Crime in Ireland: A New Architecture of Regulatory Enforcement*. Manchester University Press.

whistle-blowers, and significantly increasing penalties for administrative sanctions.[142] Pan-sectoral whistle-blowing legislation was introduced by the Protected Disclosures Act 2014.[143] The Companies Acts were also updated and consolidated in 2014, placing directors' duties on a statutory footing and categorising and standardising criminal punishments for offences contrary to criminal law.[144]

Similarly to Australia, this was also a time of increased scrutiny and reflection in Ireland, as various bodies commissioned research to explore whether regulators and enforcers had sufficient tools and powers to address white-collar crime effectively. Leading the charge, the Office of the Director of Corporate Enforcement (ODCE) called for the creation of new offences, such as reckless trading and mail and wire fraud; clarity on the test for corporate criminal liability; an ability to impose administrative sanctions on a wider field of wrongdoing; and the introduction of deferred prosecution agreements.[145] Subsequently, the Law Reform Commission released an Issues Paper in which it sought views on a range of issues, including the fortification of civil and administrative sanctions, the further criminalisation of corporate misconduct to address deficiencies in the law, clarifying the test for corporate criminal liability, and new alternatives to criminal prosecution and conviction, e.g. non-prosecution and deferred prosecution agreements.[146]

The government subsequently announced its own research paper, which included, amongst other things, proposals to streamline white-collar trials and establish the ODCE as an agency with more autonomy.[147] Shortly thereafter, the Law Reform Commission published a two-volume report, spanning over 900 pages, providing a systemic, root and branch review of Irish corporate enforcement. It called for a new agency with enhanced powers

---

[142] See McGrath, J. (2020). "Walk Softly and Carry No Stick": Culture, Opportunity, and Irresponsible Risk-Taking in the Irish Banking Sector. *European Journal of Criminology*, 17(1), 86–105.

[143] See Grennan, C., & Furlong, K. (2019). Ireland's Long and Winding Road to Adequate Whistle-Blower Protection. In McGrath, J. ed., *White-Collar Crime in Ireland: Law and Policy*. Clarus Press.

[144] See McGrath, J. (2018). Twenty Years Since the McDowell Report: A Reflection on the Powers and Performance of the Office of the Director of Corporate Enforcement. *Irish Jurist*, 60(60), 33–66.

[145] ODCE. (2010). Submission on White-Collar Crime. Dublin: Office of the Director of Corporate Enforcement, 2010, available at: http://www.odce.ie/Portals/0/EasyDNNNewsDocuments/525/ODCE_Submission_en_White_Collar_Crime_30-11-2010.pdf.

[146] Law Reform Commission. (2016). Issues Paper: Regulatory Enforcement and Corporate Offences (LRC IP 8 - 2016).

[147] Measures to Enhance Ireland's Corporate, Economic and Regulatory Framework, available at https://merrionstreet.ie/MerrionStreet/en/ImageLibrary/20171101_Measures_to_Enhance_Regulatory_Framework.pdf.

to address white-collar criminality, and for the introduction of new measures like Deferred Prosecution Agreements, amongst others.[148]

Similarly, there were a number of significant reports on the financial services sector which reviewed the role and effectiveness of the Central Bank and Financial Services Authority of Ireland (CBFSAI).[149] This flurry of official research was significant; it indicated that white-collar criminality was firmly on the State's political and legislative agenda.[150]

Traditionally, however, white-collar crime was the subject of inertia and apathy in Ireland. Although corporate regulations were often underpinned by criminal law enforcement mechanisms, white-collar crime was very rarely prosecuted in Ireland before the GFC.[151] Insider trading, for example, has never been prosecuted successfully and there was an attempt to do so on only one occasion.[152] Similarly, though possessing the power since 1971 to prosecute summary offences of breaches of banking requirements, the Central Bank seems to have exercised this power only once.[153]

Nevertheless, as Ireland transitioned from a rural state with relatively low levels of corporate activity to a highly open, internationally attractive centre for commerce and finance, a process which crystallised in the 1990s with an economic boom, a new model of corporate and financial regulation emerged. Ireland moved from a command and control model of corporate enforcement, which was formally punitive but practically lenient because the law wasn't enforced, to a much more responsive model of enforcement. In effect, the CBI adopted a "responsive" model of enforcement based on a modified application of the regulatory pyramid.[154] It is also the explicit approach of

---

[148] Law Reform Commission. (2018). Report: Regulatory Powers and Corporate Offences (LRC 119–2018).

[149] Regling, K. & Watson, M. (2010). A Preliminary Report on the Irish Banking Crisis; Honohan, P. (2010). The Irish Banking Crisis and Regulatory and Financial Stability Policy 2003–2008; a Report to the Minister for Finance by the Governor of the Central Bank. Central Bank of Ireland; Nyberg, P. (2011). Misjudging Risk: Causes of the Systemic Banking Crisis in Ireland. Report of the Commission of Investigation into the Banking Sector in Ireland.

[150] McGrath, J. (2018). Twenty Years Since the McDowell Report: A Reflection on the Powers and Performance of the Office of the Director of Corporate Enforcement. *Irish Jurist*, 60(60), 33–66.

[151] McGrath, J. (2015). *Corporate and White-Collar Crime in Ireland: A New Architecture of Regulatory Enforcement*. Manchester University Press.

[152] Ibid.

[153] On 13th March 1995, following an investigation by the Central Bank of Ireland, The Wise Finance Company was convicted of breaching Section 27 of the Central Bank Act, 1971 and fined £150 at Dublin District Court. By contrast, over the past decade, the DPP has prosecuted some of Ireland's most senior bankers for wrongdoing which came to light after the financial crisis. See further: McGrath, J. (2018). Twenty Years Since the McDowell Report: A Reflection on the Powers and Performance of the Office of the Director of Corporate Enforcement. *Irish Jurist*, 60(60), 33–66.

[154] CBI. (2018). Response to the Law Reform Commission Issues Paper "Regulatory Enforcement and Corporate Offences". Central Bank of Ireland, para. 37.

other regulatory agencies in Ireland, including the Office of the Director of Corporate Enforcement (ODCE) when enforcing Irish company law.[155] Both the CBI and the ODCE relied on their softer powers prior to the GFC. Reflecting on the unwillingness of the CBI to escalate up the enforcement pyramid, Honohan stated that it would "walk softly and carry no stick".[156] Similarly, although the ODCE had prosecuted some minor regulatory offences, and although civil orders like restriction and disqualification were employed to good effect, it had not referred a case to the DPP for prosecution on indictment until after the onset of the GFC.[157] As noted below, however, both the ODCE and the CBI subsequently demonstrated a willingness to escalate up the enforcement pyramid.

Significant civil powers are also available to address misconduct in the financial services sector. The CBI, in particular, may also draw on a variety of civil powers and impose a range of sanctions to achieve its enforcement mandate. The administrative sanction is arguably one of the most significant powers possessed by the CBI. The CBI may impose fines of up to €1 million on individuals and up to €10 million (or 10% of turnover, whichever is higher) on entities for "prescribed contraventions", which include breaches of any enactment, code, condition, or obligation, under Part IIIC of the Central Bank Act 1942, as amended. The CBI has regularly employed its administrative sanctions powers since the GFC, with total annual fines rising relatively consistently, albeit with some annual fluctuations, from €3.7 million in 2008,[158] to €30.2 million in 2019.[159] As of March 2021, the CBI has imposed more than €128 million in fines in over 140 cases in accordance with its administrative sanctions procedure.[160] Its highest single fine to date was imposed in March 2021, when it fined Ulster Bank Ireland DAC almost

---

[155] Appleby, P. (2010). Compliance and Enforcement—The ODCE Perspective. In Kilcommins, S., & Kilkelly, U., *Regulatory Crime in Ireland*. First Law, 177–191. See also: McGrath, J. Twenty Years Since the McDowell Report: A Reflection on the Powers and Performance of the Office of the Director of Corporate Enforcement. *Irish Jurist*, 60(60), 33–66; McGrath, J. (2015). *Corporate and White-Collar Crime in Ireland: A New Architecture of Regulatory Enforcement*. Manchester University Press.

[156] Honohan P. (2010). *The Irish Banking Crisis: Regulatory and Financial Stability Policy*. Dublin: Central Bank, 55. See further: McGrath, J. (2020). "Walk Softly and Carry No Stick": Culture, Opportunity, and Irresponsible Risk-Taking in the Irish Banking Sector. *European Journal of Criminology*, 17(1), 86–105.

[157] McGrath, J. (2018). Twenty Years Since the McDowell Report: A Reflection on the Powers and Performance of the Office of the Director of Corporate Enforcement. *Irish Jurist*, 60(60), 33–66.

[158] Central Bank of Ireland. (2009). Annual Report 2008. CBI, p. 77.

[159] Central Bank of Ireland. (2020). Annual Report 2019 and Annual Performance Statement. CBI, p. 124.

[160] Statement of Derville Rowland, available at: https://www.oireachtas.ie/en/oireachtas-tv/video-archive/committees/. For the figures as of 2019, see: The Case for the Senior Executive Accountability Regime—Director General, Financial Conduct Derville Rowland, 22 October 2019, available at: https://centralbank.ie/news/article/speech-senior-executive-accountability-regime-derville-rowland-22-oct-2019.

€38 million for "serious failings in the treatment of its tracker customers".[161] Furthermore, the CBI also imposed tough alternatives to fines in some cases. One individual was disqualified in 2015 for 10 years (from being concerned in the management of the financial services provider) for filing false accounts with the CBI and misrepresenting the provider's financial position.[162]

In terms of prosecutions, both the ODCE and the Garda National Economic Crime Bureau (GNECB) play significant roles concerning financial crime. These agencies, rather than the CBI, prepared the cases ultimately prosecuted by the Director of Public Prosecutions (DPP) against former executives at Irish banks, including Anglo Irish Bank, considered by some to be the "the world's worst bank".[163] These prosecutions were undertaken for breaches of the Companies Acts and criminal justice legislation, rather than for breaches of banking law, per se. Senior executives were prosecuted for breaching laws on providing finance for the purchase of a bank's own shares, hiding accounts to conceal tax obligations, conspiracy to defraud investors, fraudulent trading, and false accounting.[164] Whilst some of these cases demonstrated that continued legacy issues remain, particularly with regard to under-resourcing of regulators, the prosecutions were still a significant symbolic statement of the more intrusive contemporary approach to corporate enforcement in practice. Moreover, they resulted in more individuals being convicted than acquitted.[165]

The State persevered over a decade-long investigation, despite limited resources and considerable difficulties securing evidence, to prosecute serious breaches of the Companies Acts against some of Ireland's most senior bankers. In some cases, the State had proven its case beyond a reasonable doubt and secured convictions against some of the most senior figures in Irish banking,

---

[161] CBI. (2021). Enforcement Action Notice: Ulster Bank Ireland DAC reprimanded and fined €37,774,520 by the Central Bank of Ireland for regulatory breaches affecting tracker customers, available at: https://www.centralbank.ie/news/article/press-release-enforcement-action-notice-ulster-bank-reprimanded-and-fined-37-774-520-by-central-bank-of-ireland-for-regulatory-breaches-affecting-tracker-customers-25-march-2021.

[162] Central Bank of Ireland. (2016). Annual Report 2015 (CBI), p. 34.

[163] Lewis M. (2011). *Boomerang: Travels in the New Third World.* W. W. Norton, 84.

[164] DPP v McAteer; Whelan and Fitzpatrick (Dublin Circuit Criminal Court), 31 July 2014; DPP v O'Mahoney [2016] IECA 111; DPP v Maguire [2015] IECA 350; DPP v Bowe [2017] IECA 250; People (DPP) v McAteer, Dublin Circuit Criminal Court, 23 January 2017; People (DPP) v Drumm (Dublin Circuit Criminal Court, 29 June 2018); People (DPP) v Drumm (Dublin Circuit Criminal Court, 10 July 2018).

[165] McGrath, J. (2018). Twenty Years Since the McDowell Report: A Reflection on the Powers and Performance of the Office of the Director of Corporate Enforcement. *Irish Jurist*, 60(60), 33–66.

finally "pulling the trigger on the big gun". Nevertheless, much of the positive work undertaken by the ODCE was undermined by the collapse of the criminal trial of Sean Fitzpatrick, the former CEO and subsequently the former Chairman of Anglo Irish Bank. In this case, the court directed the jury to acquit Mr Fitzpatrick on all counts on the basis of serious failings in the investigation carried out by the ODCE which denied Mr Fitzpatrick his right to a fair trial. The ODCE was criticised for failing to conduct impartial investigations, coaching witnesses, and destroying evidence that might have been exculpatory.[166] This damaged public confidence in the State's ability to enforce the law, and engulfed the ODCE in allegations of ineffectiveness and incompetence. The Companies (Corporate Enforcement Authority) Bill 2018 was subsequently drafted to reform the ODCE into a new agency and enhance Ireland's regulatory framework.

In concluding on this section, the Irish government also enhanced its legislative framework to make it easier to detect, investigate, and prosecute financial crime. In stark contrast to the traditional political and legislative apathy that characterised corporate enforcement, this was a time of sustained review and reflection on the Irish architecture of corporate enforcement. Moreover, serious financial crimes were prosecuted and, whilst the results were mixed, some former bankers were convicted. Other forms of financial misconduct met with significant administrative fines.

4   Acting Out, Tooling Up, but Sanctions Are No Silver Bullet

Gathering together the common threads across these three jurisdictions, it is clear that there has been an increased emphasis on further criminalisation, increased maximum punishments, and the deployment of both criminal and civil sanctions to address corporate wrongdoing. In the UK, new offences addressing corporate misconduct were created and some white-collar crimes, like insider trading, were prosecuted for the first time, after the GFC and more regularly thereafter. The State also prosecuted significant numbers of individuals and one bank for misconduct associated with the GFC, including the manipulation of LIBOR, EURIBOR, and illegal capital raising activities.

Nevertheless, the majority of these cases did not result in convictions, though those that did resulted in custodial sentences. Although the State persevered over extended periods and invested significant resources, it is clear

---

[166] DPP v FitzPatrick (Circuit Criminal Court (Judge Aylmer), 23 July 2017), available at: https://static.rasset.ie/documents/news/sean-fitzpatrick-full-ruling.pdf.

it faced an uphill battle in proving its cases, where the facts of the wrongdoing were sometimes highly complex, occurring in large complex organisations, where well-resourced defendants vigorously contested their cases, and where it is challenging to convince juries that "common business practice" should lead individuals to be convicted and incarcerated. The requirements for imposing corporate criminal liability, where it must be proven that the wrongdoing was committed by the directing mind and will of the organisation, also provided too great a hurdle to prosecute Barclays Bank.

On their face, civil sanctions proved more successful, resulting in some significant fines and high costs for financial services providers. On closer inspection, however, they provided little in the way of individual accountability for senior managers. Ireland also scrutinised the powers and performance of its regulators in the wake of the GFC. It enhanced its legislative framework and provided enforcers with new powers to detect, investigate, and punish white-collar criminality. White-collar crime remained firmly on the criminal justice agenda as some of Ireland's highest profile bankers were prosecuted for a variety of criminal offences arising from the GFC. As was the case in the UK, these cases met with mixed results but demonstrated the State's sustained willingness, over a series of cases and many years, to fire the "big gun" firmly in the direction of the financial services community for the first time in the history in the State.[167] Nevertheless, procedural failings in one of its investigations tarnished the otherwise impressive work completed by enforcers, bringing the system of corporate enforcement into disrepute, and resulted in plans for an institutional overhaul of the architecture of enforcement once again.

By contrast, criminal prosecutions were not a significant feature in the landscape of enforcement in Australia post-GFC, perhaps because the more intrusive regulatory approach there before the GFC had been effective in preventing misconduct. Nevertheless, civil sanctions in Australia also resulted in extended investigations, proceedings, and appeals, with relatively small fines imposed for significant harm. The appetite for more stringent sanctions grew after the GFC, and there was an uptick in prosecutions for certain forms of financial misconduct, like insider trading, perhaps because these types of cases are typically self-contained and are less likely to raise issues pertaining to decision-making and responsibility that arise in complex, hierarchical organisations. More significantly, this was a time of intense scrutiny and reflection

---

[167] See however the view of King, C., & Lord. N. (2020). Deferred Prosecution Agreements in England & Wales: Castles Made of Sand? *Public Law*, 307–330. They question whether the UK can really escalate to criminal prosecutions in appropriate cases for a variety of ideological and practical reasons.

in Australia because various bodies started to investigate whether its regulatory agencies were effective. A series of reports subsequently argued in favour of increased powers for ASIC and the CDPP, and agitated for the ratcheting up of maximum punishments in both criminal and civil cases.

In all three of these jurisdictions, white-collar crime was politicised after the GFC, and in all three jurisdictions politicians sought to boost the enforcement powers of enforcement agencies to act out for public approval. To the extent, however, that the trigger was pulled on the big gun to prosecute serious financial crimes, sanctions did not provide a silver bullet. In high-profile criminal prosecutions, there were often fewer hits than misses.

The foregoing sections, and particularly the benchmark manipulation cases, also demonstrate that cultural contexts can facilitate wrongdoing and can provide the conditions within which it may flourish. Continuing issues and recidivist activities also demonstrate how sanctions may have a limited impact on organisational and cultural contexts. Tougher laws and enforcement practices do not prevent repeated wrongdoing in organisations with bad cultures. This is especially true when enforcers take action and lose. As a form of post-hoc regulation, sanctions may not provide the necessary introspection and moral deliberation required to produce ethical decisions at the moment they are made,[168] especially when the organisational culture within which they are immersed is one that helps them to rationalise and normalise bad practices.[169]

Law alone is a limited instrument for achieving cultural change. This is an important point developed in subsequent sections of this monograph, which argue that organisations and business leaders must accept more responsibility in pursuing pro-social purposes and raising professional standards on an industry-wide basis. This is not to say that sanctions do not play some part in deterring bad behaviour but it is argued that sanctions alone are not sufficient for the purpose of achieving cultural change. They play important instrumental and expressive regulatory roles, but even these functions are attenuated in circumstances where there is an inability to secure individual accountability. In those cases, the public desire for retribution goes unsated. More importantly, it continues to undermine confidence in the State's ability to regulate the banking sector.

---

[168] Painter-Morland, M. (2006). Redefining Accountability as Relational Responsiveness. *Journal of Business Ethics*, 66(1), 89–98.

[169] McGrath, J. (2021). Self-Deception as a Technique of Neutralisation: An Analysis of the Subjective Account of a White-Collar Criminal. *Crime, Law and Social Change*, 1–18; McGrath, J. (2020). "Walk Softly and Carry No Stick": Culture, Opportunity, and Irresponsible Risk-Taking in the Irish Banking Sector. *European Journal of Criminology*, 17(1), 86–105.

5   Early Attempts at Individual Accountability: The Fit and Proper Test

Arguably, one of the core civil supervisory strategies in regulation is the ability to license or authorise only "fit and proper" persons to perform senior management roles in the financial services industry. Ongoing engagement is also necessary to ensure that those appointed to senior positions remain appropriately skilled for their posts and continue to maintain appropriate ethical standards. The fit and proper requirements were first proposed in 1997 by the Basel Committee on Banking Supervision (BCBS) in its Core Principles for Effective Banking.[170] The third principle stated that the licencing process "at a minimum, should consist of an assessment of ... the fitness and propriety of Board members and senior management". The Core Principles Methodology further elaborated that

> The fit and proper criteria include: [1] skills and experience in relevant financial operations commensurate with the intended activities of the bank and [2] no record of criminal activities or adverse regulatory judgements that make a person unfit to uphold important positions in a bank.[171]

In a review of its compliance with the Basel Principles, Australia determined that whilst it was in compliance or broadly in compliance with many of these principles, it was not in compliance with the "fit and proper" requirements. It announced its intention to implement the "fit and proper" criteria, both at authorisation and on an ongoing basis.[172] In a Consultation Paper on the issue in 2004, it noted that mismanagement and incompetence was a key cause of the failure of financial institutions.[173] In a discussion paper published the following year, it emphasised that the board of directors and senior managers bore the responsibility for effective and sensible management of financial institutions.[174] In making these observations, these consultations

---

[170] Basel Committee on Banking Supervision, Basel Core Principles for Effective Banking Supervision, 22 September 1997, available at: https://www.bis.org/basel_framework/chapter/BCP/01.htm?inforce= 20191215, paras. 01.72, 01.73.

[171] Basel Committee on Banking Supervision. (1999). Core Principles Methodology. BCSC, p. 16, available at: https://www.bis.org/publ/bcbs61.pdf.

[172] Reserve Bank of Australia. (2001). Core Principles for Effective Banking Supervision: Self-Assessment for Australia, available at: https://www.rba.gov.au/publications/bulletin/1997/dec/1.html. For more on the background to the fit and proper test, see: https://www.aph.gov.au/Parliamentary_B usiness/Committees/Senate/Economics/Completed_inquiries/2002-04/fslab/report/c02.

[173] APRA. Fit and Proper Person Requirements: Consultation Paper, March 2004.

[174] APRA. Discussion Paper: Fit and Proper Requirements, June 2005.

and discussions were making the case for an appointments regime that would ensure only suitable people performed key management role in banks.

Though the fit and proper proposals received some push-back from industry,[175] APRA introduced prudential standard "CPS 520" to implement new fit and proper standards, which was most recently updated in 2018.[176] In accordance with Prudential Standard CPS 520, institutions regulated by APRA are required to determine whether their senior managers are fit and proper for their role and functions, before appointment to the role. Prudential Standard CPS 520 is clear in specifying that the ultimate responsibility for ensuring that the responsible persons are fit and proper for their roles rests with the board. It also specifies that entities must maintain a fit and proper policy, approved by the board, and assess senior management prior to appointment and on an annual basis thereafter, document the assessment of their competence and character. In determining whether the individual meets the criteria for appointment, the authorised deposit-taking institutions (ADIs) must examine the competence, character, diligence, honesty, integrity and judgement of the individual in order to determine if he or she can properly perform properly his or her duties. Also, APRA retains the power to disqualify persons that are not fit and proper.

Peters, commenting on an earlier CPS 520 issued by APRA, notes that the purpose of CPS 520 is not merely to determine who could take up senior management roles in financial services entities. The requirements are designed to generate positive cultural change in the financial services sector by requiring that only persons with particular characteristics could be employed at senior levels therein. Peters suggests that CPS 520 "sends a message" to banks that they need good governance protocols on the appointments process. In theory, he noted that only those persons who will manage risk prudently will be appointable and this should better protect stakeholders but that, in reality, "personalities and corporate politics" are hard to manage and predict.[177]

In the UK, the Approved Persons Regime (APER) provided ongoing engagement in relation to the fit and proper requirements. Introduced prior to the GFC, in the Financial Services and Markets Act 2000, the regime required that people in controlled functions apply to the regulator for

[175] Pearson, G. (2009). *Financial Services Law and Compliance in Australia.* Cambridge University Press.

[176] Australian Prudential Regulatory Authority. Prudential Standard CPS 520 (APRA, 2018), available at: https://www.legislation.gov.au/Details/F2018L01390.

[177] Peters, M. K. (2010). Corporate Governance of Australian Banking: A Lesson in Law Reform or Good Fortune? UNSW Australian School of Business Research Paper, p. 11 *et passim*, available at: https://ssrn.com/abstract=1567726.

approval to perform these roles. As part of this process, the regulator considered whether the person was "fit and proper" to perform their functions, having regard to their honesty, integrity, and reputation; competence and capability; and financial soundness. Even if granted, approval may also be subsequently withdrawn by the regulator, and it may impose fines on those who act in an approved function without permission. In 2018/2019, for example, the FCA used its fitness and probity powers to prohibit seven individuals.[178] In one of those cases, it fined an individual £29,300 for submitting misleading evidence of his qualifications.[179]

The PCBS Report was highly critical of the APER. It criticised the coverage of the APER, noting that it applied to less than 10% of people working in banking in the UK.[180] It also didn't apply to many individuals who contributed to prudential failings and other misconduct. It noted, for example, that the staff who submitted LIBOR data were not subject to the APER. Moreover, the Statements of Principle applied only to approved persons so others who breached the principles were not subject to enforcement action, unless they were engaged in money laundering, insider trading, or committed wrongdoing which was sufficiently serious so as to be subject to a prohibition order.

The PCBS Report further noted that the regime was not designed to assign responsibilities and was "ineffective in identifying responsibilities within banks of significance when things go wrong".[181] This was a barrier to effective enforcement because, as noted by Martin Wheatley, the then CEO of the FCA, "you have to be able to show the clear evidential trail from a senior figure, a particular abusive decision, to what actually happened. … [I]n many large organisations it is very hard to provide that evidential trail".[182] Additionally, it described regulatory oversight under the APER as being a "one shot approach", in which it exercised the most muscle in either approving or refusing an appointment.[183] Whilst individuals had to remain fit and proper whilst in their posts, the regulator found it more difficult to remove someone who was already in place and lacked the power to require individuals of

---

[178] Financial Conduct Authority (2019). Enforcement Annual Performance Report 2018/19. FCA, p. 17, available at: https://www.fca.org.uk/publication/corporate/annual-report-2018-19-enforcement-performance.pdf.

[179] Financial Conduct Authority. (2018). Final Notice Darren Cummings, available at: https://www.fca.org.uk/publication/final-notices/darren-colvin-cummings-2018.pdf.

[180] Parliamentary Commission on Banking Standards, Changing Banking for Good. (2013). The Stationery Office Limited, para. 55.

[181] PCBS Report, Vol. II, para. 553.

[182] PCBS Report, Vol. II, para. 555.

[183] PCBS Report, Vol. II, para. 557.

concern to be subjected to ongoing learning and development plans. The APER, it concluded, was a "complex and confused mess".[184] It was eventually replaced by the Senior Managers and Certification Regime, discussed further in Chapter 5.

In 2005, an Irish parliamentary committee proposed that new fitness and probity requirements be adopted in Ireland.[185] At that time, as noted by Honohan, "Whilst fit and proper requirements already existed these varied by type of financial institution and in any event needed updating and modernising".[186] The Financial Regulator undertook this task, issuing two consultation papers in 2005 and 2006,[187] and the new standardised requirements for directors and managers became effective in 2007,[188] though they were not placed on a statutory footing at the time.[189] The Irish legislature introduced statutory fitness and probity requirements in 2010, under the Central Bank Reform Act 2010 (2010 Act).[190]

There are three pillars to the Irish fitness and probity regime under the 2010 Act. With regard to the first pillar, there are on-going obligations on firms to ensure that all of their employees in a so-called controlled function (CF) role comply with fitness and probity standards. Firms must not permit a person to perform a CF role unless they are satisfied on reasonable grounds that the person complies with standards of fitness and probity set out in a CBI code.[191] The 2010 Act gives powers to the CBI to prescribe CF functions.[192] These include roles that would give an individual significant influence within the organisation and customer-facing roles. The 2010

[184] PCBS Report, Vol. II, para. 564.

[185] Dáil Eireann, Joint Committee on Finance and the Public Service, Interim Report on the Policy of Commercial Banks concerning Customer Charges and (2005).

[186] Honohan, P., Donovan, D., Gorecki, P., & Mottiar, R. (2010). The Irish Banking Crisis: Regulatory and Financial Stability Policy. Central Bank of Ireland, para. 4.27.

[187] Irish Financial Services Regulatory Authority. (2005). Financial Services Regulation: Comprehensive Framework of Standards for testing the probity and competence of Directors and Managers of Financial Services Firms, Consultation Paper 11. IFSRA; Irish Financial Services Regulatory Authority. (2006). Second Consultation on Fit and Proper Test, Consultation Paper 15, IFSRA.

[188] Irish Financial Services Regulatory Authority. (2007). Consumer Protection with Innovation, Competitiveness and Competition. Irish Financial Services Regulatory Authority. Annual Report of the Financial Regulator 2006, IFSRA.

[189] Irish Financial Services Regulatory Authority. (2008). Fit and Proper Requirements, Instructions Paper. IFSRA.

[190] Central Bank Reform Act, 2010. Fitness and probity requirements for credit unions came into effect in 2013 and operated initially on a phased basis.

[191] Central Bank Reform Act 2010, Section 21.

[192] Central Bank Reform Act 2010, Section 20. The CBI's list of CF roles is available at: https://www.centralbank.ie/docs/default-source/regulation/how-we-regulate/authorisation/fitness-probity/regulated-financial-service-providers/regulatory-requirements/gns-4-1-1-3-1-1-list-of-controlled-functions.pdf?sfvrsn=14.

Act also gives the CBI powers to adopt codes setting out required standards of fitness and probity. The relevant measures that have been adopted by the CBI under these powers include the 2017 Fitness and Probity Standards, which require persons in CF roles to be competent and capable; honest, ethical, and act with integrity; and be financially sound.[193] The CBI has also adopted a Minimum Competency Code, which sets out educational and continuing professional developments requirements for certain customer-facing staff.[194] The second pillar of the Irish fitness and probity regime is the CBI's role as a gatekeeper. The CBI has been given powers to specify senior-level CF functions (such as board member, CEO, head of control function) as a pre-controlled function (PCF). Prior written approval from the CBI is required before people can be appointed to these functions.[195]

The CBI has used this gatekeeper function to some effect. It stated that, in 2020, for example, some 20 PCF applications had been withdrawn by applicants following referral of the application to the CBI's specialist fitness and probity team in its Enforcement Division for in-depth consideration.[196] Since 2014, the ECB is exclusively competent for fitness and probity assessments of the management board and key function holders of significant credit institutions and those of all credit institutions seeking authorisation.[197] The third pillar of the regime is the CBI's powers to investigate the fitness and probity of individuals where it has reason to suspect their fitness and

---

[193] Central Bank of Ireland. (2014). Fitness and Probity Standards (Code Issued Under Section 50 of the Central Bank Reform Act 2010), available at: https://www.centralbank.ie/docs/default-source/regulation/how-we-regulate/fitness-probity/regulated-financial-service-providers/fitness-and-probity-standards.pdf?sfvrsn=6. In addition to these Fitness and Probity Standards, at EU level certain fitness & probity requirements are imposed under EU law on credit institutions and certain investment firms, in particular under the EU Capital Requirements Directive, Directive 2013/36/EU ("CRDIV") and Directive 2014/65/EU ("MiFID2").

[194] Minimum Competency Code. (2017). CBI, available at: https://www.centralbank.ie/docs/default-source/regulation/how-we-regulate/authorisation/minimum-competency/minimum-competency-code-2017.pdf?sfvrsn=4. See also, Central Bank (Supervision and Enforcement) Act 2013 (Section 48(1)) Minimum Competency Regulations 2017.

[195] Central Bank Reform Act 2010, Section 22, 23. The CBI's list of PCF roles is available at: https://www.centralbank.ie/docs/default-source/regulation/how-we-regulate/authorisation/fitness-probity/regulated-financial-service-providers/regulatory-requirements/gns-4-1-1-3-1-1-list-of-pre-approval-controlled-functions.pdf?sfvrsn=6.

[196] Speech by Derville Rowland, Director General, Financial Conduct, CBI, 10 June 2021, available at: https://www.centralbank.ie/news/article/speech-importance-of-fitness-probity-and-ensuring-responsibility-derville-rowland-10-june-2021.

[197] Council Regulation (EU) No 1024/2013 of 15 October 2013 conferring specific tasks on the European Central Bank concerning policies relating to the prudential supervision of credit institutions. See also, Guide to Fit and Proper Assessments, 2018, ECB; available at: https://www.bankingsupervision.europa.eu/ecb/pub/pdf/ssm.fap_guide_201705_rev_201805.en.pdf?3f4bf12e0963836b584ef40686cbe4c1. Also, ECB Consultation on Revised Guide to Fit and Proper Assessments, June 2021; available at: https://www.bankingsupervision.europa.eu/press/pr/date/2021/html/ssm.pr210615-443208ce35.en.html.

probity.[198] If, following investigation, the CBI has "reasonably formed the opinion" that an individual is not of such fitness and probity as is appropriate for a particular CF role (or any CF role), it may prohibit the individual from the role(s).[199] The CBI has, as of July 2021, issued nine such prohibition notices.[200] The CBI has stated that, despite the above powers available to it, "without a strengthened Individual Accountability Framework, the likelihood of profound cultural change in the regulated financial services sector is reduced".[201]

Gathering these threads together, Australia, the UK, and Ireland specify that senior managers must be fit and proper to perform their roles in the financial services sectors. Although they differ somewhat in their detail, they are each important civil supervisory strategies which aim to institutionalise good governance aimed at ensuring that only appropriately fit and proper individuals are appointed to senior roles in financial services firms. It does not follow, however, that screening and carrying out on-going due diligence for character, qualifications, and experience will always prevent bad behaviour. Even honest and honourable people, acting without malice, can be blind to misconduct that they could and should know about, and for which they are responsible.[202] In the absence of fixing personal responsibility for the wrongdoing committed by subordinates or within business areas which they manage, the need to spot irregularities or make uncomfortable inquiries risks becoming less urgent. Incrementally, risks of misconduct can accumulate over time and, in the absence of clear lines of accountability, individuals may not see their actions are neglectful or reckless when they are routine. In those circumstances, punishment after the fact does little to prevent or deter wrongdoing when the offender cannot see the wrong in the first place. This is one of the problems with punishment.

6   The Problems with Punishment

In this section, the limitations of employing sanctions in the financial services sector are outlined. Regardless of the jurisdiction, the law generally provides for criminal, civil, and administrative sanctions, depending on the seriousness

---

[198] Central Bank Reform Act 2010, Section 25.

[199] Central Bank Reform Act 2010, Section 43.

[200] See, CBI website: https://www.centralbank.ie/news-media/legal-notices/prohibition-notices.

[201] Behaviour and Culture of the Irish Retail Banks, 2018, p. 32, available at: https://www.centralbank.ie/docs/default-source/publications/corporate-reports/behaviour-and-culture-of-the-irish-retail-banks.pdf?sfvrsn=2.

[202] Heffernan, M. (2011). *Wilful Blindness: Why We Ignore the Obvious*. Simon and Schuster.

of issue in question. The most significant difference between criminal and other proceedings is that criminal proceedings, if resulting in a conviction, can result in a period of imprisonment. Offenders also experience considerable social opprobrium and collateral consequences.[203] Given the severity of this outcome, it is understandable that those who may commit crimes resist the criminal processes to the greatest extent they can. As noted by Packer:

> They ordinarily take care to avoid being caught. If arrested, they ordinarily deny their guilt and otherwise try not to cooperate with the police. If brought to trial, they do whatever their resources permit to resist being convicted. And, even after they have been convicted and sent to prison, their efforts to secure their freedom do not cease.[204]

Moreover, given the significant imbalance of power between the State and individuals who are prosecuted, individuals are provided with a panoply of due process protections to safeguard them and to protect the integrity of the criminal justice system more generally.[205] These rights act as "trumps" over policy decisions made by government in the name of public protection.[206] In general, prosecutors bear the burden of proving the case against the accused and they must prove their case beyond a reasonable doubt. In providing these rights, the State limits its own powers, curbs its own potential for abuse, and prevents the adoption of a wholly utilitarian stance by espousing and enshrining values that transcend the goal of crime prevention.[207] The presumption of innocence, the standard of proof to beyond all reasonable doubt, requiring the prosecution to discharge the burden of proof, all stand as barriers to easy conviction and represent "powerful curbs on unwise, sweeping use of the criminal sanction".[208] They stop the justice system from operating instrumentally, at maximum velocity, in recognition that the protection of the individual and the integrity of the system are more important values.[209] Therefore, the entire criminal process is characterised by

---

[203] See further: O'Malley, T. (2019). Sentencing White-Collar and Corporate Crime. In McGrath, J. ed., *White-Collar Crime in Ireland: Law and Policy*. Clarus Press, 157–194.

[204] Packer, H. L. (1964). Two Models of the Criminal Process. *University of Pennsylvania Law Review*, 113, 1–68, 2.

[205] Packer, H. (1968). The *Limits of the Criminal Sanction*. Stanford University Press.

[206] Dworkin, R. (1977). *Taking Rights Seriously*. Cambridge: Harvard University Press.

[207] Kilcommins, S., et al. (2004). *Crime, Punishment, and the Search for Order in Ireland*. Institute of Public Administration.

[208] Packer, H. (1968). *The Limits of the Criminal Sanction*. Stanford University Press, 139.

[209] McGrath, J. (2015). *Corporate and White-Collar Crime in Ireland: A New Architecture of Regulatory Enforcement*. Manchester University Press.

struggle, not just because individuals resist punishment, but because the State designs it this way to safeguard the integrity of the justice system.

Whilst criminal law is useful in addressing egregious misbehaviours, there are a number of key concerns regarding its application to the financial services sector. In the first instance, high evidential standards can create significant problems for regulatory and prosecutorial agencies addressing white-collar crime. As noted by the Australian Federal Police, sourcing the evidence to tackle financial crime is difficult because these crimes are complex and therefore difficult to detect and investigate:

> These characteristics of serious financial crime mean that investigators face significant challenges obtaining sufficient evidence to bring prosecutions. A perception that there is a low risk of being detected means that criminals are willing to take risks in committing serious financial crimes. Even if they are detected, offences may not be made out in court due to challenges associated with gathering sufficient evidence.[210]

Each jurisdiction under analysis in the monograph has made efforts to facilitate the detection, investigation, and prosecution of white-collar crimes. Nevertheless, they face an uphill battle at every stage. It is thought that white-collar criminals are far more likely to have greater resources to string out litigation and sap the resources of regulators. Haines, for example has argued that these "superior legal and financial resources can be used to wear down regulatory and prosecutorial agencies and result in a settlement that falls well short of transparent and full accountability for breaches of the law".[211] In a study of white-collar crime defence attorneys, Mann notes that they tend to be involved at a very early stage of proceedings, before the regulatory investigation has concluded or even begun, and vigorously resist any government attempts to secure evidence against their clients which might be inculpatory. Remarkably, these attorneys view a case proceeding to trial as a failure.[212]

---

[210] Australian Federal Police. (2016). Submission by the Australian Federal Police Senate Standing Committee on Economics—References Committee Inquiry into Penalties for White-Collar Crime. AFP, p. 3, available at: https://www.google.com/search?client=safari&rls=en&q=These+characteristics+of+serious+financial+crime+mean+that+investigators+face+significant+challenges+obtaining+sufficient+evidence+to+bring+prosecutions&ie=UTF-8&oe=UTF-8.

[211] Submission by Haines, F. (6 December 2016) to Australian Securities and Investments Commission, *Submission 49*, p. 17. Cited in: Senate Economic References Committee. (2017). "Lifting the Fear and Suppressing the Greed": Penalties for White-Collar Crime and Corporate and Financial Misconduct in Australia, p. 20, available at: https://www.aph.gov.au/Parliamentary_Business/Committees/Senate/Economics/WhiteCollarCrime45th/Report.

[212] Mann, K. (1985). *Defending White-Collar Crime: A Portrait of Attorneys at Work.* Yale University Press.

At trial, the ambiguity of the white-collar crime, say a complex fraud, may render it more difficult to understand than a conventional crime, like assault.

The high evidential standards which accompany criminal proceedings are not necessarily required in civil proceedings, where wrongdoers cannot be imprisoned, and cases may, for example, be proven on the balance of probabilities.[213] Although the line between civil and administrative penalties is not always clear,[214] even fewer procedural protections may accompany the imposition of administrative penalties if they may be imposed in the absence of court proceedings. In theory, it is easier for regulators to bring civil cases than criminal prosecutions because it is easier to meet the lower evidential threshold required in these cases.[215] As such, it is thought that civil liability makes it easier to enforce the law but that it lacks the moral censure and symbolic importance associated with criminal prosecution and conviction. The Macrory Report and the Law Commission in the UK concluded that greater use should be made of civil sanctions for pragmatic reasons, although they also recognised that criminal offences were still needed to address the most serious and morally reprehensible misbehaviours.[216]

In fact, however, civil sanctions are not always the panacea they appear to be. In Ireland, for example, McGrath has shown that regulators had significant difficulties securing civil sanctions, like restriction and disqualification orders, when directed against well-resourced individuals in complex organisational settings who vigorously resist proceedings.[217] Similar observations have been made in other jurisdictions where regulatory agencies have noted that "despite popular misconceptions, civil cases were often as complex, resource intensive, and difficult to prove as criminal cases, particularly when they involved white-collar offences".[218] In Australia, for example, civil proceedings are further complicated by the *Briginshaw* principle in which a higher standard of proof can be required of regulators where the allegations are serious

[213] Macrory, R. (2016). Regulatory Justice, Making Sanctions Effective. Better Regulation Executive.

[214] McGrath, J. (2010). The Traditional Court of Crime Approach to the Definition of a Crime. In Kilcommins, S., & Kilkelly, U. eds., *Regulatory Crime in Ireland*. Lonsdale, 29–61.

[215] Lynch Fannon, I. (2010). Controlling Risk Taking: Whose Job Is It Anyway? In Kilcommins, S., & Kilkelly, U. eds., *Regulatory Crime in Ireland*. First Law, 113–139.

[216] Macrory, R. (2016). *Regulatory Justice, Making Sanctions Effective*. Better Regulation Executive; Law Commission. (2010). Criminal Liability in Regulatory Contexts: A Consultation Paper. Stationery Office.

[217] McGrath, J. (2018). Twenty Years Since the McDowell Report: A Reflection on the Powers and Performance of the Office of the Director of Corporate Enforcement. *Irish Jurist*, 60(60), 33–66.

[218] Australian Securities and Investments Commission, *Submission 49*, p. 17. Cited in: Senate Economic References Committee. (2017). "Lifting the Fear and Suppressing the Greed": Penalties for White-Collar Crime and Corporate and Financial Misconduct in Australia, p. 30, available at: https://www.aph.gov.au/Parliamentary_Business/Committees/Senate/Economics/WhiteCollarCrime45th/Report.

and the consequences of the proceedings are severe.[219] Whilst the standard in civil proceedings remains the balance of probabilities, regulators alleging fraud and other serious white-collar offences will need to have strong evidence to satisfy that standard in these cases. ASIC has noted that in civil cases where white-collar crimes are alleged, "the distinction between the 'balance of probabilities' and 'beyond reasonable doubt' standard of proof is reduced".[220]

In addition, although civil cases are often considered to be faster and cheaper than criminal trials, regulators also reject this as a general proposition. A parliamentary committee investigating regulatory enforcement in Australia concluded, based on submission it received from ASIC, that:

> it was wrong to assume that civil proceedings provided a "more timely and efficient means of dealing with corporate misconduct than criminal prosecutions". In fact, ASIC submitted that civil cases frequently require even greater time, effort and resources, and were by no means a "quick and easy" alternative to criminal prosecutions. Civil procedures, ASIC explained, can be as complex as criminal procedures, particularly with regard to the commercially and legally complex cases that ASIC is often involved in.[221]

Moreover, criminally prosecuting large companies is notoriously difficult.[222] In theory, companies can be prosecuted as artificial legal persons much like natural persons are, although both the procedures at trial and mechanisms by which they are liable are different.[223] Should the company be vicariously liable for acts committed by their employees; where the "directing

---

[219] Briginshaw v Briginshaw (1938) 60 CLR 336.

[220] Australian Securities and Investments Commission, *Submission 49*, p. 18. Cited in: Australian Securities and Investments Commission, *Submission 49*, p. 17. Cited in: Senate Economic References Committee. (2017). "Lifting the Fear and Suppressing the Greed": Penalties for White-Collar Crime and Corporate and Financial Misconduct in Australia, para. 3.7, available at: https://www.aph.gov.au/Parliamentary_Business/Committees/Senate/Economics/WhiteCollarCrime45th/Report.

[221] Australian Securities and Investments Commission, *Submission 49*, pp. 17–18. Cited in: Senate Economic References Committee. (2017). "Lifting the Fear and Suppressing the Greed": Penalties for White-Collar Crime and Corporate and Financial Misconduct in Australia, para. 3.9, available at: https://www.aph.gov.au/Parliamentary_Business/Committees/Senate/Economics/WhiteCollarCrime45th/Report.

[222] Doyle, D., and McGrath, J. (2016). Attributing Criminal Responsibility for Workplace Fatalities and Deaths in Custody: Corporate Manslaughter in Britain and Ireland. In Fitz-Gibbon, K., & Walklate, S. eds. *Homicide, Gender and Responsibility: International Perspectives*. Routledge, 148–170.

[223] Farrell, R. (2019). Prosecuting Companies and Directors. In McGrath, J. ed., *White-Collar Crime in Ireland: Law and Policy*. Clarus Press, 141–157.

mind and will" of the company is blameworthy; or where corporate decision-making procedures are to blame?[224] Offences requiring intent are particularly problematic because large companies have organisational structures that can obscure the responsibility of the individual actors therein, resulting in the fragmentation of knowledge and culpability. Intention itself becomes ambiguous.[225]

Finally, the penalties on conviction also cast doubt on the value and utility of criminal prosecution as a practical matter because companies have "no soul to damn" and "no body to kick".[226] Companies can be prosecuted but not imprisoned which can make corporate criminal liability "inferior as a practical matter to an appropriate corrective measure on the civil side".[227] They can be fined but "severe penalties flow through the corporate shell and fall on the relatively blameless" through lower levels of profits for shareholders and increased prices for consumers.[228] Should they be responsible for crimes in which they may have had no involvement? Moreover, some companies, like banks, are not only too big to fail, they are also "too big to jail" where they are too economically important to be prosecuted.[229] For example, the UK has previously made representations for a DPA for the UK-based bank, HSBC, to the Department of Justice in the United States to resolve fraud allegations of money laundering in recognition of its systemic importance to its economy.[230] Therefore, in addition to problems raised by the efficacy of the criminal law generally, corporate personhood raises particular problems relating to criminal procedure and the "spill-over" effect of punishment.

It may also be particularly difficult to locate individual responsibility in large complex organisations. Senior managers may make policies or "set the tone" for activities, but lower level employees may actually execute these decisions and policies, potentially insulating senior managers from

---

[224] Gobert, J. (1994). Corporate Criminality: Four Models of Fault. *Legal Studies*, 4, 393; Sealy, L.S., & Worthington, S. (2018). *Cases and Materials in Company Law*. 8th ed. Oxford University Press, 152–163.

[225] Wolgast, E. (1992). *Ethics of an Artificial Person: Lost Responsibility in Professions and Organisations*. Stanford University Press.

[226] Coffee, J. C. (1981). "No Soul to Damn: No Body to Kick": An Unscandalised Inquiry into the Problem of corporate punishment. *Michigan Law Review*, 79(3), 386–459, available at: https://repository.law.umich.edu/cgi/viewcontent.cgi?article=3809&context=mlr.

[227] Fisher, D. R., & Sykes, A. O. (1996). Corporate Crime. *Journal of Legal Studies*, 25, 319–349, 322.

[228] Coffee, J. (1981). No Soul to Damn: No Body to Kick: An Unscandalised Inquiry into the Problem of Corporate Punishment. *Michigan Law Review*, 386–459, 387.

[229] Garrett, B. (2014). *Too Big to Jail*. Harvard University Press.

[230] Treanor, J. (2017). US Authorities Lift Threat to Prosecute HSBC. *The Guardian*, available at: https://www.theguardian.com/profile/jilltreanor.

wrongdoing.[231] In the case of PPI, the PCBS stated that "delegation and organisation distance acts to protect senior management from culpability for conduct failures within their chains of responsibility". The Head of Enforcement at the then FSA, Tracey McDermott, explained:

> Decisions were made further down the chain of command. If the delegation was appropriate (i.e. to an appropriately qualified person with suitable resources etc) the more senior individual will not be at fault. In conduct cases (although perhaps less so in prudential matters) the decisions which are made which impact adversely on customers may sometimes be made a long way from the top of the organisation and the senior management and/or board currently have relatively little visibility of them.[232]

Corporate personality can become a "Gyges ring" for company officers, giving them a convenient cloak of invisibility;[233] or, inverting the metaphor, they "promptly donned the blindfolds"[234] so the wrongdoing would be "invisible" to them.

The LIBOR scandal provides an interesting case study in how responsibility for wrongdoing can be pushed down in an organisation, even where the wrongdoing is persistent and systemic. Bob Diamond, the CEO of Barclays, blamed 14 lower-level individuals for the wrongdoing, noting that it was not reported up, saying "this bad behaviour, I am not blaming on anyone [senior]. I blame it on these individuals and they are being dealt with".[235] Nevertheless, it was found that the board was responsible for these failings, which persisted for four years, with the Treasury Committee noting, "the management of the bank turned a blind eye to the culture of the trading floor".[236] The scale and chronic nature of the wrongdoing was even more evident in UBS. Though senior management denied any knowledge of manipulations, the misconduct persisted for nine years in which 40 individuals made 900 written requests to falsify the LIBOR rate.[237]

---

[231] Jackall, R. (1988). Moral Mazes: The World of Corporate Managers. *International Journal of Politics, Culture, and Society*, 1(4), 598–614.

[232] PCBS Report, Vol. II, paras. 99, 104.

[233] Wolgast, E. H. (1992). *Ethics of an Artificial Person: Lost Responsibility in Professions and Organisations*. Stanford University Press.

[234] PCBS Report, Vol. I, para. 14.

[235] PCBS Report, Vol. II, para. 96.

[236] Treasury Committee, Second Report of Session 2012–2013, Fixing LIBOR: Some preliminary findings, HC 481, paras. 34 and 38, available at: https://publications.parliament.uk/pa/cm201213/cmselect/cmtreasy/481/481.pdf.

[237] FCA. 2012. UBS Final Notice, available at: https://www.fca.org.uk/publication/final-notices/final-notice-ubs.pdf.

The PCBS Report also noted that

> the attempted manipulation of LIBOR at Barclays, UBS and RBS was found by the FSA to have continued for a combined total of nearly 20 years, with the direct involvement of 78 individuals in nearly 1,300 documented internal requests and well over 1,000 external requests for alternations to submissions.[238]

As noted in the previous chapter, misconduct in the financial services sector is often industry-wide, not simply the result of individual "bad apples", facilitated by the broader corporate culture and regulatory environment within which individual decisions are made.[239] In this context, however, it can be difficult to prosecute wrongdoing, where individual responsibility is obscured by complex organisational structures and decision-making processes, even when individuals choose to be wilfully blind to systemic and cultural failings. If the State wants to criminally pursue individuals, not companies, it has a much tougher battle on its hands because:

> Prosecutors have far less leverage over individuals. People, unlike corporations, often face the prospect of incarceration and financial ruin in the event of a criminal conviction. As a result, individuals are more likely to test the government's legal theories and version of the facts. ... [P]rosecutors know from their interactions with lawyers for individuals that, unlike with the corporation, they are likely to have a fight on their hands if they bring charges.[240]

Moreover, even if individuals are prosecuted, this may just deflect responsibility away from broader cultural and systemic failings that remain unaddressed. The PCBS Report, whilst noting that there were some isolated cases of low-level individual bankers being sanctioned, cautioned that "This sanctioning of only a few individuals contributes to the myth that recent scandals can be seen as the result of the actions of a few "rotten apples", rather than much deeper failings in banks, by regulators and other parts of the financial services industry".[241]

---

[238] PCBS Report, Vol. II, para. 132.

[239] McGrath, J. (2020). "Walk Softly and Carry No Stick": Culture, Opportunity, and Irresponsible Risk-Taking in the Irish Banking Sector. *European Journal of Criminology*, 17(1), 86–105.

[240] Fishbein, M. E. (2014). Why Individuals Aren't Prosecuted for Conduct Companies Admit. *New York Law Journal*, 4.

[241] PCBS Report, para. 203.

7   Conclusion

Various views have been offered on legislative responses arising from high-profile regulatory scandals and corporate governance failures. Romano argues that they can give rise to knee-jerk, ill-thought out reforms.[242] Coffee, however, suggests they may be moments of opportunity in which special interest groups and legislative inertia are overcome.[243] He suggests that "a good crisis should never go to waste".[244] In this respect, Tomasic has suggested that the financial crisis was important because it "shamed regulators to be more proactive" and served to "open the door to change".[245]

The subsequent financial scandals in each jurisdiction kept the pressure on governments and agencies to follow through on misconduct with more than just rhetoric. Though the public desire for increased corporate accountability for wrongdoing has a longer trajectory, the GFC and subsequent scandals crystallised social sentiments and led to a politicisation of regulatory strategies to tackle financial crime. Politicians denounced corporate wrongdoing using zero-tolerance rhetoric, promising stiff punishments for financial crime, equating bankers with thieves and terrorists. Corporate enforcement was tooled up as politicians and regulators acted out for public approval. Legislators introduced new laws to make it easier to hold wrongdoers to account, and new enforcement practices emerged as regulators moved increasingly towards more intrusive enforcement practices. In each jurisdiction, regulators pulled the trigger on criminal and civil sanctions to punish wrongdoers. In most cases, however, they were lengthy and costly affairs and the criminal prosecutions, in particular, generated mixed results.

In the UK, although the SFO commenced criminal proceedings against a significant number of individuals for wrongdoing associated with the GFC, few of these resulted in convictions. Irish authorities arguably had more success in securing convictions but were ultimately embroiled in prosecutorial impropriety, demonstrating how fraught the investigative and prosecutorial processes can be. Large civil fines were also imposed on financial services entities but they did not sufficiently hold individuals to account or generate cultural change.

---

[242] Romano, R. (2005). The Sarbanes-Oxley Act and the Making of Quack Corporate Governance. *Yale Law Journal*, 1521–1611.

[243] Coffee, J. C. (2011). Political Economy of Dodd-Frank: Why Financial Reform Tends to Be Frustrated and Systemic Risk Perpetuated. *Cornell Law Review*, 97, 1019–1082.

[244] Ibid., p. 1020.

[245] Tomasic, R. (2011). The Financial Crisis and the Haphazard Pursuit of Financial Crime. *Journal of Financial Crime*, 7–31.

This emphasis on sanctions and punishment is not surprising given the increased social and political desire to hold corporate wrongdoing to higher standards in the wake of the GFC and subsequent scandals.[246] Criminal punishment performs an important expressive function. By asserting that financial wrongdoing is worthy of the State's strongest weapon of moral censure, criminalisation allows civil society to assert a shared sense of right and wrong and to reinforce social solidarity.[247] It acts as a call to arms to take wrongdoing seriously—a tool to mobilise actors to generate broader social change.[248] Sanctioning, particularly criminal punishment, is also an important "big gun" in the arsenal of a regulator, particularly when used sparingly and successfully.

When regulators act with a clear escalation policy and a willingness to use the big stick of the criminal law as last resort, industry realises that voluntary compliance is in its best interests and is incentivised to respond to lower levels of regulatory intervention. "Lop the tops off the pyramids", however, "and there is less prospect of self-regulation, less prospect of persuasion as an alternative to punishment".[249] This is not to say that pragmatic issues with criminal punishment do not persist. Despite claims that sanctions deter wrongdoing, they arguably do little to address the underlying systemic influences generating wrongdoing.

Ideally, regulatory intervention would focus on prevention, rather than post-hoc punishment. Regulatory strategies can help to facilitate this, especially where they embed law-abiding norms in organisations to facilitate cultures of compliance.[250] These strategies may supplement sanctioning approaches which remain available to address serious wrongdoing where regulatory strategies have failed.

---

[246] It also reflects broader international developments to criminally punish financial services providers for alleged wrongdoing. Corder, M. (2020). Dutch Court Calls for Criminal Probe into Former ING CEO. AP News (9 December), available at: https://apnews.com/article/criminal-investigations-netherlands-zurich-money-laundering-the-hague-143b16cb11e26d5626b9a78767c7d870; Polz, J. Prosecutors Arrest Three in Suspected Wirecard Criminal Racket, available at: https://www.reuters.com/article/us-wirecard-accounts/prosecutors-arrest-three-in-suspected-wirecard-criminal-racket-idUKKCN24N23V; Danish Prosecutors Drop Money Laundering Charges Against ex-Danske Bank Staff, available at: https://www.reuters.com/article/us-danske-bk-moneylaundering-idUSKBN29C0V2.

[247] Durkheim, E. (1964) The *Rules of Sociological Method*. Free Press.

[248] Carson, W. G. (1980). The Institutionalisation of Ambiguity: Early British Factory Acts. In Stotland, E., & Geis, G. eds., *White-Collar Crime: Theory and Research*. Sage, 142–173.

[249] Ayres, I. & Braithwaite, J. (1992). *Responsive Regulation: Transcending the Deregulation Debate*. Oxford University Press, 39.

[250] Larsson, P. (2012). Regulating Corporate Crime: From Punishment to Self-Regulation. *Journal of Scandinavian Studies in Criminology and Crime Prevention*, 13, 31–46.

The next chapter examines the way in which Individual Accountability Regimes (IARs) operate and the extent to which they may prevent wrong-doing and generate positive cultural change.

5

The New Individual Accountability Regimes (IARs)

1   Introduction

The previous chapter described the challenges of relying on "big stick" measures taken by the state to hold individuals to account for misconduct in financial services. It also noted that one of the key causes of misconduct identified in the 2013 UK Parliamentary Commission on Banking Standards Report (PCBS Report) was that "[t]oo many bankers, especially at the most senior levels, have operated in an environment with insufficient personal responsibility".[1] To address this problem in the UK, the PCBS Report recommended the introduction of a new regulatory framework for holding individuals to account. The UK eventually adopted a new regulatory framework, the Senior Managers and Certification Regime (SMCR), which came into force from 2016. Australia has since introduced a broadly similar individual accountability regime (IAR), the Banking Executive Accountability Regime (BEAR). There are also currently proposals to replace the BEAR with a more comprehensive Financial Accountability Regime (FAR). In Ireland, legislation to implement a new individual accountability framework, including a Senior Executive Accountability Regime (SEAR) that

---

[1] Changing Banking for Good, UK Parliamentary Commission on Banking Standards. The Stationery Office Limited, Vol. I, p. 8, available at: https://publications.parliament.uk/pa/jt201314/jtselect/jtpcbs/27/27.pdf.

© The Author(s), under exclusive license to Springer Nature
Switzerland AG 2022
J. McGrath and C. Walker, *New Accountability in Financial Services*,
Palgrave Socio-Legal Studies,
https://doi.org/10.1007/978-3-030-88715-5_5

would be broadly similar to the SMCR, is expected to be adopted in the near future.[2]

This chapter outlines the main features of the SMCR, BEAR (and forthcoming FAR), together with the proposed new IAR in Ireland, comparing and contrasting a number of features of these three broadly similar regimes. It also briefly refers to similar regimes in Hong Kong, Singapore, and Malaysia to demonstrate that there is a broader international trend to enhancing individual accountability in the financial services sector.[3] In particular, it analyses the allocation of responsibilities to individuals, the new conduct rules, and sanctions for breaches of the conduct requirements.

It also critically evaluates the prospects for success of the new IARs in the UK, Australia, and Ireland in terms of changing culture and behaviours in the financial services industry, focusing specifically on several factors: the significance of allocating accountability to identified senior individuals for specific areas of a firm's business and some potential issues with allocating accountabilities; the extent of regulators' reliance on firms to ensure individuals meet fitness and probity standards and whether this has the potential to amount to an "Achilles heel" in the new regimes; the implications of regulatory enforcement and "credible deterrence"; and the potential inherent limitations of the new IARs in terms of influencing ethical decision-making by individuals.

2   Overview of the New IARs

The PCBS Report recommended the establishment of a "senior persons regime" that would "ensure that the key responsibilities within banks are

---

[2] On 27 July 2021, the Irish government published the General Scheme of a Central Bank (Individual Accountability Framework) Bill 2021, available at: https://www.gov.ie/en/publication/d28d9-general-scheme-central-bank-individual-accountability-framework-bill/.

[3] The Hong Kong Manager in Charge Regime was introduced by way of regulatory circular from the Hong Kong Securities and Futures Commission in December 2016; see: Circular to Licensed Corporations Regarding Measures for Augmenting the Accountability of Senior Management, 16 December 2016, available at: https://apps.sfc.hk/edistributionWeb/gateway/EN/circular/intermediaries/licensing/doc?refNo=16EC68. In September 2020, the Monetary Authority of Singapore ("MAS") issued Guidelines on individual accountability and conduct (available at: https://www.mas.gov.sg/-/media/MAS/MPI/Guidelines/Guidelines-on-Individual-Accountability-and-Conduct.pdf), together with a set of FAQs (available at: https://www.mas.gov.sg/-/media/MAS/MPI/Guidelines/FAQs-on-Guidelines-on-Individual-Accountability-and-Conduct.pdf). In December 2019, the Central Bank of Malaysia, Bank Nagara Malaysia ("BNM"), issued a draft "Responsibility Mapping" document ("Proposals"), setting out proposed requirements and expectations to be introduced by the BNM in relation to individual accountability. The proposals have not yet been adopted; they are intended to come into force one year after formal adoption. The proposals are available at: Responsibility Mapping, Exposure Draft, 26 December 2019, BNM, available at: https://www.bnm.gov.my/documents/20124/52006/ed_responsibility+mapping_dec2019.pdf/73187c28-8465-fdd2-7fcf-0ddefa2e8bb2?t=1578645662143.

assigned to specific individuals, who are made fully and unambiguously aware of those responsibilities and made to understand that they will be held to account for how they carry them out".[4] Thus, having responsibility for relevant aspect of the bank's business is not sufficient; the individual must also be accountable. As stated by Brener, "[a]ccountability involves providing an explanation or rendering an account for ones' actions with the implication that they will be assessed and judged with some level of consequence".[5]

The PCBS Report also recommended a licensing regime for other personnel who were not senior managers but whose conduct could seriously harm the bank, its reputation or its customers. It further proposed the creation of a clear single set of conduct rules, the breach of which would constitute grounds for enforcement action by the regulators.[6] These recommendations were implemented in the UK in the SMCR, which came into force from 7 March 2016.[7] The licensing regime recommendation was implemented as a self-certification regime by regulated firms. Initially, it applied to most PRA-authorised firms (including banks) but it has since been progressively extended and, from 9 December 2019, it applies to all firms authorised to provide financial services in the UK.[8]

In Australia, in November 2016, the Parliamentary House of Representatives Standing Committee on Economics issued a report into the four major banks in Australia (Coleman Report).[9] The Coleman Report made a number of recommendations to address concerns regarding individual accountability in the Australian banks and noted the UK's SMCR.[10] Following on from the Coleman Report, the Australian government, in July 2017, issued a Consultation Paper on a proposed new Banking Executive Accountability

---

[4] PCBS Report, Vol. I, pp. 8–9.

[5] Brener, A. (2019). Developing the Senior Managers Regime. In *Research Handbook on Law and Ethics in Banking and Finance*. Edward Elgar Publishing, 274–301, 276.

[6] PCBS Report, pp. 8–9.

[7] Part 4 of the Financial Services (Banking Reform) Act 2013 amended Part V of the Financial Services and Markets Act 2000 to provide the legislative framework for the SMCR in the UK.

[8] The legislative basis for this extension of the SMCR regime is Section 21 and Schedule 4 of the Bank of England and Financial Services Act 2016.

[9] Review of the Four Major Banks: First Report, Australian Parliamentary House of Representatives Standing Committee on Economics, November 2016, available at: https://www.aph.gov.au/-/media/02_Parliamentary_Business/24_Committees/243_Reps_Committees/Economics/45p/Four_Major_B anks_-_First_Report/Final_-_Review_of_the_Four_Major_Banks_First_Report.pdf?la=en&hash=47D B03894D2D1642BEE77A7946B82E11B4A3F7A3.

[10] Interestingly, the Coleman Report also stated: "The committee is aware of potential problems with the [SMCR]. In particular, concerns that parts of the regime may undermine businesses' internal accountability structures and that the [SMCR] runs counter to traditional concepts of criminal and civil liability". Ibid., para. 3.31.

Regime (BEAR).[11] The BEAR proposals had "particular regard" to some elements of the SMCR because the Consultation Paper stated there was "benefit in ensuring consistency as far as possible and practicable" with individual accountability frameworks in other jurisdictions.[12] It also noted, however, that "as the particular circumstances of the Australian banking sector differ to those in the UK, the proposals in this paper do not adopt all elements of the [SMCR]".[13]

The new BEAR was adopted in February 2018, on the basis of legislation inserting a new Part IIAA in the Australian Banking Act 1959 (hereinafter the "1959 Act"). It initially applied, from July 2018, only to the four largest Authorised Deposit-taking Institutions (ADIs) in Australia. Since July 2019, it applies to all ADIs in Australia. In January 2020, for the purposes of implementing recommendations in the Australian Royal Commission Report, the Australian Government issued a Proposal Paper (hereinafter the "Proposal Paper"), which set out proposals to replace the current BEAR with a Financial Accountability Regime (FAR); in July 2021, it published draft FAR legislation and, in October 2021, the Financial Accountability Regime Bill was introduced into the House of Representatives.[14] The proposed FAR would extend the scope of the BEAR to all entities regulated by the Australian Prudential Regulation Authority (APRA) and, in particular, superannuation firms and insurance firms and would be jointly administered by APRA and the Australian Securities & Investments Commission (ASIC).[15]

In Ireland, in July 2018, the Central Bank of Ireland (CBI) published a report (CBI Report) setting out the conclusions of its review of the culture

---

[11] Banking Executive Accountability Regime, Consultation Paper, July 2017, available at: https://treasury.gov.au/sites/default/files/2019-03/c2017-t200667-BEAR_cp.pdf.

[12] Ibid., p. 3.

[13] Ibid.

[14] Implementing Royal Commission Recommendations 3.9, 4.12, 6.6, 6.7 and 6.8 Financial Accountability Regime, Australian Treasury Proposal Paper, 22 January 2020, available at: https://treasury.gov.au/sites/default/files/2020-01/c2020-24974.pdf. Draft FAR legislation available at: https://treasury.gov.au/consultation/c2021-169627. The Financial Accountability Regime Bill, introduced into the Australian House of Representatives in October 2021, available at: https://www.aph.gov.au/Parliamentary_Business/Bills_Legislation/Bills_Search_Results/Result?bId=r6801.

[15] The Proposal Paper provides that for smaller firms (referred to as "core compliance entities"), all of the relevant obligations would apply, with the exception of the obligations to submit Accountability Statements and Accountability Maps, as "Since the BEAR commenced on 1 July 2018, industry feedback suggests that the development, submission, and updating of accountability maps and statements poses a significant compliance burden on smaller entities" (Proposal Paper, p. 4). This is reflected in the July 2021 draft FAR legislation, which refers to "core notification obligations" and "enhanced notification obligations".

of the five retail banks in Ireland.[16] The CBI Report noted that the CBI's current powers were not sufficient and that "without a strengthened Individual Accountability Framework, the likelihood of profound cultural change in the regulated financial services sector is reduced".[17] It also recommended that legislation be developed to introduce a new Individual Accountability Framework, including a Senior Executive Accountability Regime (SEAR). The proposed new Individual Accountability Framework, as outlined in the General Scheme of the Central Bank (Individual Accountability Framework) Bill 2021 is modelled on the SMCR. It is anticipated that the proposed legislation will be adopted in 2022.

The following sections provide a brief overview of some of the key features of the new UK, Australian, and proposed Irish IARs. It details, in particular, the following key features: the allocation of responsibilities to individuals; the new conduct rules; and sanctions for breaches of the conduct requirements.

2.1   The Allocation of Accountability to Senior Individuals

In the UK, the SMCR is administered by the Financial Conduct Authority (FCA) and Prudential Regulation Authority (PRA).[18] Under the SMCR, the FCA or PRA may designate a function as a Senior Management Function (SMF).[19] The SMFs that have been designated include the chief executive officer, chief financial officer, chairman, chair of certain board committees (nominations, audit, remuneration, risk), senior independent director, compliance oversight, AML oversight, head of risk, and head of internal audit.[20] Furthermore, the FCA and PRA have specified certain "prescribed responsibilities" which are responsibilities which must (depending on the size of the firm) be allocated to a person in a SMF. These prescribed responsibilities include, for example, responsibility for the firm's performance of its obligations under the SMCR; responsibility for the firm's obligations for conduct rules training and conduct rules reporting; oversight of risk, audit,

---

[16] Behaviour and Culture of the Irish Retail Banks, July 2018, CBI, available at: https://www.cen tralbank.ie/docs/default-source/publications/corporate-reports/behaviour-and-culture-of-the-irish-retail-banks.pdf?sfvrsn=2.

[17] Ibid., p. 32.

[18] Section 59 Financial Services and Markets Act 2000.

[19] Ibid.

[20] For a full list of the FCA-designated SMFs, see, SUP 10C of the FCA Handbook: https://www.handbook.fca.org.uk/handbook/SUP/10C/4.html#D83; for the PRA-designated SMFs, see the Senior Management Function section of the PRA Rulebook: http://www.prarulebook.co.uk/rulebook/Content/Part/212475/06-10-2020.

and compliance; responsibility for leading the development and monitoring of effective implementation of policies and procedures for the induction, training, and professional development of all members of the firm's governing body, its SMFs and other key function holders; and acting as the firm's whistle-blower's champion.[21]

An individual cannot take up a SMF without the prior approval of the regulator,[22] except in certain very limited circumstances,[23] which will be withheld unless the regulator is satisfied that the individual is fit and proper for the SMF for which he or she has applied.[24] As part of the application process, the applicant must submit to the regulator a Statement of Responsibilities setting out the aspects of the firm's business for which the individual is to be responsible.[25] Certain types of firms, including banks, insurance companies and other so-called "enhanced firms", are also required to have a Management Responsibilities Map in place, that sets out their management and governance arrangements and all responsibilities described in the Statements of Responsibility of all SMFs to show how responsibilities within the firm are allocated across the firm.[26] The regulators have provided some general guidance on the content of Statements of Responsibilities.[27]

With regard specifically to board members of regulated financial services firms, only the chairman, senior independent director and chairs of the audit, remuneration and nomination committees have been designated as SMFs. Also, the FCA expects that certain of the above-described "prescribed responsibilities" will be assigned to non-executive director SMFs (including development of members of the governing body; oversight of internal audit, compliance, risk; whistle-blower's champion).[28] In a Supervisory Statement

---

[21] The FCA-designated prescribed responsibilities are set out in the following section of the FCA Handbook: https://www.handbook.fca.org.uk/handbook/SYSC/24/2.html?date=2020-10-06.

[22] Section 59 Financial Services and Markets Act 2000.

[23] It is permissible to appoint an individual to an SMF role on a temporary basis, for up to 12 weeks, where the appointment is to provide cover for an SMF whose absence is temporary or reasonably unforeseen (FCA Handbook, SUP 10C.3.13, available at: https://www.handbook.fca.org.uk/handbook/SUP/10C/3.html?date=2016-03-07).

[24] Section 61 Financial Services and Markets Act 2000.

[25] Section 60(2A) Financial Services and Markets Act 2000.

[26] FCA Handbook: https://www.handbook.fca.org.uk/handbook/SYSC/25/2.html#D30; also, FCA Handbook, SYSC 23 Annex 1, Definition of SMCR firm and different types of SMCR firms, available at: https://www.handbook.fca.org.uk/handbook/SYSC/23/Annex1.html?date=2021-07-21#D26.

[27] See, e.g. FCA Handbook, SUP 10C.11 and SUP 10C Annex 10D; Strengthening individual accountability in banking (2021). PRA, Supervisory Statement SS28/15, available at: https://www.bankofengland.co.uk/-/media/boe/files/prudential-regulation/supervisory-statement/2021/ss2815-june-2021.pdf?la=en&hash=156397322744C304387307613D72EB63920FBD77.

[28] FCA Handbook, SYSC 24.3.2: https://www.handbook.fca.org.uk/handbook/SYSC/24/?view=chapter.

issued in June 2021, the PRA stated that the non-executive directors that are in a SMF are not required or expected to assume any executive responsibilities. Rather, their accountability is restricted to those activities for which they are responsible.

These responsibilities are inherent in the nature of their chairmanship or senior independent director role, such as: ensuring that the board and/or the committees which they chair meet with sufficient frequency; fostering an open, inclusive discussion which challenges executives where appropriate; devoting sufficient time and attention to matters within their remit which are relevant to the firm's safety and soundness; helping to ensure that the board or committee and its members have the information necessary to perform their tasks; facilitating the running of the board or committee to assist it in providing independent oversight of executive decisions.[29] The PRA noted as examples of hypothetical scenarios where it might consider taking action against a within-scope non-executive director: the risk committee fails to assist the board in overseeing executive management's implementation of the firm's risk strategy; within-scope directors have serious concerns about an overly dominant CEO, but these concerns are not addressed, recorded or discussed by the board or with PRA or FCA supervisors.[30] For non-executive directors in certain types of firms (such as banks and insurance companies), a regulatory notification (but not pre-approval) requirement in respect of their appointment to the non-executive director role applies under PRA rules.[31]

The SMCR also introduced a new certification regime for staff whose functions are not sufficiently senior to amount to a SMF, but whose functions nevertheless give rise to a risk of "significant harm" to the firm or any of its customers.[32] The FCA and PRA may specify certain functions as "significant harm" functions.[33] The roles that have been specified as "significant harm" functions include "significant management" roles, "material risk-takers", and persons in "client-dealing" roles.[34] Staff covered by this certification regime

---

[29] Strengthening individual accountability in banking (2021). PRA, Supervisory Statement SS28/15, para. 2.31.

[30] Ibid., para. 2.32.

[31] PRA PS16/15 Strengthening individual accountability in banking: responses to CP14/14, CP28/14 and CP7/15 of July 2015, available at: www.bankofengland.co.uk/pra/Documents/publications/ps/2015/ps1615.pdf and PRA PS22/15 Strengthening individual accountability in insurance: responses to CP26/14, CP7/15 and CP13/15 August 2015, available at: www.bankofengland.co.uk/pra/Documents/publications/ps/2015/ps2215.pdf.

[32] Section 63E Financial Services and Markets Act 2000.

[33] Ibid.

[34] See, e.g. FCA Handbook, SYSC 27.7.3.

do not require prior approval from the regulator to carry out their role.[35] They are not permitted to carry out their role, however, unless their firm has certified that they are fit and proper to do so.[36] A firm can only issue such a certificate for a 12-month period.[37] This means that it must review, at least on an annual basis, the fitness and propriety of all staff falling within the certification regime. Regulated firms are also required to review the fitness and probity of all its SMFs and non-executive directors, at least on an annual basis. Furthermore, they must consider whether there are any grounds on which a regulator could withdraw the regulatory approval for the SMFs and, if so, notify the regulator of those grounds.[38]

In Australia, the BEAR equivalent of the SMFs under SMCR are "Accountable Persons", as defined in the 1959 Act, as amended.[39] Accountable Persons are persons with actual or effective senior executive responsibility for the management or control of an ADI or a significant or substantial part of the operations of an ADI. The BEAR sets out a non-exhaustive list of types of Accountable Persons.[40] Also, as is the case with the Statements of Responsibility requirements under the SMCR, ADIs are required under BEAR to have in place and provide to APRA the Accountability Statements for each of their Accountable Persons, setting out a comprehensive statement of the areas of responsibility of the individual.[41] Furthermore, similarly to the Management Responsibility Maps of the SMCR, the BEAR requires ADIs to have in place and provide to APRA an Accountability Map detailing the reporting lines and lines of responsibility across the ADI,[42] to ensure that the responsibilities of Accountable Persons cover all aspects of the operations of the entity and its significant or substantial subsidiaries.[43]

The BEAR does, however, differ in a number of respects from the SMCR, including with regard to allocation of accountability and review of fitness and probity of individuals. First, prior approval of APRA is not required for an individual to be appointed to an Approved Person role. The 1959 Act, as amended, simply provides that an individual cannot be appointed

---

[35] The FCA-specified "significant harm" functions are set out in the FCA Handbook at SYSC 27.7.3: https://www.handbook.fca.org.uk/handbook/SYSC/27/?view=chapter. For the PRA certification regime, which refers to "significant risk takers", see the PRA Rulebook at: http://www.prarulebook.co.uk/rulebook/Content/Part/212542/06-10-2020.

[36] Section 63E(1), 63F(1) Financial Services and Markets Act 2000.

[37] Section 63F(5) Financial Services and Markets Act 2000.

[38] Section 63(2A) Financial Services and Markets Act 2000.

[39] The meaning of "Accountable Person" is set out in Section 37BA Banking Act 1959.

[40] Section 37BA Banking Act 1959.

[41] Section 37(1)(a) Banking Act 1959.

[42] Section 37(1)(b) Banking Act 1959.

[43] Section 37D Banking Act 1959.

as an Accountable Person if the person has not been registered with APRA or has been disqualified.[44] Under the registration process, the applicant firm must include an Accountability Statement for the individual in question and a signed declaration that the ADI is satisfied the person is suitable be an Accountable Person.[45] APRA must register the individual as an Accountable Person if these information requirements are met.[46] In other words, APRA does not consider whether the individual in question is fit and proper for the role during the registration process. In this regard, Wayne Byres, then chairman of APRA stated to an Australian Parliamentary Committee in 2016:

> A significant and highly resource intensive part of the UK regime is, in fact, that the regulator approves senior appointments. To me, that actually undermines the accountability for appointments. The appointment should be the responsibility of the organisation. The regulator should have responsibility to veto or remove but once you have an appointment that the regulator has approved, and that individual, subsequently, proves that they should not have been in that position, well, who is at fault? Is it the organisation that appoints them or is it the regulator that allowed them there? I think it muddles the accountability. I would not advocate that sort of thing.[47]

In this regard, as outlined in the previous chapter, APRA's Prudential Standard CPS 520 requires institutions regulated by APRA to determine whether their senior managers are fit and proper for their role and functions, before appointment to the role and to assess senior management prior to appointment and on an annual basis thereafter.[48] This requirement covers senior managers and persons who exercise senior management responsibilities,[49] so is wider in scope than Accountable Persons under BEAR. As also outlined above, the Australian Government issued a Proposal Paper, which set out proposals to replace the current BEAR with a Financial Accountability Regime (FAR) and, in October 2021, the Bill to establish FAR, the Financial Accountability Regime Bill, was introduced into the Australian House

---

[44] Section 37DA(1) Banking Act 1959.

[45] Section 37HA Banking Act 1959.

[46] Ibid.

[47] Mr Wayne Byres, Chairman of APRA, Committee Hansard, 14 October 2016, available at: https://www.aph.gov.au/Parliamentary_Business/Hansard/Hansard_Display?bid=committees/commrep/558cbc94-fa24-488d-aafd-2f9fc07b540e/&sid=0001.

[48] Australian Prudential Regulatory Authority. Prudential Standard CPS 520 (APRA, 2018), available at: https://www.legislation.gov.au/Details/F2018L01390.

[49] Ibid., para. 24.

of Representatives.[50] Whilst under the January 2020 proposals APRA would have been provided with a "non-objection" power, giving it the power to veto the appointment or re-appointment of Accountable Persons, this proposed power was not included in the October 2021 draft legislation.

Secondly, the BEAR does not contain an SMCR-type certification regime, described above, for other staff who are not sufficiently senior to be Accountable Persons, but who nevertheless could cause harm to the firm or its customers (although as noted above, APRA's CPS 520 may apply to them).

A third difference between the SMCR and the BEAR relates to the scope of functions covered by the respective senior manager regimes. Whilst the respective lists of senior managers are broadly equivalent, it is interesting to note that, whereas all board directors are included as Accountable Persons under BEAR,[51] only the chairman of the board, senior independent director and chairman of key committees are deemed to be board-level SMFs under the SMCR.[52] Also, unlike the SMCR, BEAR explicitly includes as an Accountable Person the head of the HR function.[53] This latter difference might not be very significant in practice, given that under the SMCR, the Prescribed Responsibilities that must be assigned to a SMF (e.g. an SMF-18, "other overall responsibility function") include a number that are typically HR-type functions. These functions include responsibility for the firm's obligations regarding conduct rules training and reporting; leading the development and monitoring the effective implementation of the induction, training, and professional development of the firm's governing body, SMFs and key function holders.[54] More generally, it is useful to note that the BEAR does not have the equivalent of the SMCR Prescribed Responsibilities, i.e. specified responsibilities that must be allocated to an identified senior manager.

---

[50] The Proposal Paper provides that for smaller firms (referred to as "core compliance entities"), all of the relevant obligations would apply, with the exception of the obligations to submit Accountability Statements and Accountability Maps, as "Since the BEAR commenced on 1 July 2018, industry feedback suggests that the development, submission, and updating of accountability maps and statements poses a significant compliance burden on smaller entities" (Proposal Paper, ibid., p. 4).

[51] Section 37BA(3)(a) Banking Act 1959.

[52] According to the Revised Explanatory Memorandum introducing the legislation for the BEAR, "Non-executive directors for the ADI will be accountable persons, but their obligations under BEAR will reflect their oversight role for the ADI and its group. They will not be required to perform day-to-day executive and management functions to meet the obligations of the BEAR". Commonwealth of Australia, Revised Explanatory Memorandum to the Treasury Laws Amendment (Banking Executive Accountability and Related Measures) Bill 2017, para. 1.98, available at: https://www.legislation.gov.au/Details/C2017B00229/Explanatory%20Memorandum/Text.

[53] Section 37BA(3)(i) Banking Act 1959.

[54] SYSC 24.2.6 FCA Handbook, available at: https://www.handbook.fca.org.uk/handbook/SYSC/24/2.html?date=2020-10-07#D13.

It is also useful to note the respective positions under the SMCR and BEAR regarding "rolling bad apples". The "rolling bad apples" problem was recognised to be a serious problem in the financial services industry internationally and described in the following terms in a 2018 Financial Stability Board report:

> Another aspect of strengthening individual accountability relates to the problem of individuals who engage in misconduct but are able to obtain subsequent employment elsewhere without disclosing their earlier misconduct to the new employer (so-called rolling bad apples). The result is that employees are mobile, but their conduct records are not, and a valuable deterrent against misconduct – risk to future employment – is thus lost.[55]

The Financial Stability Board Report recognised, however, the complexity of the issue and that "many firms limit what they disclose to third parties about former employees due to legal risks arising from data protection, defamation, employment rights or privacy law".[56]

Under the SMCR regulatory reference requirements, regulated firms proposing to hire an individual into a SMF role or material risk-taker role must seek information from previous employers of the individual, covering at least the previous six years, that is reasonably relevant to an assessment of the individual's fitness and probity.[57] In Australia, the Australian Banking Association (ABA) has issued industry-agreed protocols in respect of prospective employees, requiring subscribing banks to carry out relevant background checks. The 2019 Australian Royal Commission Final Report into misconduct in the banking, superannuation and financial services industry (Hayne Report) recommended making the Australian ABA Protocol for financial advisors mandatory for all Australian finance service licensees whose licence authorises the provision of financial advice.[58] In July 2021, ASIC issued a Protocol, giving effect to this recommendation.[59] In Ireland, whilst the proposed new Individual Accountability Framework is modelled on the

---

[55] Strengthening Governance Frameworks to Mitigate Misconduct Risk: A Toolkit for Firms and Supervisors, Financial Stability Board, 20 April 2018, p. 32, available at: https://www.fsb.org/wp-content/uploads/p200418.pdf.

[56] Ibid., p. 33.

[57] See, SYSC 22 FCA Handbook, available at: https://www.handbook.fca.org.uk/handbook/SYSC/22/?view=chapter; PRA Rulebook, Fitness and Propriety 2.7.4; Strengthening individual accountability in banking (2021). PRA, Supervisory Statement SS28/15.

[58] Hayne Report, p. 82.

[59] See, ASIC press release, 20 July 2021; available at: https://asic.gov.au/about-asic/news-centre/find-a-media-release/2021-releases/21-180mr-asic-releases-reference-checking-and-information-sharing-protocol-for-financial-advisers-and-mortgage-brokers/.

SMCR, it appears that regulatory reference requirements along the lines of the SMCR are unlikely to be included in the proposed new regime.[60]

Under the proposals to replace BEAR with FAR, which would essentially extend the application of the regime from ADIs to all firms regulated by APRA, firms would be subject to "core notification obligations" i.e. a requirement to notify the regulator in specified circumstances e.g, where the regulated firm reasonably believes that an accountable person has breached their accountability obligations or where the firm has reduced an accountable person's variable remuneration because of the individual's failure to comply with their accountability obligations. There would also be "enhanced notification obligations", whereby firms that meet thresholds to be identified by the Minister would be required to notify accountability statements and accountability maps to the regulator.[61]   Somewhat similarly, the SMCR distinguishes in terms of scope of obligations between limited scope, core and enhanced firms.[62] Furthermore, the Australian FAR proposals intend to introduce new Accountable Person roles, including "senior executive responsibility for management of the entity's dispute resolution function (internal and external)" and "senior executive responsibility for management of the entity's end-to-end product responsibility".[63] These roles are not currently prescribed as SMFs under SMCR.

In Ireland, there are a number of elements to the proposed new Individual Accountability Regime, as set out in the General Scheme of the Central Bank (Individual Accountability Framework) Bill 2021. One of these is the proposed introduction of a Senior Executive Accountability Regime (SEAR), which is similar to the SMCR. Under the proposed SEAR, each person in a so-called Senior Executive Function would be required to have in place a Statement of Responsibilities, clearly setting out their individual role and areas of responsibility. The CBI would also have powers to prescribe responsibilities that must be allocated to a person in a Senior Executive Function.

---

[60] The Regulatory Impact Analysis that was published by the Irish government along with the General Scheme of the Central Bank (Individual Accountability Framework) Bill 2021 stated (at p. 4) "Feedback from the industry in the UK in relation to the SMCR has been broadly positive, with reservations focused on elements that are not replicated in the Irish legislation, particularly the operation of Regulatory References", available at: https://www.gov.ie/en/publication/ed2ba-regulatory-impact-assessment-central-bank-individual-accountability-framework-bill/.

[61] Financial Accountability Regime Bill 2021, October 2021; Section 31.

[62] See, e.g. FCA Handbook SYSC 23 Annex 1, available at: https://www.handbook.fca.org.uk/handbook/SYSC/23/Annex1.html?date=2021-04-07#D26.

[63] For a fuller list of the proposed roles that ASIC and APRA may prescribe as Accountable Person roles, see, "Financial Accountability Regime—List of Prescribes Responsibilities and Positions". Policy Proposal Paper. July 2021; available at: https://treasury.gov.au/sites/default/files/2021-07/c2021-169627-policy-paper.pdf.

The proposed Senior Executive Functions would cover all persons in a Pre-approval Controlled Function role (PCFs) in within-scope firms. In this regard, pursuant to the Central Bank Reform Act 2010, the CBI has powers to specify senior-level functions as PCF roles (e.g. board director, CEO) requiring prior CBI approval.[64] Interestingly, whereas as outlined above, only certain board director roles fall within the scope of the SMCR, by contrast all board directors, including all non-executives, of within-scope firms would fall within the scope of the SEAR. Within-scope firms would be required to provide the CBI with Responsibility Maps, documenting key management, and governance arrangements in a comprehensive, accessible, and clear single source of reference. It is intended that SEAR would initially apply only to certain types of regulated financial services firms, such as credit institutions, insurance undertakings, and certain types of investment firms.[65]

The proposed new regime also includes an annual fitness and probity certification process. This will be broadly along the lines of the UK certification regime under the SMCR. Accordingly, firms would certify on an annual basis that all persons in a so-called Controlled Function role in their firm meet the applicable fitness & probity standards. Under the current fitness & probity legislation, the CBI may designate specified roles as Controlled Function roles. In essence, roles that the CBI has designated as Controlled Function roles would cover all those in a Senior Executive Function together with many in more junior roles including customer-facing roles.[66]

2.2   The New Conduct Rules for Individuals

One of the recommendations of the UK PCBS Report, in the context of its recommendations relating to the introduction of a new senior managers

---

[64] Central Bank Reform Act 2010, Sections 22, 23. The CBI's list of PCF roles is available at: https://www.centralbank.ie/docs/default-source/regulation/how-we-regulate/authorisation/fitness-pro bity/regulated-financial-service-providers/regulatory-requirements/gns-4-1-1-3-1-1-list-of-pre-approval-controlled-functions.pdf?sfvrsn=6.

[65] Specifically, it is intended that SEAR would initially apply to: credit institutions (excluding credit unions); insurance undertakings (excluding reinsurance undertakings, captive (re)insurance undertakings and insurance Special Purpose Vehicles); investment firms which underwrite on a firm commitment basis and/or deal on own account and/or are authorised to hold client monies/assets; third country branches of these types of entities.

[66] For a list of the roles designated by the CBI as Controlled Function roles, see: https://www.centralbank.ie/docs/default-source/regulation/how-we-regulate/authorisation/fitness-probity/regulated-financial-service-providers/regulatory-requirements/gns-4-1-1-3-1-1-list-of-controlled-functions.pdf?sfvrsn=14.

regime, was that the existing framework of statements of principle and associated codes of conduct "which are incomplete and unclear in their application" be replaced by a single set of banking standards rules.[67] This recommendation has been addressed in the SMCR, which gives the FCA and PRA powers to adopt conduct rules.[68] Pursuant to these powers, the FCA Handbook has been amended to include a Code of Conduct and associated guidance (the PRA has the same conduct rules in its Rulebook).[69] It contains two tiers of conduct rules for individuals. The first tier applies to essentially all staff (other than ancillary staff) of regulated firms and the second tier applies essentially only to those in SMF roles.[70] This first tier of conduct rules is as follows:

Rule 1: "You must act with integrity".
Rule 2: "You must act with due skill, care, and diligence".
Rule 3: "You must be open and cooperative with the FCA, the PRA and other regulators".
Rule 4: "You must pay due regard to the interests of customers and treat them fairly".
Rule 5: "You must observe proper standards of market conduct".

The further tier of conduct rules, applicable only to those in SMF roles, is as follows:

SC1: "You must take reasonable steps to ensure that the business of the firm for which you are responsible is controlled effectively".
SC2: "You must take reasonable steps to ensure that the business of the firm for which you are responsible complies with the relevant requirements and standards of the regulatory system".
SC3: "You must take reasonable steps to ensure that any delegation of your responsibilities is to an appropriate person and that you oversee the discharge of the delegated responsibility effectively".
SC4: "You must disclose appropriately any information of which the FCA or PRA would reasonably expect notice".

---

[67] PCBS Report, p. 9.

[68] Section 64A Financial Services and Markets Act 2000, as amended.

[69] FCA Code of Conduct; FCA Handbook; see: https://www.handbook.fca.org.uk/handbook/COCON.pdf. The Code of Conduct was adopted pursuant to Section 64A Financial Services and Markets Act 2002. The PRA has in place the same conduct rules, as set out in its Rulebook; see: https://www.prarulebook.co.uk/rulebook/Content/Part/302382/08-04-2021.

[70] SC4, requiring information to be disclosed appropriately to the FCA or PRA in certain circumstances also applies to non-executive directors, who do not have a SMF, of specified PRA-regulated firms. See, Strengthening individual accountability in banking (2021). PRA, Supervisory Statement SS28/15, 5.21.

The BEAR in Australia does not have the equivalent of this two-tiered set of conduct standards. Rather, it has a single list of "accountability obligations" imposed on Accountable Persons. They must carry out their functions by "acting with honesty and integrity, and with due skill, care, and diligence"; "dealing with APRA in an open, constructive, and cooperative way"; and by "taking reasonable steps in conducting those responsibilities to prevent matters from arising that would adversely affect the prudential standing or prudential reputation of the ADI".[71]

The BEAR does not explicitly include an equivalent of the SMCR individual conduct rule to pay due regard to the interests of customers and treat them fairly, and to observe proper standards of market conduct. Also, it does not explicitly include the equivalent of the SMCR conduct rule requiring persons in a SMF role to disclose appropriately any information of which the regulator would reasonably expect notice. An ADI must, however, notify APRA of any breach of accountability obligations by an Accountable Person.[72]

Under the proposal to replace BEAR with FAR, the Australian government proposes that a further "accountability obligation" be added. Specifically, it proposes that Accountable Persons take "reasonable steps" in conducting their responsibilities as an accountable person to prevent matters from arising that would (or would be likely to) result in a material contravention by the regulated firm of specified financial services legislation.[73]

What does the obligation to take "reasonable steps" involve? In the UK, the FCA's Handbook provides some general guidance (see the sanctioning factors outlined below).[74] In Australia, the legislation specifically provides that the taking of reasonable steps in relation to a matter includes having "appropriate governance, control and risk management in relation to that matter"; and "safeguards against inappropriate delegations of responsibility in relation to that matter"; and "appropriate procedures for identifying and remediating problems that arise or may arise in relation to that matter"; the draft FAR legislation adds to this list, the taking of appropriate action in response to non-compliance or suspected non-compliance.[75]

---

[71] Section 37CA Banking Act 1959.

[72] Section 37FC (d)(ii) Banking Act 1959.

[73] Financial Accountability Regime Bill 2021, October 2021; Section 21.

[74] FCA Handbook, COCON 4.2.

[75] Section 37CB Banking Act 1959; Financial Accountability Regime Bill 2021, October 2021; Section 22.

In Ireland, the proposed Individual Accountability Framework sets out common conduct standards to be applied to all staff in regulated firms. It also sets out additional conduct standards for all in a PCF role, together with "other persons who exercise significant influence on the conduct of a [regulated firm's] affairs".[76] The common conduct standards are similar to the above first tier of conduct rules under the SMCR. Interestingly, the proposed Irish standards require individuals to be co-operative with the regulators and deal with them "without delay" (this is not explicitly stated in SMCR conduct rules). Also, whereas these SMCR conduct rules require individuals to "pay due regard to the interests of customers and treat them fairly", the Irish equivalent requires individuals to "act in the best interests of customers and treat them fairly and professionally". It may well, however, be that there is no material difference in the implementation and enforcement of these respective requirements.

The additional conduct standards that apply to persons in PCF roles and "other persons who exercise significant influence on the conduct of a [regulated firm's] affairs" are similar to the above further tier of conduct rules that apply to SMFs under the SMCR. Interestingly, the Irish conduct standards include a requirement to "participate effectively in collective decision-making", which is not explicitly included under SMCR. Also, whereas the SMCR rules require individuals to take "reasonable steps" to meet the relevant requirements, this phrase is not included in the equivalent Irish version; the Irish version provides, however, that it is a defence to a CBI enforcement action "if the person can show that he or she acted reasonably in all of the circumstances of the case, and to provide a non-exhaustive list of matters that may be relevant to assessing whether a person acted reasonably".[77] It will be interesting to see whether this difference in wording has any significance in practice and gives rise to differences of approach in terms of where the burden of proof lies.

2.3   Sanctions on Individuals for Breaches of the Conduct Rules

The UK FCA and PRA have wide powers to sanction individuals for breaches of the above-outlined SMCR conduct rules, including: public censure (in effect, a public reprimand), financial penalty "of such amount as it considers appropriate", suspension for up to two years or restriction on activities for

---

[76] General Scheme of a Central Bank (Individual Accountability Framework) Bill 2021, p. 1.
[77] Ibid., p. 15.

up to two years.[78] Separately, the FCA or PRA may withdraw their SMF approval in relation to an individual if they are no longer satisfied that the individual has the requisite fitness and probity.[79]

The FCA's Handbook provides that an individual will only be considered to be in breach of the conduct rules if he or she is "personally culpable". This standard is reached when their conduct is deliberate or when their standard of conduct is "below that which would be reasonable in all the circumstances".[80] The FCA Handbook provides the examples of factors that it would take into account in assessing this, including "whether they exercised reasonable care when considering the information available to them"; "whether they reached a reasonable conclusion upon which to act"; "the knowledge they had, or should have had, of regulatory concerns, if any, relating to their role and responsibilities".[81]

Furthermore, individuals in a SMF role under the SMCR are subject to a new statutory "duty of responsibility", breach of which gives rise to the above-described potential sanctions. Pursuant to this duty of responsibility, if the individual's firm breaches regulatory requirements and the individual is responsible for the area in which the breach occurred, the individual can be held accountable if he or she "did not take such steps as a person in [the senior manager's] position could reasonably be expected to take to avoid the contravention occurring (or continuing)".[82] The burden of proof lies with the regulator to show that the individual in the SMF role did not take the steps a person in their position could reasonably be expected to take to avoid the firm's breach occurring.

To date, the FCA and PRA have imposed a sanction for breach of the SMCR individual conduct requirements in only one case. In that case, the FCA and PRA imposed fines totalling £642,430 on Mr Jes Staley, CEO of Barclays Group, for breach of the conduct rule requiring him to "act with due skill, care, and diligence".[83]

---

[78] Section 66 Financial Services and Markets Act 2000.

[79] Section 63(1) Financial Services and Markets Act 2000.

[80] FCA Handbook COCON 3.1.3G, available at: https://www.handbook.fca.org.uk/handbook/COCON/3/?view=chapter.

[81] Ibid.

[82] Section 66A, 66B Financial Services and Markets Act 2000. For guidance on the factors the FCA would likely take into account in assessing whether a breach has arisen in particular circumstances, se, FCA Handbook, Decision Procedure and Penalties Manual (DEPP), para. 6.2.9, available at: https://www.handbook.fca.org.uk/handbook/DEPP/6/2.html.

[83] FCA Press Release, 11 May 2018, available at: https://www.fca.org.uk/news/press-releases/fca-and-pra-jointly-fine-mr-james-staley-announce-special-requirements. Mr. Staley attempted to identify the author of two letters which raised concerns about an employee, the process for hiring that employee and Mr Staley's role in dealing with the concerns about the employee at a previous employer. The

In Australia, under the BEAR, where an Accountable Person breaches his or her accountability obligations, the regulator currently has no powers to fine the individual, but may disqualify the individual from acting as an Accountable Person for "a period that APRA considers appropriate".[84] Under the FAR proposals, whilst the January 2020 proposal paper had proposed that individuals be subject to civil penalties for breaches of their accountability obligations, this proposal was not contained in the July 2021 draft FAR legislation - the October 2021 Bill that was introduced into the Australian House of Representatives provided for civil penalties for any person (whether or not an accountable person) who e.g. attempts to contravene or aids, abets, counsels or procures a contravention of a civil penalty provision of the Bill or is knowingly concerned in such contravention; furthermore, the regulator could disqualify an accountable person and the legislative proposals would enable the regulator to issue directions to the firm to address concerns, where the regulator has reasonable grounds to believe that the firm or Accountable Person has breached obligations.[85]

In Ireland, under the General Scheme of the Central Bank (Individual Accountability Framework) Bill 2021, the CBI would be able to impose sanctions on an individual for breach of the proposed conduct standards. The sanctions that could be imposed would be those currently in place under the CBI's Administrative Sanctions Procedure, under which individuals may be e.g. fined up to €1 million and disqualified.[86] Under current legislation, the

---

letters were treated by Barclay's Compliance department as potential whistle-blows. The FCA found that Mr Staley's actions to be in breach of the conduct rule in question for a number of reasons, including that he failed to identify a conflict of interest in relation to his actions; he failed to be objective by distancing himself from the internal investigation being carried out into the substance of the allegations in the whistle-blows and he failed to maintain the independence of the internal investigation by trying to identify the author. The FCA's decision noted that, given the crucial role of the CEO, the standard of behaviour expected of Mr Staley under this conduct rule is more exacting than for other employees. The level of sanction imposed by the FCA on Mr Staley was widely criticised. It was, for example, referred to as a "feeble sanction" in a *Financial Times* article (Ford, J. [2018]. Regulators Need to Show They Care About Whistle-Blowers, *Financial Times*, 13 May); an Article in *Forbes* criticised the FCA's "lack of spine" for allowing Mr Staley to keep his job (Kelton, E. [2018]. UK Decision About Jes Staley in Barclays Whistle-Blower Case Is a Disaster. *Forbes*, 7 May, available at: https://www.forbes.com/sites/erikakelton/2018/05/07/uk-decision-about-jes-staley-in-barclays-whistleblower-case-is-a-disaster/#33ccdbcd394c). In November 2021, Mr Staley stepped down from his role in Barclays in light of a separate FCA investigation relating to his alleged links with Mr. Jeffrey Epstein; see: https://www.theguardian.com/business/2021/nov/01/barclays-jes-staley-steps-down-fca-investigation.

[84] Section 37J Banking Act 1959.

[85] Financial Accountability Regime Bill 2021, October 2021; Exposure Draft. Sections 42, 65, 81.

[86] For an overview of the CBI's Administrative Sanctions Procedure, see the CBI's Outline of the Administrative Sanctions Procedure, 2018, available at: https://www.centralbank.ie/docs/default-source/regulation/how-we-regulate/enforcement/administrative-sanctions-procedure/legislation-and-guidance/outline-of-the-administrative-sanctions-procedure.pdf?sfvrsn=8.

CBI could only impose such sanctions on individuals under the Administrative Sanctions Procedure if they are a person concerned in the management of a firm that has infringed relevant requirements and 'participated' in the breach. Thus, a breach by the firm first needs to be established before the individual can be sanctioned.[87] Under the proposed new legislation, however, the CBI could sanction the individual without the necessity of any prior finding against the individual's firm. The sanctioning powers under the Administrative Sanctions Procedure are separate to the powers the CBI has under the Fitness & Probity regime to prevent or approve the appointment of an individual to a specified senior management role, or to prevent an individual from continuing in a role if the CBI is not satisfied as to the individual's fitness and propriety for the role.[88]

For potential breaches of the common conduct standards in Ireland, the proposed legislation provides that the individual has a full defence to any potential CBI enforcement action if they "can show that they acted reasonably in all the circumstances of the case".[89] Also, as outlined above, for potential breaches of the additional conduct standards, individuals would have a full defence to any potential CBI enforcement action against them if they can show that they acted reasonably in all the circumstances and "provide a non-exhaustive list of matters that may be relevant to assessing whether a person acted reasonably".[90]

Furthermore, the proposed Irish legislation also includes a duty of responsibility, very similar to the above SMCR duty of responsibility, pursuant to which persons in Senior Executive Functions have a legal duty to take "reasonable steps" to avoid their firm committing a contravention "in relation to the areas of the business for which they are individually responsible".[91] Where the individual's firm has breaches of regulatory requirements and the individual has not complied with this "duty of responsibility", the individual may be sanctioned under the Administrative Sanctions Procedure.

It is useful to note that senior managers in the financial services industry are also subject to regulatory requirements in relation to remuneration,

---

[87] See, CBI Report, p. 38.

[88] See, Central Bank Reform Act 2010, as amended. From 4 November 2014, the European Central Bank is exclusively competent as the authority for fitness and probity assessments of the management board and key function holders of credit institutions that are designated by the ECB as significant credit institutions, together with the management board and key function holders of all credit institutions seeking authorisation; see, generally, Fitness & Probity—Frequently Asked Questions, CBI, 2018, available at: https://www.centralbank.ie/docs/default-source/regulation/how-we-regulate/authorisation/fitness-probity/fitness-and-probity---frequently-asked-questions-2018.pdf?sfvrsn=6.

[89] General Scheme of a Central Bank (Individual Accountability Framework) Bill 2021, p. 10.

[90] Ibid., p. 15.

[91] Ibid., p. 6.

including variable remuneration, that can negatively impact them in the event of their misconduct. Thus, for example, in the UK, the PRA and FCA have issued a policy statement on remuneration (hereinafter the Policy Statement).[92] The Policy Statement sets out detailed rules in relation to, for example, the proportion of total remuneration that may be composed of variable remuneration and minimum periods that must elapse before a specified portion of the variable remuneration can vest. It also contains various provisions for the non-vesting of variable remuneration or claw-back of variable remuneration that has been awarded, where there is evidence of employee misbehaviour.[93] Similarly, in Ireland, the CBI applies, in particular, various European Union requirements relating to remuneration and non-payment of variable remuneration in the event of misconduct by staff.[94] In Australia, the BEAR includes specific requirements relating to the deferral of a proportion of variable remuneration for a minimum period.[95] It also includes the requirement on firms to have a remuneration policy in force that requires that, if an Accountable Person has failed to comply with his or her accountability obligations, the person's variable remuneration is to be reduced "by an amount that is proportionate to the failure".[96]

2.4   Other IARs

The focus of this monograph is on the new IARs in the UK and Australia, together with the proposed new IAR in Ireland. It is, nevertheless, useful to note in passing a few points of comparison with other recently-adopted IARs in the financial services sector in Hong Kong and Singapore, together with the forthcoming regime in Malaysia. The new IARs in these Asian countries

---

[92] Strengthening the Alignment of Risk and Reward: New Remuneration Rules, PRA and FSA Policy Statement, PRA PS 12/15, FCA PS 15/16, available at: https://www.fca.org.uk/publication/policy/ps15-16.pdf.

[93] See, e.g., Peer review of the United Kingdom, 14 April 2021, Financial Stability Board ("FSB"), an FSB peer review of financial sector compensation reforms in the UK. Its recommendations include: "The Authorities should review the interaction between the [SMCR] and remuneration framework, including how the interplay between the [SMCR] and remuneration rules/codes reward diligent and proactive risk management" (p. 5), available at: https://www.fsb.org/wp-content/uploads/P140421.pdf.

[94] See, e.g. the European Banking Authority's Guidelines on Sound Remuneration Policies Under Articles 74(3) and 75(2) of Directive 2013/36/EU and disclosures under Article 450 of Regulation (EU) No 575/2013, available at: https://www.eba.europa.eu/sites/default/documents/files/documents/10180/1314839/1b0f3f99-f913-461a-b3e9-fa0064b1946b/EBA-GL-2015-22%20Final%20report%20on%20Guidelines%20on%20Sound%20Remuneration%20Policies.pdf. More generally, see, e.g. de Andres, P., et al. (2019). European Banks' Executive Remuneration Under the New European Union Regulation. *Journal of Economic Policy Reform*, 22, 208–225.

[95] Part IIAA Division 4 Banking Act 1959.

[96] Section 37E Banking Act 1959.

indicate a broader trend internationally towards an increased regulatory focus on the accountability of individuals to generate cultural change in financial services firms.

In Hong Kong, the Hong Kong Securities and Futures Commission ("SFC") introduced a new Manager in Charge of Core Functions regime ("Manager-in-Charge Regime"), by way of regulatory circular in December 2016.[97] This regime, which covers all firms licensed by the SFC, has been fully in force since October 2017.[98] The stated aim of the Manager-in-Charge regime is to "heighten the accountability of the senior management" of licensed firms and to "promote awareness of senior management obligations under the current regulatory regime".[99] Under this regime, licenced firms are required to identify Managers-in-Charge for specified areas of the firm. A Manager-in-Charge must, inter alia, be of sufficient authority within the firm to make decisions in their core function in question, and report directly and be accountable to the board or the Manager-in-Charge with overall management oversight. Somewhat similarly to the Statements of Responsibility and the Management Responsibility Maps under the SMCR, licensed corporations are required, pursuant to the SFC Circular, to set out in a document approved by their board, the management structure and roles, responsibilities and reporting lines of senior management. The document must set out the details regarding the specific responsibilities of each Manager-in-Charge. The Manager-in-Charge regime does not, however, have the equivalent of the SMCR certification regime for less senior personnel. Also, it does not introduce any new conduct standards or sanctioning powers, but does serve to clarify where individual responsibility may lie in the event of misconduct arising.

Also, in broad alignment with the Manager-in-Charge regime, on 16 October 2017 (the day the transition period for the full implementation of the Manager-in-Charge regime expired), the Hong Kong Monetary Authority (HKMA), which regulates banking in Hong Kong, issued a circular to "elucidate the expectations" of the HKMA regarding management accountability. The circular, described as a Management Accountability Initiative, covered the regulated activities of banks registered with the HKMA.[100] The HKMA

---

[97] See: Circular to Licensed Corporations Regarding Measures for Augmenting the Accountability of Senior Management, 16 December 2016, available at: https://apps.sfc.hk/edistributionWeb/gateway/EN/circular/intermediaries/licensing/doc?refNo=16EC68.

[98] Ibid.

[99] SFC Press Release Announcing the SFC Circular, 16 December 2016, available at: https://www.sfc.hk/edistributionWeb/gateway/EN/news-and-announcements/news/doc?refNo=16PR143.

[100] Circular Letter from the HKMA, 16 October 2017, available at: https://www.hkma.gov.hk/media/eng/doc/key-information/guidelines-and-circular/2017/20171016e1.pdf.

circular and accompanying guidance (hereinafter 2017 Guidance) clarify that the HKMA does not intend to introduce a new layer of regulatory requirements on regulated banks.[101] Rather, the Management Accountability Initiative is intended to clarify the HKMA's expectations and improve the arrangements for gathering information on regulated activities and individual businesses. The 2017 Guidance sets out requirements on registered firms, including in relation to the identification of individuals who are principally responsible for identified functions and information relating to lines of responsibility that are broadly analogous to the Statements of Responsibility and Responsibility Maps under the SMCR.

In Singapore, in September 2020, the Monetary Authority of Singapore (MAS), which regulates financial institutions in Singapore, issued Guidelines on individual accountability and conduct (Guidelines),[102] together with a set of FAQs.[103] The Guidelines have been effective since 10 September 2021. The Guidelines, which are to apply to essentially all financial institutions regulated by MAS, note that "embedding a strong culture of responsibility and ethical behaviour in [financial institutions] requires individual accountability on the part of senior managers and a supportive governance framework".[104] They set out five "outcomes" relating to accountability and conduct that regulated financial institutions are expected to achieve. The aim of the Guidelines is to set out a framework for firms rather than detailed prescriptive rules. The first three identified outcomes in the Guidelines relate specifically to senior managers. Regulated firms must ensure that: first, senior managers responsible for managing and conducting the firm's core management functions are clearly identified; second, the senior managers are fit and proper for their role (and held responsible for the actions of their employees and the conduct of the business under their purview); third, the firm's governance framework supports senior managers' performance of their roles and responsibilities, with a clear and transparent management structure and reporting relationships, a clear statement in place of the responsibilities of each senior manager (the equivalent of a Statement of Responsibilities under

---

[101] Management Accountability at Registered Institutions, Frequently Asked Questions, available at: https://www.hkma.gov.hk/media/eng/doc/key-information/guidelines-and-circular/2017/20171016e 1a1.pdf.

[102] Guidelines on Individual Accountability and Conduct, MAS, 10 September 2010, available at: https://www.mas.gov.sg/-/media/MAS/MPI/Guidelines/Guidelines-on-Individual-Accountab ility-and-Conduct.pdf.

[103] Frequently Asked Questions (FAQs) on Guidelines on Individual Accountability and Conduct, MAS, 10 September 2020, available at: https://www.mas.gov.sg/-/media/MAS/MPI/Guidelines/FAQs-on-Guidelines-on-Individual-Accountability-and-Conduct.pdf.

[104] Guidelines on Individual Accountability and Conduct, MAS, p. 2.

the SMCR), and a clear delineation of the overall management structure (the equivalent of Management Responsibility Maps under the SMCR).[105]

The fourth outcome set out in the Guidelines requires regulated firms to ensure that Material Risk Personnel (MRP) in their firm, whom they must identify, are fit and proper for their role (this must be assessed prior to appointment and on an on-going basis) and subject to appropriate risk governance and oversight. This is somewhat equivalent to the certification regime under the SMCR, although formal "certification" of MRPs is not required under the Guidelines. The fifth stated outcome in the Guidelines requires regulated firms to have in place a framework of policies, procedures, and practices that promotes and sustains the desired conduct by all staff in the firm.

In December 2019, the Central Bank of Malaysia, Bank Nagara Malaysia (BNM), which regulates financial institutions in Malaysia, issued a draft "Responsibility Mapping" document ("Proposals"),[106] setting out proposed requirements and expectations to be introduced by the BNM in relation to individual accountability. The proposals have not yet been adopted; they are intended to come into force one year after formal adoption.[107] They are aimed at complementing existing governance arrangements to promote a corporate culture that reinforces ethical, prudent, and professional behaviour by individuals in leadership positions because "[c]larity on the expectations will encourage individuals in these positions to take greater ownership of the areas under their purview and set the appropriate tone from the top".[108]

The Proposals set out four principles. Under the first principle, the boards of regulated financial services firms are required to oversee and ensure an effective process for identifying and assigning "responsibility areas" to individuals and the responsibility areas are to be clearly identified and mapped onto the firms' organisational structure. This is equivalent to the Management Responsibility Maps requirements under the SMCR. The second principle requires CEOs of these firms to ensure that all identified "responsibility areas" are allocated to individuals at an appropriately senior level, who have the professional competence, authority, and accountability to manage these areas. There is no requirement for prior approval of the BNM for the appointment of senior executives. Under the third principle, individuals to whom

---

[105] Ibid., pp. 9–10.

[106] Responsibility Mapping, Exposure Draft, 26 December 2019, BNM, available at: https://www.bnm.gov.my/documents/20124/52006/ed_responsibility+mapping_dec2019.pdf/73187c28-8465-fdd2-7fcf-0ddefa2e8bb2?t=1578645662143.

[107] Ibid.

[108] Ibid.

responsibilities are allocated must act in good faith, and take "reasonable steps" to ensure that their responsibility area is managed effectively and in line with relevant legal and regulatory requirements; also, they must exercise sound professional judgement, diligence, and due care, adhere to the code of ethics of the financial institution and act with integrity. The fourth principle requires the CEO to maintain a complete, comprehensive and up-to-date register of each individual's responsibilities. This is equivalent to the Statements of Responsibilities under the SMCR.

With regard to enforcement against individuals, the Proposals state that BNM looks to the financial institutions to ensure that a material failure by responsible individuals is met with appropriate consequences and that "except in cases of serious misconduct committed with intent, the Bank generally does not expect to take enforcement actions as an immediate response to events of individual misconduct or poor behaviour".[109]

3   Are the New IARs Likely to Succeed in Improving Behaviours in the Financial Services Industry?

The SMCR and the BEAR have only been in place a short period of time. This makes it difficult to reach reliable conclusions as to whether they are likely to succeed in improving the culture of financial services firms. Nevertheless, some early research surveying their reception and effectiveness is valuable. In 2019, the FCA published a "stocktake report" on the SMCR since its inception in the banking sector. This involved interviews with senior individuals in the industry. It stated that banks told the FCA that the SMCR enabled firms to improve their controls environment, "which they expect to lead to improved behaviours" but "[i]t is not clear to what extent the regime has been linked to culture".[110] A more recent evaluation of SMCR in December 2020 by the PRA is, however, a bit more positive. It surveyed firms and concluded that the SMCR "is widely considered to have had a positive impact on culture and behaviour".[111] The UK industry body, UK Finance, published a report in 2019 on the impact of the SMCR since its

---

[109] Ibid., p. 2.

[110] Senior Managers and Certification Regime Banking Stocktake Report, FCA, August 2019, available at: https://www.fca.org.uk/publications/multi-firm-reviews/senior-managers-and-certification-regime-banking-stocktake-report.

[111] Evaluation of the Senior Managers and Certification Regime, PRA, December 2020, p. 25, available at: https://www.bankofengland.co.uk/-/media/boe/files/prudential-regulation/report/evaluation-of-smcr-2020.pdf?la=en&hash=151E78315E5C50E70A6B8B08AE3D5E93563D0168.

introduction. This was also based on interviews with senior managers and managers in control functions in the industry. It stated:

> Our report shows that since the introduction of the SMCR there has been a meaningful and tangible change in culture, behaviour and attitudes towards risk within firms. For senior managers, the evidence shows that the SMCR has focused minds, with a clear emphasis on what each person is individually responsible for, and how they could be held accountable. However, there is rather less evidence of such a tangible impact throughout the rest of a firm. Some respondents were also critical, expressing the view that the changes have created too much complexity and engendered a focus on recording decisions and actions, rather than looking at culture more holistically.[112]

In Australia, a December 2020 review by APRA of the implementation of BEAR frameworks in Australia by the ADIs found that all of the large ADIs had implemented adequate frameworks and that the actions taken by these ADIs have "delivered a stronger understanding of the end-to-end accountability obligations of accountable persons at the ADIs, have sharpened challenge by boards on executive accountable persons' actions, and facilitated more targeted engagement with APRA to achieve prudential outcomes".[113] It also made some recommendations for improvements. It noted, for example, that the large ADIs could benefit from better monitoring the actions taken by accountable persons to fulfil their accountability obligations and that executive Accountable Persons could consider how they can more deliberately align their actions and records with the ADI's expectations about what constitutes reasonable steps to deliver accountability obligations.[114] Also, a December 2020 review of the implementation of BEAR in Australia by Sheedy and Canestrari-Soh, suggests that the BEAR has given rise to improvements in governance culture. They noted that there were benefits to clarifying individual's obligations.[115] They found that "[a]ccountability has an empowering effect so decisions get made, problems get resolved and there is greater care and diligence. Risk/compliance functions are getting a bigger say as their line one colleagues consult them more. Directors and assurance teams also find

---

[112] SMCR: Evolution and Reform, UK Finance, September 2019, p. 8, available at: https://www.ukf inance.org.uk/system/files/SMCR%20-%20Evolution%20and%20Reform.pdf.

[113] Implementation of the Banking Executive Accountability Regime (BEAR), Information Paper, APRA, 11 December 2020, p. 4, available at: https://www.apra.gov.au/sites/default/files/2020-12/BEAR%20information%20paper%20December%202020.pdf.

[114] Ibid.

[115] Sheedy, E. A., & Canestrari-Soh, D. (2020). Regulating Accountability: An Early Look at the Banking Executive Accountability Regime (Bear), available at: https://doi.org/10.2139/ssrn.3775275.

it easier to do their jobs because they can ascertain who is accountable when things go awry".[116] They concluded:

> The study supports a link between accountability and risk culture. The majority of participants (65%) report an improvement in organisational culture since the introduction of the BEAR. We observed the most favourable risk culture scores in the organisation that has been most successful in embedding accountability over time.[117]

Nevertheless, whilst it appears that the SMCR has led to significant investment in new processes and procedures within firms to ensure compliance with SMCR, together with associated changes in behaviours, it is perhaps too early to assess whether the intended shift to an increasing internalisation by firms and individuals of the norms of behaviour expected by the regulator is occurring.

The success of the new IARs will depend not so much on whether regulated firms implement effectively the required processes and procedures, but rather on whether they lead to improvements in the culture and behaviour of firms. In this regard, as stated in the above December 2020 APRA review of the implementation of BEAR, "[t]he objectives of the BEAR are to drive significant improvements in the operating culture of ADIs through increasing transparency and accountability, and reinforcing the standards of conduct expected of the banking industry by the Australian community".[118]

The process of culture and behaviour change in the financial services industry is a longer-term process and assessing success will be difficult. The following section discusses a number of factors that will likely impact on the future success of the new IARs: first, the significance of allocating identified responsibilities to particular individuals; second, potential concerns around the extent of reliance on firms to ensure compliance with conduct standards under the IARs; third, the sanctioning of individuals as a "credible deterrence" tool; and fourth, potential inherent limitations of the new IARs, in terms of influencing ethical decision-making by individuals.

---

[116] Ibid., p. 6.

[117] Ibid.

[118] "Implementation of the Banking Executive Accountability Regime (BEAR)", Information Paper, APRA, 11 December 2020, p. 8, available at: https://www.apra.gov.au/sites/default/files/2020-12/BEAR%20information%20paper%20December%202020.pdf.

3.1   The Significance of Allocating Accountability to Individuals for Specific Areas of a firm's Business

The main aim of allocating accountability to named individuals for areas of a firm's business is to address the problem, identified in the PCBS Report, of senior individuals being wilfully blind to misconduct that may often be in the short-term commercial interests of the firm, and suffering no negative consequences for such wilful blindness. In other words, it is intended to address the problem that "a culture exists in banking which diminishes a sense of personal responsibility".[119] In principle, the allocation of accountabilities to specified individuals should focus the minds of these individuals on the behaviours expected of them. At a minimum, it is more likely to make the requirements and expectations of the regulator more salient to senior individuals and influence their individual decision-making "choice architecture" when faced with decisions on what actions to take (or not take).[120]

This is particularly relevant for large, complex, firms with multiple layers of management, including matrix management structures and management across multiple jurisdictions. In these environments, the temptation is greater, absent clear individual accountability, for senior individuals not to raise awkward ethical questions about commercially profitable activities or to go along with practices in the firm that are tolerated, but which raise ethical implications. As noted by the Dutch regulator, De Nederlandsche Bank (DNB), holding individuals to account typically causes them to change their behaviours or decision-making processes. This is because "accountability fuels the basic human need for approval from others" and "makes people want to perform well in the eyes of their supervisors".[121]

Furthermore, regulated firms have a commercial interest in ensuring that their firm is well governed, which includes ensuring that there is clarity within the firm as to who is accountable for particular aspects of the firm's business. Accordingly, at least to some extent, there is an alignment of interests as between regulated firms and their regulator to ensure clarity regarding individual accountabilities within the firm. As noted in an FCA stock-take report

---

[119] PCBS Report, Vol. II, para. 538.

[120] For a discussion on the importance of salience and influencing choice architecture for purposes of achieving regulatory compliance, see, e.g. Behaviour and Compliance in Organisations, Occasional Paper 24, FCA, December 2016, available at: https://www.fca.org.uk/publication/occasional-papers/op16-24.pdf.

[121] Supervision of Behaviour and Culture: Foundations, Practice & Future Developments, DNB, p. 309, available at: https://www.dnb.nl/media/1gmkp1vk/supervision-of-behaviour-and-culture_tcm46-380398-1.pdf.

on implementation of the SMCR in the banking industry, which was based on interviews with industry representatives, "[f]irms described the initial stages of implementation as challenging but came to see clear definition of accountability as beneficial".[122]

In other words, clarifying individual roles and responsibilities within financial services firms is an integral element of good corporate governance, even in the absence of the detailed provisions of IARs. Thus, for example, the 2015 Basel Corporate Governance Principles for Banks provides that regulatory supervisors should establish guidance or rules requiring banks to have robust corporate governance in place, including "a clear allocation of responsibilities, accountability, and transparency amongst the members of the board and senior management and within the bank".[123] This principle is enshrined in various ways in legislative instruments and regulatory requirements in various jurisdictions. In the EU, for example, the Capital Requirements Directive (CRDIV),[124] which deals with the prudential supervision of credit institutions and investment firms, requires that within-scope firms have robust governance arrangements in place, "which include a clear organisational structure, with well-defined, transparent, and consistent lines of responsibility".[125]

Additionally, a 2018 report from the G20 Financial Stability Board, aimed at providing regulators and firms with a "toolkit" for addressing governance and misconduct risk, recommended assigning key responsibilities to specified individuals, which could then be used to develop a "responsibilities map". The proposed responsibilities map is the equivalent of a Management Responsibility Map under SMCR, setting out how key responsibilities are allocated across a firm. It stated, "[t]he identification and assignment of key responsibilities may be achieved through legislative or regulatory requirements, firm-driven decisions on their preferred structure, or both".[126] An EU Commission Consultation on implementing the Basel Committee on Banking Supervision's Basel III framework referred to this "toolkit" and invited comments, *inter alia,* on whether an amended EU Capital Requirements Directive should incorporate these ideas, so that firms falling within the scope of the Directive would be required to have in place a statement

---

[122] Senior Managers and Certification Regime Banking Stocktake Report, 5 August 2019, FCA.

[123] Basel Committee on Banking Supervision, Corporate Governance Principles for Banks, 2015, para. 158, available at: https://www.bis.org/bcbs/publ/d328.pdf.

[124] Capital Requirements Directive, EU Directive 2013/36, as amended by EU Directive 2019/878.

[125] Article 74(1), CRDIV, Directive 2013/36/EU.

[126] Strengthening Governance Frameworks to Mitigate Misconduct Risk: A Toolkit for Firms and Supervisors, FSB, 20 April 2018, p. 6, available at: https://www.fsb.org/wp-content/uploads/P200418.pdf.

of responsibilities for their board members and key function-holders, clearly identifying the activities for which they are responsible.[127] It may also be the case that financial services regulators in other jurisdictions have powers under their existing regulatory frameworks to require firms regulated by them to identify and assign key responsibilities to holders of specified roles within the firm.

It should be noted, however, that even under the IARs, the issue of allocating accountabilities to individuals can sometimes raise governance and HR issues, particularly in large, multi-national, financial services firms, where pre-existing internal management structures are not sufficiently clear and the new IARs involve individuals taking on new responsibilities (or having responsibilities removed from them). Also, in specific areas, such as IT risk, where issues of adequacy of available internal expertise to manage the identification and mitigation of all aspects of the potentially very serious risks that could materialise, great care may be needed to ensure effective governance is in place and that individuals do not take on accountabilities beyond their capacities.[128]

More generally, the issue of allocating accountability to individuals for managing risks can be more complex than might seem to be the case on the basis of job titles. The standard framework for allocating responsibilities for risk governance is the "three lines of defence" (3LoD) model. The 3LoD model has been endorsed, for example, in the 2015 Basel Corporate Governance Principles for Banks as the appropriate risk governance model for banks to use.[129] Under this model, the customer-facing business units are the first line of defence; they "own" the risks and are accountable for them, as they take on the risks as part of their functions in carrying on the business. The second line of defence includes the internal Risk function, which monitors and reports on risks, and the internal Compliance function, which advises on and monitors compliance with regulatory requirements. The third line of defence is Internal Audit, which is intended to provide internal review and assurance on the quality and effectiveness of the internal control systems and practices. More recently, the term "three lines model", which moves

---

[127] Implementing the Final Basel II Reforms in the EU, Public Consultation, European Commission, 11 October 2019, p. 53, available at: https://ec.europa.eu/info/sites/info/files/business_economy_euro/banking_and_finance/documents/2019-basel-3-consultation-document_en.pdf.

[128] For IT risk in the context of BEAR, see, Manwaring, K., & Hanrahan, P. F. (2019). BEARing Responsibility for Cyber Security in Australian Financial Institutions: The Rising Tide of Directors' Personal Liability. *Journal of Banking and Finance Law and Practice*, 30(1), 20–42.

[129] Basel Committee on Banking Supervision. (2015). Corporate Governance Principles for Banks, paras. 13, 38, 39.

away from a conception of "defence" to more constructive purposes of this structure, is generally used to describe the structure.[130]

This distinction in respective roles in the 3LoD is recognised in the SMCR (and BEAR and proposed SEAR), which includes as SMFs (Accountable Persons under BEAR) first line roles (such as head of key business area), together with second line roles (chief risk officer, compliance oversight) and third line (head of internal audit).

In principle, this demarcation of respective roles should enable each of the respective individual role-holders to be sufficiently clear on their respective roles and accountability for any failures in risk governance. In practice, however, the demarcation of respective roles is not so clear-cut. As noted by Brener, "[t]he theory sounds conceptually attractive but it is difficult to operate successfully".[131] The PCBS Report was particularly critical of the 3LoD model, "which has been adopted by many banks with the active encouragement of the regulators", as "it appears to have promoted a wholly misplaced sense of security".[132] It suggested that the 3LoD model is a form of "fashionable management school theory" which has "lent undeserved credibility to some chaotic systems". It stated:

> Responsibilities have been blurred, accountability diluted, and officers in risk, compliance and internal audit have lacked the status to challenge front-line staff effectively. Much of the system became a box-ticking exercise whereby processes were followed, but judgement was absent.[133]

A number of commentators have noted that there is still some disagreement over where the boundaries between the three lines should be drawn and considerable divergence in the manner of its operationalisation within firms.[134] Often, for example, it can be unclear to what extent the compliance's role extends beyond assisting the first line functions to manage compliance, to also involve overseeing the first line functions. Also, the model

---

[130] See, e.g. UK Chartered Institute of Internal Auditors: https://www.iia.org.uk/resources/corporate-governance/application-of-the-three-lines-model/.

[131] Brener, A. (2019). Developing the Senior Managers Regime. In Russo, C. A., Lastra, R. M., & Blair, W. eds. *Research Handbook on Law and Ethics in Banking and Finance*. Edward Elgar Publishing, 274–301, 276.

[132] PCBS Report, Vol. 2, para. 143.

[133] Ibid.

[134] See, e.g. Davies, H., & Zhivitskaya, M. (2018). Three Lines of Defence: A Robust Organising Framework, or Just Lines in the Sand? *Global Policy*, 9, 34–42; Brener, A. (2019). Developing the Senior Managers Regime. In Russo, C. A., Lastra, R. M., & Blair, W. eds. *Research Handbook on Law and Ethics in Banking and Finance*. Edward Elgar Publishing, 274–301.

can lead to rigid operational silos which can give rise to issues of inadequate information flows between the silos about risks.[135]

On the other hand, the new IARs may serve to force the individuals in each of the three layers of functions to ensure that there is sufficient clarity in relation to their particular areas of accountability. The regimes might also assist the individuals in second and third line control functions to increase their status within their firm. By comparison with their revenue-generating front-line business colleagues, individuals in second and third line internal control functions are sometimes perceived to have a lesser status within their firm.

The dynamic around this may shift, however, if individuals in these internal control functions become more assertive in addressing potential misconduct issues to protect themselves against the risk of individual sanctions. In this regard, individuals in second and third line control functions often have much less to gain (in particular, in terms of performance bonuses) and much more to lose (where any finding against their integrity in a specialised professional control function may be career-ending) through engaging in or tolerating misconduct.[136] This view is supported by a recent study on the implementation of BEAR in Australia, which determined that "Risk/compliance functions are getting a bigger say as their line one colleagues consult them more".[137] Also, although it determined that there were difficulties regarding accountability for first line functions (the customer-facing business units), it concluded:

> The BEAR appears to be having a favourable impact on risk governance by bringing home Line 1 accountability. Executives are grasping the concept that if there is a problem in their area of accountability, they alone will be answerable. Because they are concerned about their standing within the organisation, along with possible financial consequences, executives are more likely to be proactive in risk management. When problems emerge, the response is faster and more thorough. In other words, the risk culture is more proactive.[138]

---

[135] See, e.g., The Three Lines of Defence, Institute of Internal Auditors, June 2019, available at: https://fna.theiia.org/about-ia/PublicDocuments/3LOD-IIA-Exposure-Document.pdf.

[136] In this regard, it is interesting to note that, as part of the various regulatory responses to the Wells Fargo misconduct (referred to in Chapter 2 of this monograph), in January 2020 the US Office of the Comptroller of the Currency commenced litigation to prohibit and impose significant fines on the former Chief Risk Officer of Wells Fargo's Community Bank, Head of Internal Audit and General Counsel of Wells Fargo (see: https://www.occ.gov/static/enforcement-actions/eaN20-001.pdf).

[137] Sheedy, E. A., & Canestrari-Soh, D. (2020). Regulating Accountability: An Early Look at the Banking Executive Accountability Regime (Bear), p. 6, available at: https://papers.ssrn.com/sol3/papers.cfm?abstract_id=3775275.

[138] Ibid., p. 29.

In summary, whilst the allocation of accountabilities for key aspects of a firm's functions to named individuals within a firm is very much in line with good corporate governance and may enhance the status and influence of the internal control functions within the firm, there are a number of circumstances where the delineation of precise accountabilities may well not be a straightforward exercise.

3.2   The "Achilles Heel" of Meta-Regulation? The Extent of Reliance on Firms to Ensure Individuals Meet Fitness and Probity Standards

An important feature of the new IARs is the emphasis they place on the role of firms to satisfy themselves as to the fitness and probity of their staff, both prior to taking them on for a role (whether or not pre-approval from the regulator is also required) and on an on-going basis.

The FCA had identified a problem with the approved persons regime (APER) that the SMCR replaced, which relied more heavily on the regulator to vet individuals and gave rise to the risk of "moral licensing":

> While moral considerations act as a check on wrongdoing in some situations, this can be overridden if people feel that they have absolved themselves of the need to hold themselves to higher standards. Pre-financial crisis regulation relied on the FSA assessing firms' employees' fitness and propriety, rather than firms doing this themselves. It is possible that removing responsibility for vetting staff ethics from firms constituted a form of moral licensing.[139]

A potential benefit of the increasing focus on the role of firms to vet staff under the new IARs is that it might encourage firms to "internalise" the required standards of fitness and probity, in particular through devoting internal resources to further developing appropriate internal processes, procedures and practices to vet their internal staff appropriately. On the other hand, there is always the risk that at least some firms might treat the requirements as an elaborate procedural "box-ticking" exercise.

The broad regulatory approach adopted, of not prescribing how firms should comply with the regulatory requirement and, instead, relying on regulated firms to develop their own systems for ensuring and demonstrating compliance is a well-established approach, discussed further in Chapter 2

---

[139] Behaviour and Compliance in Organisations, Occasional Paper 24, December 2016, FCA, p. 6; https://www.fca.org.uk/publication/occasional-papers/op16-24.pdf.

of this monograph, that has been described in the regulatory literature as "management-based regulation" or "meta-regulation".[140]

To a certain extent, meta-regulation is a necessary and practical approach to achieving regulatory objectives, given that the resources of the regulator are limited and there are practical reasons for firms to develop systems and processes to vet the fitness and probity of their staff and directors that fit within their already-established human resources and other internal processes. This type of regulatory approach, however, as with any regulatory approach, has its Achilles heel. It is that firms' internal systems and controls are designed to achieve their own goals; not necessarily those of the regulator.[141] As Black has argued, the "fundamental" weakness of meta-regulation:

> is paradoxically the element which is also its potential source of strength: that it relies on firms' processes, systems, controls and internal cultures to work, messy, fragmented and contested though they may be. This is a necessary reliance, but that which is a potential source of strength can also be its Achilles heel.[142]

As Black has argued, a successful management-based regulatory strategy is fundamentally reliant on the simultaneous presence of four elements: (i) firms have to have the appropriate culture and organisational capacity to support the compliance systems which are put in place; (ii) firms need to have the right incentives to pursue public objectives as well as private profits; (iii) regulators need to possess sufficient skills and industry experience to evaluate firms; (iv) regulators need to have sufficient courage and political support to challenge firms.[143]

In implementing the new conduct standards described above, regulators and regulated firms will also need to have a sufficiently clear mutual understanding of what "reasonable steps" senior individual are expected to take to ensure compliance. As noted by MacNeil, the SMCR conduct requirements relating to taking reasonable steps, "rely considerably on the discretion and risk tolerance of the regulator, which can be expected to vary over time and to be influenced by the economic cycle as well as political pressure".[144]

---

[140] Black, J. (2015). Regulatory Styles and Supervisory Strategies. In Moloney, N., Ferran, E., & Payne, J. eds. *The Oxford Handbook of Financial Regulation.* Oxford University Press, 217–253, 227.

[141] Ibid.

[142] Black, J. (2012). Paradoxes and Failures: "New Governance" Techniques and the Financial Crisis. *The Modern Law Review,* 75(6), 1037–1063, 1048.

[143] Black, J. (2015). Regulatory Styles and Supervisory Strategies. In Moloney, N., Ferran, E., & Payne, J. eds. *The Oxford Handbook of Financial Regulation.* Oxford University Press, 217–253, 228.

[144] MacNeil, I. (2018). Regulating Instead of Punishing: The Senior Managers Regime in the UK. In Ligeti, K., & Tosza, S. eds., *White-Collar Crime: A Comparative Perspective.* Bloomsbury, 225–252, 238.

Black has noted that none of her above four elements was present in the pre-global financial crisis era in the UK, which has since adopted a more intrusive supervision approach, including in relation to individual account-ability (and increasing focus by the regulator on interviewing applicants during the pre-approval process).[145] It is useful to bear in mind these four elements in the context of regulators' reliance on firms to vet the fitness and probity of staff on an on-going basis, in particular in the context of the new IARs. A key question looms: whilst regulated firms may have the rele-vant processes, procedures, and internal documentation in place to suggest compliance with the new IARs, do they have the appropriate culture to ensure that the substantive requirements, as well as the procedural require-ments, of the new IARs are met? In this regard, regulators may need to pay attention to issues such as whether firms have the right incentives to take disciplinary action against individuals, particularly senior executives, who engage in misconduct but who are also perceived within the firm as instrumental in the commercial success of the firm.

Firms are required to carry out appropriate due diligence on the fitness and probity of their staff, throughout the life-cycle of the individual staff member's employment with the firm, from initial on-boarding, through to reviews during employment (including any disciplinary action in the event of misconduct) and, potentially, providing a reference to potential new employers when the individual moves on. In Ireland, the CBI issued a "Dear CEO" letter to all regulated firms in 2020, in which it criticised the level of fitness and probity due diligence being carried out by firms under the current fitness and probity regime.[146] This "Dear CEO" letter, which was based on a thematic review and inspection by the CBI of firms' compliance with fitness and probity requirements, stated that the area which was most "consistently weak" across the majority of firms was due diligence, which "was not sufficiently robust to evidence compliance with the requirements of the F[itness] & P[robity] Standards".[147]

The letter also set out a number of expectations, including an annual self-declaration by affected individuals that they meet the applicable standards as

[145] Black, J. (2015). Regulatory Styles and Supervisory Strategies. In Moloney, N., Ferran, E., & Payne, J. eds. *The Oxford Handbook of Financial Regulation*. Oxford University Press, 217–253, 228.
[146] CBI. (2020). "Dear CEO" Letter to Regulated Firms, 17 November, available at: https://www.centralbank.ie/docs/default-source/regulation/how-we-regulate/fitness-probity/news/dear-ceo-letter---thematic-inspections-of-compliance-with-obligations-under-the-fitness-and-probity-regime.pdf?sfvrsn=4.
[147] Ibid., p. 3.

"the minimum expected".[148] Once the new individual accountability framework is implemented in Ireland, it is expected that regulated firms will be required to certify on an annual basis that individuals in Controlled Function roles are fit and proper persons to perform their functions. Controlled Function roles, under the current fitness and probity legislation and implementing regulations, cover all those in a senior, Pre-approval Controlled Function role together with many in more junior roles including customer-facing roles.[149]

In accordance with the SMCR, regulated firms must certify on an annual basis the fitness and probity of all of their staff falling within the certification regime. They must also review the fitness and probity of all their SMFs, at least on an annual basis and consider whether there are any grounds on which a regulator could withdraw the regulatory approval for the individual and, if so, notify the regulator of those grounds.[150] In the absence of comprehensive guidance for the industry, combined with a regulatory focus on minimum required standards, there is a risk that at least some firms will focus on procedural compliance with the required minimum legal requirements, rather than internalising good governance and applying evolving best industry practice. The issues are potentially complex, including in the context of the individual's employment law rights and, in Ireland, constitutional rights. Thus, for example, complex issues may arise in relation to assessing an individual's non-financial misconduct (such as bullying, harassment, and discrimination)[151] and the individual's conduct outside of work.[152] This complexity

---

[148] Ibid., p. 4.

[149] For a list of the roles designated by the CBI as Controlled Function roles, see: https://www.centra lbank.ie/docs/default-source/regulation/how-we-regulate/authorisation/fitness-probity/regulated-financ ial-service-providers/regulatory-requirements/gns-4-1-1-3-1-1-list-of-controlled-functions.pdf?sfvrsn=14 and, for designated Pre-approval Controlled Function roles, see: https://www.centralbank.ie/docs/def ault-source/regulation/how-we-regulate/authorisation/fitness-probity/regulated-financial-service-provid ers/regulatory-requirements/gns-4-1-1-3-1-1-list-of-pre-approval-controlled-functions.pdf?sfvrsn=6.

[150] Section 63(2A) Financial Services and Markets Act 2000.

[151] See, e.g. FCA "Dear CEO" letter regarding non-financial misconduct in wholesale general insurance firms, 6 January 2020, available at: https://www.fca.org.uk/publication/correspondence/dear-ceo-letter-non-financial-misconduct-wholesale-general-insurance-firms.pdf. Also, as stated in an FCA speech, "In our judgement, the way a senior manager approaches issues around diversity may be relevant to our assessment of their competence and character. And the way firms handle non-financial misconduct, including allegations of sexual misconduct, is potentially relevant to our assessment of that firm, in the same way that their handling of insider dealing, market manipulation or any other misconduct is. This is a message industry needs to hear". Speech by Christopher Woolard, FCA, 19 December 2018, available at: https://www.fca.org.uk/news/speeches/opening-and-speaking-out-div ersity-financial-services-and-challenge-to-be-met.

[152] An interesting example of the issues that can arise is a 2014 decision of the FCA to ban the then managing director of an asset management company from the industry, for not being fit and proper. Specifically, the FCA found that the individual did not meet the standards of honesty and integrity expected, as he had, for a period, regularly evaded paying the required train fare on his commuting journeys to work. Although he reached a financial settlement with the train company and was not

reflects the practical constraints on regulators that meta-regulation identifies: the reliance regulators have to place on firms' internal processes, systems,
controls, and internal cultures to achieve regulatory objectives.

This monograph contends that it would benefit the financial services
industry itself to develop more comprehensive guidance to assist all firms in
the industry to obtain reliable information about best practices and to internalise "good" practices, rather than overly focusing on meeting minimum
procedural requirements. Useful steps have been taken in this direction in the
UK by the UK Financial Services Culture Board (FSCB), an industry-funded
body whose aim is to "promote high standards of behaviour and competence
across UK banks and building societies".[153] The FSCB has issued Statements of Good Practice and supporting guidance on fitness and propriety
assessments under the certification regime and on regulatory references.[154]
As stated by the Financial Services Culture Board:

> The regulations set a baseline, but can only be the starting point. To this end,
> we worked with our members to explore some of the challenges of implemen-
> tation, and how best to overcome them. In doing so, we wanted to help firms
> implement the rules in a way that was practical, while ensuring fairness and
> proportionality to individuals affected. The [Financial Services Culture Board]
> has since produced four pieces of good practice guidance intended to help firms
> reference their own policies and procedures against a statement of what 'good'
> looks like. This guidance facilitates the practical application of the rules in a
> way that respects both the purpose and spirit of the regulation. They show the
> value of collective efforts to raise standards through the pooling of knowledge
> and expertise.[155]

In due course, there would also be benefit to industry co-operation to raise
standards and identify "what 'good' looks like" regarding a range of other
issues, such as the interpretation and application of the substantive conduct
rules. Indeed, this was recommended in the UK Finance report, referred to
above, which argued for the adoption of further guidance on such issues;
it noted that such guidance is "unlikely to be provided by the regulators and

---

prosecuted, he admitted to this behaviour in an interview with the FCA in interview (see, https://
www.fca.org.uk/publication/final-notices/jonathan-paul-burrows.pdf).

[153] UK Financial Services Culture Board website; see: https://bankingstandardsboard.org.uk/what-is-
the-bsb/.

[154] UK Financial Services Culture Board website; see: https://financialservicescultureboard.org.uk/the-
senior-managers-and-certification-regime-bsb-publishes-full-suite-of-good-practice-guidance/.

[155] Ibid.

may be an action for industry to pursue itself".[156] In the absence of clear and specific guidance, provided to staff in a manner that is salient to them, individuals may interpret the behavioural standards expected of them in a manner that fits with the firm's short-term commercial goals rather than that intended by the regulator, particularly in the context of the multitude of grey areas faced by senior business managers on a daily basis. This is discussed further in Chapter 6 of this monograph, in the context of a suggested trajectory towards professionalisation of the industry.

3.3   Individual Accountability and "Credible Deterrence"

As noted in the Introduction to this chapter, it is too early, at this stage in the evolution of the various new IARs, to reach any reliable conclusions about how regulators are likely to use the powers available to them under these regimes. Their approaches will likely depend on the particular market, institutional, political, and social context in each jurisdiction. Much will also likely depend on the actions taken by regulated firms in response to the new regulatory requirements. Regulators in different jurisdictions may, for example, move between constructive engagement with regulated firms and more forceful measures, in accordance with a "responsive regulation" strategy (discussed further in Chapter 2 of this monograph), depending on the actions of firms they regulate.[157]

One important question is: to what extent are regulators likely to focus more on sanctioning individuals for breaches of behavioural standards under the applicable IAR? In the UK, following the global financial crisis, the FCA articulated a new regulatory strategy aimed at "credible deterrence", involving increased focus on sanctioning firms and individuals to encourage behavioural change in the industry.[158] The FSA stated that "[t]o achieve credible deterrence, wrongdoers must not only realise that they face a real

---

[156] SMCR: Evolution and Reform, UK Finance, September 2019, p. 5, available at: https://www.ukfinance.org.uk/system/files/SMCR%20-%20Evolution%20and%20Reform.pdf.

[157] Ayres, I., & Braithwaite, J. (1992). *Responsive Regulation: Transcending the Deregulation Debate.* Oxford University Press; See, also, Black, J., & Baldwin, R.. (2010). Really Responsive Risk-Based Regulation. *Law & Policy*, 32, 181–213.

[158] See, generally, Black, J. (2012). Paradoxes and Failures: "New Governance" Techniques and the Financial Crisis. *The Modern Law Review*, 75(6), 1037–1063. Also, Georgosouli, A. (2019). What Makes Deterrence Credible. In Russo, C. A., Lastra, R. M., & Blair, W. eds., *Research Handbook on Law and Ethics in Banking and Finance*. Edward Elgar Publishing, 302–316.

and tangible risk of being held to account, but must also expect to face a meaningful sanction".[159]

Whilst a regulator's sanctioning powers are an essential part of its tool-kit, and firms and individuals need to be held to account for regulatory failures, there is a potential concern that an over-focus on the use of sanctioning powers might tend in the direction of an overly-aggressive and potentially unfair "heads-on-spikes" regulatory approach to dealing with breaches by individuals. This might undermine the regulators' goals of working with the financial services industry to improve behaviours. In addition, this approach may not be effective in deterring poor behaviours.[160]

How likely is it that this potential concern might materialise? It is interesting to note that, since the initial coming into force of the SMCR in March 2016, the UK regulatory authorities have imposed a sanction for breach of the SMCR individual conduct requirements in only one case. In that case, the FCA and PRA imposed fines totalling £642,430 on Mr Jes Staley, CEO of Barclays Group, for breach of the conduct rule requiring him to "act with due skill, care, and diligence".[161] Accordingly, there is no clear evidence to date of this potential concern arising, at least in the context of the SMCR.

This issue has not arisen to date under the BEAR in Australia, because of the lack of powers to sanction individuals .[162]

In Ireland, whilst the CBI currently has powers to impose fines on individuals under its Administrative Sanctions Procedure, these powers have only been used to fine individuals on a few occasions since 2010.[163]

---

[159] Enforcement Annual Performance Account 2012/13, FSA, p. 5, available at: https://www.fca.org.uk/publication/annual-reports/fsa-enforcement-performance-account-2012-13.pdf.

[160] As argued by Hodges and Steinholtz, "The deterrence policy can only go in the direction of increasing penalties, whether on firms or individuals, which will ultimately be seen as unfair and ineffective in achieving behavioural change"; Hodges, C., & Steinholtz, R. (2018). *Ethical Business Practice and Regulation: A Behavioural and Values-Based Approach to Compliance and Enforcement*. Bloomsbury, 184.

[161] FCA Press Release, 11 May 2018, available at: https://www.fca.org.uk/news/press-releases/fca-and-pra-jointly-fine-mr-james-staley-announce-special-requirements.

[162] Speech by APRA Deputy Chair, Helen Rowell, 20 February 2020, available at: https://www.apra.gov.au/news-and-publications/deputy-chair-helen-rowell-speech-to-australian-institute-of-company-directors.

[163] See, the following CBI public notices regarding enforcement action against individuals: June 2021 (disqualification for 15 years and fine of €200,000) imposed (see: https://www.centralbank.ie/docs/default-source/news-and-media/legal-notices/settlement-agreements/public-statement-relating-to-enforcement-action-against-gary-mccollum.pdf?sfvrsn=4) June 2020 (disqualification for 8 years 4 months, together with a fine of €70,000) imposed (see: https://www.centralbank.ie/docs/default-source/news-and-media/legal-notices/settlement-agreements/public-statement-relating-to-enforcement-action-against-rory-o'connor-former-executive-director-and-chief-financial-officer-of-rsa-ireland-insurance-dac.pdf?sfvrsn=6); December 2018 (disqualification for 18 years and fine of €23,000) imposed (see: https://www.centralbank.ie/docs/default-source/news-and-media/legal-notices/settlement-agreements/public-statement-relating-to-an-enforcement-action-against-tom-mcmenamin.pdf?sfvrsn=6); February

Furthermore, enforcement cases against individuals can be far more complex, resource-intensive for regulators and adversarial in nature than enforcement cases against firms. Whereas firms may be inclined to settle a case in order to maintain a constructive strategic relationship with their regulator, individuals may be much more inclined to consider that a sanction from the regulator may be career limiting or ending for them. Therefore, they may be more likely to adopt an adversarial approach to a regulatory investigation. The FCA has recognised this. It notes that the SMCR will lead to a new enforcement dynamic, which involves "more contest and more litigation".[164]

In this regard, it should be noted that regulatory investigations of individuals are also likely to raise potentially complex regulatory issues for the individual's firm. This may arise where the regulator investigates both the firm and individuals within the firm for regulatory breaches. The FCA has recognised that this may lead to a firm being less willing to settle cases against them where their senior managers may also be in the cross-hairs of the regulator.[165] Inevitably, firms are interested parties in any actions against their employees, particularly where the regulator's assessment of the reasonableness of steps the individual may have taken (or not taken) will likely have to take account of the relevant processes, systems and controls put in place by the employee's firm to assist their senior managers to take "reasonable steps".[166] This SMCR-type situation is quite different to the situation that might arise in other criminal or regulatory investigations of individuals (e.g. for insider trading) where the issue of the potential responsibility of the firm is unlikely to arise to the same extent.

Accordingly, regulators may be less inclined to use their sanctions tool against individuals, other than in clear cases of misbehaviour by individuals that might undermine the regulatory agenda if the regulator did not seek to impose a sanction. Therefore, whilst IARs are a key tool to ensure that senior managers are held to account for their failures, the use of the sanctioning powers against individuals under these SMCR and similar-type

---

2018 (disqualification for 3 years and fine of €23,000) imposed (see: https://www.centralbank.ie/docs/default-source/news-and-media/legal-notices/settlement-agreements/public-statement-relating-to-settlement-agreement-between-central-bank-of-ireland-and-michael-p--walsh.pdf?sfvrsn=6). In May 2017, the CBI imposed disqualification for 10 years on an individual; the CBI's public notice stated that its proposed fine of the individual was not imposed due to bankruptcy of individual (see: https://www.centralbank.ie/docs/default-source/news-and-media/legal-notices/settlement-agreements/mr-tadhg-gunnell.pdf?sfvrsn=8).

[164] Speech by Mark Steward, Director of Enforcement and Market Oversight, FCA, 19 January 2017, available at: https://www.fca.org.uk/news/speeches/practical-implications-us-law-eu-practice.

[165] Steward speech, ibid.

[166] See, Jordanoska, A. (2021). Regulatory Enforcement Against Organisational Insiders: Interactions in the Pursuit of Individual Accountability. *Regulation & Governance*, 15(2), 298–316.

regimes might form only a limited part of the overall regulatory strategy to improve behaviours in the industry.

On the other hand, in those jurisdictions where prior regulatory approval is required before an individual can take up specified types of senior management functions, regulators may make increasing use of their powers of refusal to approve in order to achieve their deterrence goal. This can readily be done, through making the application process more rigorous, including through an individual interview process, in which the regulator can, at a minimum, convey its expectations regarding conduct standards, and can refuse applications where there is evidence that these high standards have not been met.

In Ireland, for example, the CBI has stated that in 2020 that some 20 applications under the current fitness and probity regime for senior positions had been withdrawn following referral of the application to the CBI's specialist fitness and probity team in its Enforcement Division.[167] It is likely that individuals would generally prefer to withdraw their application, rather than have the CBI adopt a formal negative decision in respect of their fitness and probity. The European Central Bank (ECB) has also announced its intention of implementing "stricter and more intrusive fit and proper assessments" of applicants to board positions in banks; a number of the banks in Ireland fall within this scope.[168]

A benefit of this approach for regulators is that it is likely to be an effective means for educating senior executives of the expectations of the regulator regarding individual conduct, in a manner that is salient for the senior executives. This is in line with a "responsive regulation" approach to enforcement, in accordance with which the regulator can get important messages out to industry about the standards of behaviour it expects and can escalate the level of actions it takes as appropriate.[169] Individuals who have gone through a rigorous interview process with their regulator, during which they have had

---

[167] Speech by Derville Rowland, Director General, Financial Conduct, CBI, 10 June 2021, available at: https://www.centralbank.ie/news/article/speech-importance-of-fitness-probity-and-ensuring-responsibility-derville-rowland-10-june-2021.

[168] ECB Raises the Bar on Bank Governance, Opinion Piece, Yves Mersch, ECB, 1 October 2020, available at: https://www.bankingsupervision.europa.eu/press/interviews/date/2020/html/ssm.in2 01001~1f7f9235a4.en.html. From 4 November 2014, the ECB has been exclusively competent to assess whether directors of "significant credit institutions" (i.e. credit institutions specified as significant by the ECB) and directors of all firms applying to the ECB for authorisation as a credit institution meet minimum standards of fitness and probity in order to take up the role of director. See, generally, Guide to Fit and Proper Assessments, ECB, May 2017, available at: https://www.bankingsupervision.europa.eu/ecb/pub/pdf/ssm.fap_guide_201705.en.pdf.

[169] Ayres, I., & Braithwaite, J. (1992). *Responsive Regulation: Transcending the Deregulation Debate.* New York: Oxford University Press; See, also, Black, J., & Baldwin, R. (2010). Really Responsive Risk-Based Regulation. *Law & Policy*, University of Denver, 32(2), 181–213.

to justify actions taken (or not taken) by them, are likely to remember the experience for some time and it is likely to influence their future behaviours. Furthermore, individuals are likely to be influenced in their behaviours by this process, in particular where they know they will likely have to seek regulatory approval for a role at some future stage in their career in the financial services industry. A further benefit for regulators is that, unlike a sanctioning process, a fitness and probity application process typically requires the applicant to satisfy the regulator of the applicant's fitness and probity—in effect, a reversal of the burden of proof.[170]

3.4   Individual Accountability and Influencing Ethical Decision-Making

The new conduct rules under the IARs are intended to provide clear guidance on the standards of conduct expected of individuals in the industry, which are underpinned by a regime of individual accountability for failure to comply with these conduct standards. The IARs, in particular the UK SMCR, have been described as marking "a decisive and positive shift in the on-going challenge to improve not only firm behaviour but also how those entrusted with senior management responsibilities perceive the nature of those obligations and the consequences when they are not met".[171]

An inherent limitation of the IARs, however, is that they rest on a partial view of the factors influencing individual decision-making. Behaviour is shaped by a complex interplay of individual factors, like financial incentives; organisational cultures in particular firms; and broader structural factors, within which these organisations and individuals operate.[172] In order to influence individual decision-making effectively, not only must the context of the individual and the individual's firm be considered, but also wider industry and societal factors. Omarova employs the metaphor of the Russian nesting doll, the Matryoshka, to describe this multi-layered culture of finance. In this metaphor, the behaviour of individual actors is the inner-most doll, which is

---

[170] In the UK, the relevant provision is set out in Section 61(1) Financial Services and Markets Act 2000; in Ireland, the relevant provision is Section 23(5) Central Bank Reform Act 2010. There is currently no equivalent pre-approval process in Australia.

[171] Speech by M. Steward, Director of Enforcement and Market Oversight, FCA, 3 April 2017, available at: https://www.fca.org.uk/news/speeches/expanding-scope-individual-accountability-corporate-misconduct.

[172] Black, J. (2012), "New Governance" Techniques and the Financial Crisis. *Modern Law Review*, 75, 1037–1063, 1058. See also, McGrath, J. (2020). Why Do Good People Do Bad Things: A Multi-level Analysis of Individual, Organizational, and Structural Causes of White-Collar Crime. *Seattle University Law Review*, 43(2), 525–553.

held within various further dolls of progressively larger size, from the individual's firm to wider market dynamics. In this regard, as noted by Omarova, "[a] critically important source of firms' internal systems of norms, incentives, and behavioral patterns is the market in which these firms compete and the industry which they collectively compose".[173]

IARs are important tools to generate better organisational cultures, but they do not as such address the broader structural conditions affecting firms' culture and individual decision-making. IARs focus on holding senior individuals to account, in order to generate improved firm culture. They do this because regulators clearly recognise the relationship between the behaviours of individuals and the culture of the firm. In the language of organisational psychologists, they target bad apples and the barrels in which those apples are formed.[174] Nevertheless, the on-going debate about whether poor behaviours result from "bad apples" or "bad barrels" often ignores the wider market, political and social context in which "barrels" are formed. Often "[e]thical problems in organizations originate not with 'a few bad apples' but with the 'barrel makers'".[175]

Chapter 3 of this monograph considered a number of structural factors which give rise to misconduct in the financial services industry. Some of these factors are not specific to the financial services industry. The factors include the issue of the "morals of the marketplace", in which it is broadly expected and considered legitimate in the commercial world that an individual's firm pursue profits on the basis of freely-negotiated and, importantly, self-interested, exchange.[176] These "morals of the marketplace" are linked to an important extent to the shareholder value norm. The shareholder value norm, as articulated by Friedman, provides that managers should maximise profits for shareholders, so long as they stay within the rules.[177] In this context, poor customer outcomes and misconduct may well arise, in particular, where there is limited market competition and where there is information asymmetry as between the financial services firm and their customers (particularly in retail

---

[173] Omarova, S. T. (2017). Ethical Finance as a Systemic Challenge: Risk, Culture, and Structure. *Cornell Journal of Law and Public Policy*, 27, 797–839, 825.

[174] Scholten, W., & Ellemers, N. (2016). Bad Apples or Corrupting Barrels? Preventing Traders' Misconduct. *Journal of Financial Regulation and Compliance*, 24(4) 366–382.

[175] O'Toole, J., & Bennis, W. (2009). A Culture of Candor. *Harvard Business Review*, 87(6), 54–61, 54.

[176] Omarova, S. T. (2017). Ethical Finance as a Systemic Challenge: Risk, Culture, and Structure. *Cornell Journal of Law and Public Policy*, 27, 797–839, 810.

[177] Friedman, M. (1962). *Social Responsibility of Capital and Labor. Capital and Freedom.* The University of Chicago Press.

markets where consumers may not have a sophisticated understanding of financial products).

The IARs do not, by design, address these wider structural factors, even though they are likely to have an important influence on how senior managers interpret and apply the individual conduct rules for which they are held individually to account under the IARs. The following chapter considers one of the mechanisms that may assist in addressing these structural factors: a "trajectory towards professionalisation" in the industry.[178] The chapter argues that this mechanism would assist in fostering a pro-social norm amongst individuals in financial services firms; in other words, a recognition that they have broader obligations to society that go beyond simply short-term profit-maximisation for their firms.

4   Conclusion

The introduction of the new individual accountability frameworks in the UK and Australia, together with the forthcoming introduction of such a framework in Ireland, are important steps towards developing a culture in financial services in which senior individuals take responsibility for their actions (or failures to act). This should assist in raising the standards of compliance with regulatory requirements and ethical norms in the industry. The core elements of the new regimes involve, first, clarifying individual roles and responsibilities at a senior level within organisations. This is, in any event, a principle of good governance as outlined in the 2015 Basel Corporate Governance Principles for Banks. As large financial services firms also have a clear commercial interest in ensuring internal clarity around allocation of individual senior-level accountabilities, this convergence of interests, to some extent, between them and their regulators should facilitate the successful implementation of these requirements. There remain, however, some areas of uncertainty regarding roles and responsibilities, for example, in relation to management of risk, including conduct risk, as between the three lines of defence.

The second core element of the new regimes involves clarification of the required standards of individual behaviour. For these required standards of behaviour to become salient and part of the everyday expected behaviours within firms, regulators will need to continuously engage with firms and the wider industry to articulate the expected standards in detail and provide clear examples of the types of behaviours that are/are not acceptable. This links to

---

[178] PCBS Report, Vol. 1, para. 94.

the third core element of the new regimes, which involves holding individuals to account for failures to comply with the required standards of behaviour. It is argued that the new regimes are likely to be more successful if regulators adopt a "responsive" regulatory approach, in which the focus is on education and persuasion and where sanctioning individuals for breaches of the conduct standards is a last resort.

Also, in those jurisdictions in which individuals require the approval of the regulator to take on a senior position, the approval process provides the regulator with a particularly useful opportunity to educate individuals, encourage them to engage in relevant self-reflection in relation to the required conduct standards, get appropriate messages out to the wider industry about the required standards of behaviour, and, in limited circumstances, prohibit individuals from taking up the senior position in question, where there is clear evidence that the individual does not meet the expected standards of behaviour.

Finally, individual decision-making is shaped by a complex interplay of factors at the level of the individual, the individual's firm and wider industry and social structures and norms. Whilst the IARs are intended to influence decisions at individual and firm level, the influence of wider industry and social structures and norms must also be considered if the aims of the IARs are to be achieved. One of the mechanisms to address this, the "trajectory towards professionalisation", is considered in the following chapter.

6

Professionalising Banking: A Trajectory Towards the Internalisation of Norms

1   Introduction

As discussed in the previous chapter, individual accountability regimes (IARs) represent significant and valuable efforts to re-engineer individuals' decision-making processes and organisational cultures, but they are not designed to address the broader structural conditions which shape these contexts. As previously noted, there are many structural factors, like short-term profit-maximisation norms, that "incentivise, and then spread, misconduct across the financial services industry".[1] This chapter argues that a "trajectory towards professionalisation" will serve, at least to some extent, to address the industry-wide norms that influence firms' cultures and individual behaviours.[2] It contends that professionalisation will help to develop bankers with a professional, pro-social identity, in which there is a recognition of broader obligations to society, that exist independently of the profit-driven nature of

---

[1] Skinner, C. P. (2016). Misconduct Risk. *Fordham Law Review*, 84, 1559–1610, 1577. See also: Zaring, D. (2017). The International Campaign to Create Ethical Bankers. *Journal of Financial Regulation*, 3(2), 187–209, McGrath, J. (2019). Why Do Good People Do Bad Things: A Multi-level Analysis of Individual, Organizational, and Structural Causes of White-Collar Crime. *Seattle University Law Review*, 43, 525; Omarova, S. (2018). Ethical Finance as a Systemic Challenge: Risk, Culture, and Structure. *Cornell Journal of Law and Public Policy*, 27(3), 797–839.

[2] Parliamentary Commission on Banking Standards, Changing Banking for Good, Vol. I. The Stationery Office Limited, para. 94.

© The Author(s), under exclusive license to Springer Nature Switzerland AG 2022
J. McGrath and C. Walker, *New Accountability in Financial Services*, Palgrave Socio-Legal Studies, https://doi.org/10.1007/978-3-030-88715-5_6

banking and the hierarchy of their own firms.[3] These industry-wide norms can potentially "shape individual choice and action, within an organisation, in an endless feedback loop that includes both 'tone from the top' as well as 'echo from the bottom'".[4] Just as individuals may learn misconduct on the job, they may also learn positive behaviours by observing and interacting with the group to which they belong.[5] Over time, these patterns and ways of knowing become routine so that "what is common is moral".[6]

In this regard, as argued by the former Governor of the Bank of England, Mark Carney, an approach based on total regulation and large ex post sanctions is "bound to fail because it promotes a culture of complying with the letter of the law, not its spirit and because authorities will inevitably lag developments in fast-changing markets".[7] He argues that a "more comprehensive, lasting solution combines public regulation with private standards"; this would involve three components: aligning compensation with values, increasing senior management accountability and "renewing a sense of vocation in finance".[8] Thus, renewing a sense of vocation in finance is a key element in improving conduct and culture in the industry. This chapter argues specifically in favour of further professionalising the retail banking sector. Whilst the arguments set out have broader application throughout the banking industry and the wider financial services industry, this chapter does not seek to engage in issues such as delineations of specific sectors within the fast-changing financial services industry. This is probably best reserved for more detailed work on implementation. The focus of the discussion here is to explain why a trajectory towards increasing professionalisation in the banking industry is important and worthwhile for the purposes of improving individual behaviour and culture in the industry. Whilst this chapter notes a number of steps that have been and could be take in this direction, any detailed consideration of the steps that should be taken are not within the scope of this monograph. In this regard, the authors recognise that there

---

[3] Grant, A. M., & Berg, J. M. (2012). Prosocial Motivation. In Cameron, K. S., & Spreitzer, G. M. eds., *The Oxford Handbook of Positive Organizational Scholarship*. Oxford University Press, 28–44; Grant, A. M. (2007). Relational Job Design and the Motivation to Make a Prosocial Difference. *Academy of Management Review*, 32(2), 393–417.

[4] Cook, K., & Malone, T. (2021). Social Capital & Superminds. In Starling Compendium, Culture & Conduct Risk in the Banking Sector. Why It Matters and What Regulators Are Doing to Address It, p. 59, available at: https://starlingtrust.com/the-starling-compendium/.

[5] Ellemers, N. (2012). The Group Self. *Science*, 336(6083), 848–852.

[6] Lindström, B., Jangard, S., Selbing, I., & Olsson, A. (2018). The Role of a "Common Is Moral" Heuristic in the Stability and Change of Moral Norms. *Journal of Experimental Psychology: General*, 147(2), 228–242.

[7] Carney, M. (2021). *Values: Building a Better World for All*. Signal, 204.

[8] Ibid., pp. 204–205.

are significant challenges in professionalising banking. These include how the banking industry could be encouraged in practice to raise its standards above those that can be enforced by regulation, and whether there is a need for legislation to facilitate this.

The chapter further argues that efforts to professionalise banking should challenge and empower bankers themselves to take concrete industry-wide steps to establish and develop professional structures in which an educational formation inculcates a sense of ethical values and social purpose to banking which goes beyond profit-maximisation for the individual's firm. This training should be completed either before bankers begin to practice in firm settings or shortly thereafter so that their ethical identity is primed at an early stage. Continuing professional development (CPD) requirements should be imposed, at all levels within banks, to reinforce this training. In addition, to reinforce a professional identity, the banking community itself, as a potential moral anchor for its members, should design an industry-wide code of ethics, to articulate in detail the expected standards of behaviour within the industry and thereby reinforce a common sense of right and wrong.[9] Such industry codes could be recognised by the regulator and serve as a "safe harbour" for individuals who act in accordance with them (as is the case in the UK) or could be legally enforceable by the regulator (as is the case in Australia).

It is recognised that the professions are not without their challenges. There are concerns, for example, that other professions, like medicine, are becoming more like businesses, and that professional discipline is less about accountability and more about maintaining the respectability of the profession, especially when professionals are sanctioned for wrongdoing in only the most egregious of cases.[10] Professionalisation will not be a panacea and it is not argued that professionalisation or any form of self-regulation should displace governmental regulation in any way. Instead, professionalisation should be considered an enhancement to the second side of the regulatory pyramid, existing in parallel but distinctly from government regulation. The government still performs core regulatory functions, setting out rules and requirements, approving of codes of ethics, and punishing wrongdoing using criminal and civil sanctions in appropriate circumstances. Professionalising the financial services sector further serves to "decentre" regulation away from

---

[9] Ellemers, N. (2017). *Morality and the Regulation of Social Behaviour: Groups as Moral Anchors.* Psychology Press.

[10] Montgomery, J. (1989). Medicine, Accountability, and Professionalism. *Journal of Law and Society*, 16(3), 319–339.

State-led enforcement.[11] The network of professionals forming and enforcing norms creates "webs of influence", even in the absence of official laws and state punishments.[12] In this system, the State performs the role of a meta-regulator, in which businesses themselves are required to implement proper and effective systems of internal control, but with oversight exercised by regulators to ensure that they work properly.[13]

The purpose of this chapter is not to prescribe in precise detail the enabling framework that would establish the meta-regulation of this profession. Instead, it seeks to challenge and embolden bankers and other stakeholders to explore how banking can encourage pro-social goals, improving banking culture at a structural level for the benefit of society. It sets out the case for a trajectory towards professionalisation, in the first instance, by defining the characteristics of a profession. It then proceeds by analysing the extent to which banking maps onto these core characteristics and the extent to which governments have considered and furthered the process of professionalisation. Finally, it identifies existing gaps in the trajectory towards professionalisation and examines the merits of further professionalising banking beyond the steps already taken, critically evaluates the challenges and benefits of professionalisation, and argues in favour of professionalisation.

2   What Is a Profession?

Increasing professionalism in banking is not an entirely new concept. In the 1930s, American bankers mourned for "the good old days" when a banker "felt that he was a quasi-public servant and fiduciary" and when bankers' "code of ethics was on a plane much higher than that of business or industry".[14] Bank failures during the Great Depression, however, reminded bankers that despite their aspirations to professional standards, banking was,

---

[11] Black, J. (2001). Decentring Regulation: Understanding the Role of Regulation and Self-Regulation in a "Post-regulatory" World. *Current Legal Problems*, 54(1), 103–146.

[12] Rhodes, R. (1997). *Understanding Governance*. Open University; Rose, N. (1997). *Powers of Freedom: Reframing Political Thought*. Cambridge University Press.

[13] Parker, C. (2002). *The Open Corporation: Effective Self-Regulation and Democracy*. Cambridge University Press.

[14] Lamport, A. M. (1931). Banking—Business or Profession? *Bankers' Magazine*, 122(3), 317, available at: https://archive.org/stream/sim_bankers-magazine_1931-03_122_3/sim_bankers-mag azine_1931-03_122_3_djvu.txt.

It is possible that Lamport was harkening back to a purer time which never really existed. There is, however, evidence that this view of bankers as professionals who are "honest and reliable men of business" was also held in other jurisdictions. See Bache & Co (London) Ltd v Banque Vernes et Commercial de Paris [1973] 2 Lloyd's Rep. 437. Of course, the view of bankers may have evolved in different ways at different times and in different jurisdictions.

at its core, a business.[15] Nevertheless, the banking community said that it had learned from its mistakes and understood that respectable hardworking individuals, in the absence of banking education, were insufficient for successful and responsible banking.[16] Successful banking operations depended not just on financial strength and public trust, but on the ability of bankers.

Though these perspectives were offered almost a century ago, there are parallels with the statements of some bankers giving evidence to Parliamentary Inquiries after the recent GFC, who professed that they had learned from past mistakes, and argued in favour of higher conduct standards and the professionalisation of the financial services sector. The decline of professionalism in banking and elsewhere, Ariely notes, is associated with an increasing emphasis on "the laws of commerce, and the urge for wealth, and with it disappeared the bedrock of ethics and values on which the professions had been built".[17]

Whilst not a new concept, the status and expectations of professionals in society have changed substantially over time. Societal hierarchies have shifted from conferring status based on the ownership of property in pre-industrial times, to one based on managed capital in an industrial society, to the professional society based on human capital (where property and industry still matter).[18] In the professional society, educational qualifications, specialised training, and expertise give rise to class, power, and status. As the professional society has advanced and progressed, it has become easier to identify the contemporary features of the professions. This section argues that a profession is defined by four core characteristics. Specifically, a profession is characterised by (1) academic training in a body of specialised knowledge to exercise skilled judgements, (2) members' commitment to serve a positive social purpose, that goes beyond profit-maximisation (3) mechanisms for members to be disciplined by their community for failing to honour those duties, and (4) an underlying code of ethics. In the paragraphs below, these core characteristics are analysed under four subheadings for the ease of the reader. This is an important framework which is used in subsequent parts of this chapter to analyse the benefits of professionalising the banking sector.

---

[15] Meredith, L. D. (1932). Banking—Business or Profession? *Bankers' Magazine*, 124(4), 393.

[16] Mayham, R. E. (1938). Banking a Profession. *Bankers' Magazine*, 136(1), 23.

[17] Ariely, D. (2009). *Predictably Irrational, Revised, and Expanded Edition: The Hidden Forces That Shape Our Decisions*. Harper Collins, 209.

[18] Perkin, H. (1990). *The Rise of Professional Society: England Since 1880*. Routledge.

2.1   Specialist Training to Make Skilled Judgements

A profession is characterised as one where the training is "intellectual in character".[19] Drawing on early research on the medical profession,[20] scholars have argued that the specialist skills of professions are internally organised into a body of theory or series of abstract propositions that guide the conduct of the professional in concrete circumstances.[21] These theories are taught in formal academic settings in circumstances where on-the-job training alone would be inadequate. This education gives professionals the authority to make skilled judgements but also requires them to not use their position to take advantage of their clients. It has been argued that the professions themselves must not only play an important role in setting their own training and educational standards but that the "association must be in the van-guard. The standards it sets must be more exacting than those with which the lay public might be content".[22] The understanding of a specialist body of knowledge goes beyond an acquisition of skills and goes to "the mastery of the traditions of this particular occupation, an appreciation of its contribution and the will to continue this tradition".[23] This is an ongoing process in which the professions continuously strive for higher standards, and which brings the profession esteem and standing. It also gives the profession credibility when it seeks to work with the government to formulate the legislative policy that affects it. Some professions are well established and recognised as such, like medicine and law. They have clear qualification requirements and training pathways. Other highly skilled and well-paid occupations do not always require formal educational qualifications and they do not have the clearly delineated training pathways that usually characterise a profession.[24]

2.2   Serving a Positive Social Purpose

Professions appeal to a higher purpose, "pursued largely for others", and where "the amount of the financial return is not the accepted measure of

---

[19] Brandeis, L. B. (1912). Business—A Profession. Address at Brown University Commencement.

[20] Hall, O. (1948). The Stages of a Medical Career. *American Journal of Sociology*, 53(5), 327–336; Hall, O. (1949). Types of Medical Careers. *American Journal of Sociology*, 55(3), 243–253; Hall, O. (1951). Sociological Research in the Field of Medicine: Progress and Prospects. *American Sociological Review*, 16(5), 639–644.

[21] Greenwood, E. (1957). Attributes of a Profession. *Social Work*, 2(3) 45–55, 45.

[22] Merton, R. K. (1958). The Functions of the Professional Association. *The American Journal of Nursing*, 58(1), 50–54, 52.

[23] Despotidou, L., & Prastacos, G. P. (2012). Professionalism in Business: Insights from Ancient Philosophy. In *Leadership Through the Classics*. Springer, 437–455, 438.

[24] Greenwood, E. (1957). Attributes of a Profession. *Social Work*, 2(3), 45–55.

success".[25] With regard to medical and legal professionals, the higher purpose may be healing the sick or fighting for justice. In some instances, there is a vocational aspect to joining a profession so that the character and identity of the professional is fused with the work they do.[26] Professions develop "social and moral ties amongst its members who enter a community of purpose".[27] They have shared goals, common understandings for achieving those goals, and preserve continuity by transmitting these beliefs socially from one generation of members to the next, both formally through training and informally by custom.[28] They are most characterised by their function, not their structures, "designed in the first instance, to work through their specialised competences for the welfare of the community in general and of their respective clienteles in particular".[29] Conflicts may arise between professional interests and the public interest but it would be a mistake to think that the professions merely pay lip service to social values. Broader social norms must be respected because "Society's granting of power and privilege to the professions is premised on their willingness and ability to contribute to social well-being and to conduct their affairs in a manner consistent with broader social values".[30] This is not to say that professional activities cannot be lucrative, but these matters are expected to be pursued within the confines of the wider social purpose of the profession.

2.3   Self-Policing

Although there may be lay representation on a disciplinary board and some government oversight, the community's ability to regulate and police itself is an inherent and vital aspect of its professional status.[31] If a professional fails honestly and effectively to discharge his or her responsibilities to the client, he or she can be formally or informally disciplined by the community to which he or she belongs. It may exercise this policing power in the first instance by

---

[25] Brandeis, L. B. (1912). Business—A Profession. Address at Brown University Commencement.

[26] Buijs, J. A. (2005). Teaching: Profession or Vocation? *Journal of Catholic Education*, 8(3), 326–345.

[27] Merton, R. K. (1958). The Functions of the Professional Association. *The American Journal of Nursing*, 50–54, 52.

[28] Camenisch, P. F. (1983). *Grounding Professional Ethics in a Pluralistic Society*. Haven Publications.

[29] Merton, R. K. (1958). The Functions of the Professional Association. The *American Journal of Nursing*, 50–54, 50.

[30] Frankel, M. S. (1989). Professional Codes: Why, How, and with What Impact? *Journal of Business Ethics*, 8(2), 109–115, 110.

[31] Kaye, R. P. (2006). Regulated (Self-)Regulation: A New Paradigm for Controlling the Professions? *Public Policy and Administration*, 21(3), 105–119; Adams, T. L. (2017). Self-Regulating Professions: Past, Present, Future. *Journal of Professions and Organization*, 4(1), 70–87.

undertaking a gatekeeping role, by managing its own professional training, and by controlling admission to the profession (though the ability to screen for ethics prior to admission is generally underused).

The ability to self-regulate in this way is a privilege conferred by society so the profession must exercise its powers and privileges in the public interest. As noted previously, a profession is a community with a common purpose. To foster and maintain this common purpose, its members must demonstrate an ongoing commitment to policing its ideals and standards so that "each practitioner is his brother's keeper".[32] The members operate through organisations or professional associations generating a learning culture in which collective understandings and ethical aims are formed and reinforced.[33] These ongoing associations are cemented through the expression of values, norms, and symbols that express the culture of the profession. To observe these norms is to acquire individual prestige and social privilege.[34] To betray them is to betray one's culture and oneself, and become deviant. Deviance is not however entirely negative; enforcing the rules against a rogue operator cements the social solidarity of the group and fortifies a common sense of right and wrong.[35]

Self-regulation poses advantages and disadvantages.[36] On the one hand, self-regulation is advantageous when industry is in a better position than government to know and understand its internal operations and is better placed to act on them; when formal legal instruments are inadequate; and because it has the potential to save the money that taxpayers would otherwise have to spend on public enforcement. Interestingly, when discipline is exercised by the group to which an individual belongs (the in-group), it may be more effective in deterring misconduct, than that exercised by regulators and the government (out-groups), when the relationship with outsiders is characterised by mistrust.[37]

On the other hand, it can potentially create circumstances where groups acquire powers that are outside the usual democratic accountability processes, and where rule-making, adjudication, and enforcement displace functions

---

[32] Merton, R. K. (1958). The Functions of the Professional Association. *The American Journal of Nursing*, 58(1), 50–54, 52.

[33] Raiborn, C. A., & Payne, D. (1990). Corporate Codes of Conduct: A Collective Conscience and Continuum. *Journal of business Ethics*, 9(11), 879–889; Doig, A., & Wilson, J. (1998). The Effectiveness of Codes of Conduct. *Business Ethics: A European Review*, 7(3), 140–149.

[34] Caplow, T. (1954). *The Sociology of Work*. University of Minnesota Press.

[35] Durkheim, E. (1964). *The Rules of Sociological Method*. Free Press.

[36] Ogus, A. (1995). Rethinking Self-Regulation. *Oxford Journal of Legal Studies*, 15(1), 97–108.

[37] Mooijman, M., Van Dijk, W. W., Van Dijk, E., & Ellemers, N. (2017). On Sanction-Goal Justifications: How and Why Deterrence Justifications Undermine Rule Compliance. *Journal of Personality and Social Psychology*, 112(4), 577–588.

that should be the preserve of the State. In the United States, where self-regulatory organisations are one element of a broader mix of actors which regulate the financial services sector, albeit with government oversight, it has been argued that these organisations tend to pursue more lax enforcement policies, and government intervention generally prompts only enough action to fend off government enforcement.[38] Even those who argue in favour of self-regulation in the financial services sector acknowledge its deficiencies and know that it is a controversial hard sell, but suggest that it may be palatable where it is possible to "responsibilise" the industry into more effectively managing systemic risks, curb its profit-seeking tendencies, and make it act in the long-term public interest.[39]

2.4   Codes of Ethics/Conduct

Professions demonstrate their commitment to acting ethically by devising and observing a code of conduct.[40] The enforceability of codes of conduct is made possible through regulatory structures. Some suggest that the code of conduct for a profession is "its most visible and explicit enunciation of its professional norms. A code embodies the collective conscience of a profession and is testimony to the group's recognition of its moral dimension".[41]

Professional codes perform various functions. They may be aspirational in setting expectations for members; educational in providing guidance on how to deal with ethical quandaries, and regulatory in detailing rules and disciplinary procedures.[42] Some parts of a code are merely virtue signalling that are designed to reassure society of its moral fibre and are not meant to be taken seriously. They are "merely costumes the profession puts on to impress outsiders".[43] Codes also remind the members that their actions have real significance for those who breach their social licence and pursue individual's interests at the expense of the collective interests of the profession. The code of conduct promotes "decisions towards consequences that are cumulatively best, but unlikely to be achieved by individual well-intentioned agents acting

---

[38] DeMarzo, P. M., Fishman, M. J., & Hagerty, K. M. (2005). Self-Regulation and Government Oversight. *The Review of Economic Studies*, 72(3), 687–706.

[39] Omarova, S. T. (2010). Rethinking the Future of Self-Regulation in the Financial Industry. *Brooklyn Journal of International Law*, 35, 665–706.

[40] Frankel, M. S. (1989). Professional Codes: Why, How, and with What Impact? *Journal of Business Ethics*, 8(2), 109–115.

[41] Ibid., p. 110.

[42] Ibid.

[43] Gibb, C: 1976, *Hidden Hierarchies: The Professions and Governments*. Greenwood Press, 242.

on their own".[44] In addition, a professional code of ethics may be seen as the price professions pay for a certain degree of autonomy over their own affairs. The public grants this privilege provided the profession exercises its powers in conformity with broader prevailing social values.

Codes of conduct are both descriptive and normative in that they reflect an ethical consensus and set the expectations for a profession. Nevertheless, they will not in themselves generate ethical conduct or even legal compliance. Enron's code of conduct, for example, committed it to the highest ethical standards but its corporate culture was one where ethical boundaries were breached when they were considered barriers to success.[45] In professional contexts, however, where cultural norms anchor the identity of its members in the moral fibre of the code, where breaches are subject to disciplinary measures by a community of peers, there is the possibility that professionals will respect its provisions.[46] Even if the code is occasionally breached, it still sets expectations and standards that professionals should measure themselves against.[47]

Where codes raise societal expectations of the profession, and where the professions strive to live up to the standards in these codes, the result is a "virtuous circle" that gives a profession standing.[48] This is an iterative process, taking place over time. The goal is that professionals internalise social expectations. Where a gap emerges between expectations and practices, the members themselves should be able to speak up and reassert their values, provided there is psychological safety amongst its members and a culture of transparency and introspection. The profession will only have standing when its members stand for something, even when they do so by speaking out against their own.[49]

Gathering these threads together, whilst it is acknowledged that the professions are not without controversy and that defining them is challenging, it has been argued that they are characterised by certain core features. A profession is one where there is a strong emphasis on training in a core body of knowledge that allows its members to make skilled judgements. There

---

[44] Goldman, A. H. (1980). *The Moral Foundations of Professional Ethics*. Rowman and Littlefield, 23.

[45] Sims, R. R., & Brinkmann, J. (2003). Enron Ethics (or: Culture Matters More Than Codes). *Journal of Business Ethics*, 45(3), 243–256.

[46] Ellemers, N. (2017). *Morality and the Regulation of Social Behaviour: Groups as Moral Anchors*. Psychology Press.

[47] Khurana, R., & Nohria, N. (2008). It's Time to Make Management a True Profession. *Harvard Business Review*, 86(10), 70–77.

[48] Romme, A. G. L. (2019). Revitalizing the Quest for Professionalism in Business and Management: Purpose, Knowledge, Behaviour, and Expectation. *International Business Research*, 12(5), 40–52, 42.

[49] Wolgast, E. H. (1992). *Ethics of an Artificial Person: Lost Responsibility in Professions and Organizations*. Stanford University Press.

are clear educational pathways into the professions and they set high standards for their members. The professions can be lucrative but financial gain is not the sole measure of their success. The professions are unified by the common expectation that they serve a higher goal than money. They must act in the public interest. In doing so, society grants professionals standing and certain privileges. One such privilege is self-regulation. The professions generally police their own members. This policing occurs on an informal basis, through common expectations and peer pressure, and through formal disciplinary actions. Members may, for example, be disciplined where they breach the profession's code of ethics. The code is an explicit expression of the standards of the profession and observing the code is the price that professionals pay for a certain amount of self-regulation. They work best when they require standards that exceed regulatory expectations and where professionals strive to uphold them. The next section analyses the case for professionalising banking. Drawing particularly on official inquiries, it examines the extent to which banking is already characterised by these core attributes, the case for further professionalisation, and the concrete steps taken in this direction, where they exist.

3   A "Trajectory Towards Professionalisation"

This section draws on formal inquiries in both the UK and Australia which have analysed the extent to which banking is a profession, and have examined the extent to which its further professionalisation would create a more ethical industry. These discussions are at a less advanced stage in Ireland. Irish inquiries into the banking crisis, whilst discussing the need for professionalism in a loose sense, did not express views on establishing banking as a formal profession,[50] though there were suggestions that bankers should engage in continuing educational development.[51] This section critically describes how both the UK and Australian inquiries have urged that banking move along a "trajectory towards professionalisation".

---

[50] Honohan P. (2010). *The Irish Banking Crisis: Regulatory and Financial Stability Policy*. Central Bank of Ireland; Nyberg, P. (2011). *Commission of Investigation into the Banking Sector in Ireland*. Government Publications Office; Regling, K., & Watson, M. (2010). *A Preliminary Report on the Sources of Ireland's Banking Crisis*. Government Publications Office.

[51] Report of the Joint Committee of Inquiry into the Banking Crisis, January 2016, available at: https://inquiries.oireachtas.ie/banking/wp-content/uploads/2016/01/02106-HOI-BE-Report-Volume1.pdf.

3.1   UK

To what extent is banking already a profession? Bankers often have specialised skills and knowledge. Due to this expertise, there is an information asymmetry between banker and customer so the customer places a high degree of trust and confidence in the banker.[52] Banking is also key to the successful operation of the economy so there is a strong public interest aspect to its operation.[53] The banking relationship, however, is primarily based on contract law, and bankers do not owe their customers fiduciary duties, like doctors and lawyers do, unless exceptional circumstances arise.[54] In the UK, the PCBS Report received a number of conflicting submissions on the status of banking as a profession.[55] Some, like the Chartered Banker Institute, argued that banking was already a profession.[56] Others (including former bankers) contested this, saying that banking was unlike the professions of law and medicine; it was more concerned with generating profit and clients were interacting with corporate entities, not individuals providing knowledge and services.[57]

The PCBS Report specified that professional status was built on four pillars: qualifications; on-going education; ethics and integrity; and professional standards bodies.[58] In the first instance, it noted that there were no formal requirements to be a banker, no common qualification held by those in banking, and that there was some evidence that the level of qualifications held by bankers had declined since the 1980s.[59] It received submissions from interested parties that a common qualification for bankers would be inappropriate because bankers performed a wide variety of different roles and provided very different services.[60] As such, a single qualification for bankers would not reflect the complexity of the banking trade. Some suggested,

---

[52] Järvinen, R. A. (2014). Consumer Trust in Banking Relationships in Europe. *International Journal of Bank Marketing*, 32(6), 551–566.

[53] Thakor, A. V. (2019). *The Purpose of Banking: Transforming Banking for Stability and Economic Growth*. Oxford University Press.

[54] Glover, J. (1995). Banks and Fiduciary Relationships. *Bond Law Review*, 7(1), 50–65; Edelman, J. J. (2010). When Do Fiduciary Duties Arise? *Law Quarterly Review*, 126, 302–327; Corcoran, E. (2020). Fiduciary Duties and Financial Services Providers. *The Irish Jurist*, 63(63), 1–27.

[55] Changing Banking for Good, UK Parliamentary Commission on Banking Standards. The Stationery Office Limited, Vol. I, available at: https://publications.parliament.uk/pa/jt201314/jtselect/jtpcbs/27/27.pdf; Vol. II available at: https://www.parliament.uk/globalassets/documents/banking-commission/Banking-final-report-vol-ii.pdf.

[56] PCBS Report, Vol. II, para. 568.

[57] Ibid., para. 569.

[58] Ibid., para. 567.

[59] Ibid., para. 571.

[60] PCBS Report, Vol. II, para. 575.

however, that whilst a single qualification would be misguided, there was, nevertheless, a shared core of knowledge which characterised both retail and wholesale banking and that some banks were reemphasising the importance of formal qualifications.[61]

There was also conflicting evidence on the importance of common codes of conduct or ethics. Some submissions called for such codes and suggested that they should be embedded in formal training.[62] Others noted that bankers had not lacked such codes in the past. One submission noted that Goldman Sachs had a code that emphasised integrity and honesty but that the code stated that its provisions could be waived "from time to time".[63] It also noted the Worshipful Company of International Bankers' Principles of Good Business Conduct. This code set high standards but the organisation did not seem to promote the code in any way except when its members were "reminded of the Principles at each annual banquet as they are reproduced in full on the menu card for the event".[64]

A professional code, the PCBS Report noted, is important in setting standards and measuring performance but not when it is "a document which employees simply sign and then forget about".[65] Instead, codes can only be effective when they are enforceable. With the professions of medicine and law, the professionals themselves exert authority over their members. If codes are breached, members are disciplined and may even by struck off the register which permits them to practice.[66] A representative of the FSA enthusiastically embraced the idea of professional discipline noting that it "gets round all the legal problems about criminal sanctions and civil sanctions".[67] The PCBS Report was more cautious, noting that a representative body that sought to promote and advance standards amongst its members could experience difficulties when seeking to enforce those standards. It noted that in the professions of medicine, law and accounting, "there is normally a clear distinction between functions such as professional development and the mechanism for investigating breaches and imposing sanctions, with the latter

---

[61] Ibid.

[62] Ibid., para. 577.

[63] Ibid., para. 579.

[64] Ibid., para. 579.

[65] Ibid., para. 581.

[66] The Financial Stability Board has suggested that addressing "rolling bad apples" is particularly important. They are individuals who continue to engage in bad behaviour in new posts by not disclosing that prior misconduct. See FSB. (2018). Strengthening Governance Frameworks to Mitigate Misconduct Risk: A Toolkit for Firms and Supervisors, available at: https://www.fsb.org/wp-content/uploads/P200418.pdf.

[67] PCBS Report, Vol. II, para. 582.

being on a statutory basis".[68] Within banking, there was no such body and no corresponding distinction. It was sceptical that any form of disciplinary body could be created in the short or medium term. If the PCBS Report had taken a directive approach and proposed the introduction of a new code and proposed creating a professional standards body to enforce it, this would have had the difficulty that would not be an organic, bottom-up, grass roots led, industry initiative. It would not, in itself, create cultural change and could create confusion if it overlapped with more formal regulatory functions.[69]

The PCBS Report did not consider banking to possess the core characteristics of a profession. It covered too wide a range of activities, lacked a common core of learning, and responsibilities to clients did not trump self-interest. It recommended, however, that bankers should embark on the "trajectory towards professionalisation".[70] The banking community should demonstrate its willingness, under its own steam, to develop its own professional body and set standards and expectations of its members that exceeded existing regulatory standards. It also encouraged and challenged the banking community by setting milestones which it should meet on this journey. The professional standards body should be able to "claim comprehensive coverage of all banks with operations in the UK" and not limit itself to the retail banks at the expense of the wholesale banking sector, or focus on new entrants or junior, customer-focusing staff at the expense of more senior operators.[71]

The PCBS Report was particularly strong on the need for the profession to adopt and require professional educational standards, particularly amongst managers. It stated bluntly, "The fact that individuals can run banks and take decisions involving significant prudential risks without being required to have any formal qualification or background in the field is a particularly notable gap".[72] It stated that the banking community must identify the common skills required of all those who work in banking and not permit its most senior staff to neglect their professional development. It noted,

> A set of expected qualifications which forces bank clerks to night school for years to come, but gives a free pass to those working in wholesale banking or at more senior levels—the groups which most conspicuously failed in recent years—would ignore the lessons of the crisis.[73]

---

[68] Ibid., para. 589.

[69] Ibid., paras. 596–598.

[70] PCBS Report, Vol. I, para. 94.

[71] PCBS Report, Vol. II, paras. 599–611.

[72] Ibid., para. 607.

[73] Ibid., para. 607.

There are regulatory requirements in the UK in relation to education and CPD for individuals working in financial services, but the more specific on-going regulatory requirements, including in relation to CPD, largely focus on customer-facing staff and do not tend to cover more senior personnel.[74] The banking community, the PCBS Report suggested, must commit itself to its own development. It should set up and fund its own professional standards body, set its own governance standards and disciplinary processes. Crucially,

> The body must never allow itself to become a cosy sinecure for retired bank chairmen and City grandees. Just as importantly, it must eschew from the outset and by dint of its constitution any role in advocacy for the interests of banks individually or collectively.[75]

The subsequent Lambert Review found that "there is a strong case for a collective effort to raise standards of behaviour and competence in the banking sector, and that the best way to deliver this is by setting up a new and independent body to drive the process forward".[76] This prompted the creation of the UK Banking Standards Board (BSB) in 2015, which was subsequently expanded into the Financial Services Culture Board (FSCB) in 2021 to encompass non-banking members. It is a non-statutory, industry-funded body, and is governed by an independent board with a majority of non-practitioner members. Its aim is to help raise standards of behaviour and competence across the industry.[77] It is not a representative body, as such, and has no regulatory or enforcement powers.[78] It operates by conducting analyses and assessments to "provide firms with an independent picture of their individual cultures, [and] enable them to benchmark themselves against sector peers and track progress over time".[79] Its CEO, Alison Cottrell, has stated that it takes an outcomes-based approach to measuring culture, where those outcomes include profits, revenues, and share prices, but that it is motivated to improve the service provided to customers, not in driving the sector's financial performance.[80]

---

[74] See generally, e.g. FCA Handbook on Training and Competence, available at: https://www.handbook.fca.org.uk/handbook/TC/.

[75] PCBS Report, Vol. II, para. 611.

[76] Lambert, R. (2014). Banking Standards Review, p. 2, available at: https://financialservicescultureboard.org.uk/pdf/banking-standards-review.pdf.

[77] See, https://financialservicescultureboard.org.uk/who-we-are/.

[78] Goff, S. (2014). Sir Richard Lambert Launches UK Banking Standards Council. *Financial Times* (19 May), available at: https://www.ft.com/content/40acded2-df38-11e3-a4cf-00144feabdc0. Lambert stated it is "absolutely not a regulatory body—it needs to stay out of the way of the FCA".

[79] See: https://financialservicescultureboard.org.uk/what-we-do/.

[80] Cottrell, A. (2018). The UK Banking Standards Board: An Outcome-Based Approach to Assessing Organisational Culture. *Journal of Risk Management in Financial Institutions*, 11(1), 47–56.

The Board has set out a framework of nine characteristics, pertaining to various ethical behaviours and competences, and uses this framework to assess banks, drawing on data from employee surveys, focus groups, interviews, and other submissions. To date, these reviews, available on the Board's website, have demonstrated a mismatch between the stated values of UK banks and the way in which their employees understand their cultures.[81] Whilst these British efforts reflect industry-led initiatives to identify issues in banking culture and promote ethical behaviours, they do not provide, by design, the self-policing that one would expect of a profession.

3.2   Australia

In Australia, the Hayne Report categorised the financial services industry as one which had insufficiently transitioned "from an industry dedicated to the sale of financial products to a profession concerned with the provision of financial advice".[82] It considered this to be concerning because clients often did not appreciate this distinction and placed a significant degree of trust and confidence in their skills and expertise, whereas, in reality, financial advisors were something between salespersons and professional advisors. The Report identified two solutions to this situation: recognise advisors as either sales-persons or as a profession. It noted the latter was in the public interest to protect clients, stating: "It is a necessary step to protect those who seek finan-cial advice … clients place their trust in advisers on the basis that they will behave like professionals".[83]

Whilst noting that some measures had been taken to professionalise the sector, the Hayne Report argued that three further steps were required. Firstly, it argued that the financial services industry lacked the public respect and trust that are necessary for it to act as a profession and that this trust could not be acquired until the industry stopped charging fees "for no service", and dealt with those who had done so in the past. Secondly, conflicts of interest were not only pervasive, they were tolerated. This was not the case in other professions and often resulted in financial services advisors giving bad advice. Thirdly, the industry lacked effective self-disciplinary procedures that charac-terised a profession, including the capacity to expel a rogue operator from the profession.

---

[81] Financial Services Culture Board website, available at: https://financialservicescultureboard.org.uk.

[82] Hayne, D. M. (2018). Final Report of the Royal Commission into Misconduct in the Banking, Superannuation and Financial Services Industry, p. 119.

[83] Ibid., p. 135.

The Hayne Report noted that whilst ASIC has the power to ban financial services advisors, it may not always exercise the power when this would be disproportionate to the harm committed and when it must direct its limited resources to more pressing wrongdoing. Accordingly, it does not address all circumstances when financial services providers fail to act with integrity and honesty. In making these observations, the Report argued that the financial services industry needed to do more to police itself effectively. Ideally, this would include a disciplinary system in which each financial advisor is registered as a precondition to providing advice, and that a single centralised body could impose a range of disciplinary actions up to and including the cancellation of the individual's registration (i.e. expulsion from the profession). Moreover, licensed operators should be obliged to report their serious compliance concerns and misconduct to this body. Industry associations and clients could make voluntary notifications about the conduct of financial services providers to this body. This would provide it with the necessary knowledge to police its members.

As further noted by the Hayne Report, however, steps had already been taken to professionalise the sector prior to this report,[84] though they gathered further momentum thereafter. In 2012, legislation implemented the Future of Financial Advice reforms (FoFA).[85] The reforms required financial services advisors to act in the best interests of their retail clients when giving advice, banned conflicted remuneration (thereby moving remuneration from a commission-based model to a fee for service model), and created greater transparency on fees for advice. The Report noted that these measures "represented an important step towards making financial advice a profession".[86]

In 2017, the Australian government also announced plans to introduce compulsory education requirements, supervision for new advisors, a code of ethics, and industry exams and professional development obligations on an annual basis.[87] The Corporations Amendment (Professional Standards of Financial Advisers) Act 2017 established the Financial Adviser Standards

---

[84] Ibid., p. 135.

[85] The Corporations Amendment (Future of Financial Advice Act 2012 and Corporations Amendment (Further Future of Financial Advice Measures) Act 2012, as amended by the Corporations Amendment (Revising Future of Financial Advice) Regulation 2014; Corporations Amendment (Financial Advice) Regulation 2015; and the Corporations Amendment (Financial Advice Measures) Act 2016.

[86] Hayne, D. M. (2018). Final Report of the Royal Commission into Misconduct in the Banking, Superannuation and Financial Services Industry, p. 131.

[87] The Hon Kelly O'Dwyer MP, Minister for Revenue and Financial Services, Higher Standards for Financial Advisers to Commence. Media Release, 9 February 2017.

and Ethics Authority (FASEA).[88] FASEA sets the education, training, and ethical standards of licensed financial advisers in Australia.[89] These requirements came into force on 1 January 2019. They transform the landscape of financial services advice. New entrants to this budding profession must have a qualifying degree, complete a one-year training period (called the "professional year"), and complete an entrance exam, the Financial Advisor Exam, before they are eligible to practice as a financial advisor or financial planner.

Regarding qualifying degrees, FASEA detailed an accreditation process relating to the core knowledge areas on the curriculum and the standards it expects, and specifically lists the degrees, courses, qualifications, and educational providers it recognises. Higher education providers are required to contact FASEA to have their qualifications accredited. In addition, upon completing the professional year, financial services advisors must complete 40 hours of CPD training on an annual basis. Existing advisors are not exempted from these educational requirements. They have until 1 January 2022 to pass the Financial Advisor exam. In addition, they must have reached an educational standard that is equivalent to an approved degree by 1 January 2026.

Regarding ethical standards, FASEA also issued a Code of Ethics, covering all financial advisors, which came into operation on 1 January 2020. Under section 921E of the Corporations Act, all relevant providers must comply with the Code of Ethics. This principles-based code is designed "to shape and reinforce ethical conduct and encourage a deeper engagement by the individual with their duties to their client as well as wider society".[90] It sets standards for ethical behaviours, client care, quality processes, and professional standards. It also emphasises the values of trustworthiness, competence, honesty, fairness, and diligence. The impact of this code, it states, is that "those who formerly provided a commercial service, are now committed to offering a professional service".[91] Financial advisors and financial planners must not merely serve their own financial interests but also the common good. As stated in the code, "While the ethos of "the market" legitimises the pursuit of self-interest through the satisfaction of others' wants, the ethos of

---

[88] See generally Treasury, Financial Adviser Standards and Ethics Authority Limited (FASEA), available at: https://treasury.gov.au/programs-and-initiatives-banking-and-finance/financial-adviser-standards-and-ethics-authority-limited-fasea/.

[89] ASIC, Professional Standards for Financial Advisers—Reforms, 17 June 2018, available at: http://asic.gov.au/regulatory-resources/financial-services/professional-standards-for-financial-advisers-reforms/. Corporations Act Ch 7 Pt 7.6 Div 8A.

[90] FASEA, Code of Ethics Standard Commences 1 January 2020, available at: https://www.fasea.gov.au/code-of-ethics/.

[91] Ibid.

"the professions" aims to secure the public good through the subordination of self-interest in favour of serving the interests of others".[92] At the end of 2020, the Australian government announced that it will move the standard-making functions of FASEA to Treasury and that the standards will be set by legislative instrument. FASEA's other functions will be transferred to ASIC and FASEA will be wound up. It suggested that this will "further streamline the number of bodies involved in the oversight of financial advisers".[93]

At present, breaching the code results in neither a criminal offence nor a civil penalty.[94] Instead, the explanatory statement for the Code of Ethics explains that all relevant providers are required by Division 8B of Part 7.6 of the Corporations Act 2001 to be covered by a compliance scheme approved by ASIC. This requires a monitoring body to oversee compliance with the Code of Ethics. If the monitoring body determines that a provider has breached the code, it may issue a warning or reprimand; require additional training; require additional supervision; require specified corrective action; require an independent compliance audit of the provider (if it is a licensee); and require the provider to provide the services to the client again at no cost, or to reduce or waive fees.

If the breach is sufficiently serious, where for example, the provider does not comply with the disciplinary measures imposed by the monitoring body, it may be excluded from coverage of the monitoring body's compliance scheme. As it is a statutory requirement under Division 8B of Part 7.6 of the Corporations Act 2001 that providers must be covered by an approved scheme, this will, in effect, remove them from the profession. As it happened, however, the code monitoring bodies were never established by the industry associations and the Australian government announced that it would replace the code monitoring bodies with a new disciplinary system and a single disciplinary body for financial advisers, as recommended by the Hayne Report.[95] Until then, ASIC monitors compliance with the Code. Moreover, it may be noted that even when this separate disciplinary system for financial advisors

---

[92] FASEA, Financial Planners and Advisers Code of Ethics 2019, section 5, available at: https://www.legislation.gov.au/Details/F2019L00117.

[93] The Hon Josh Frydenberg MP, Treasurer of the Commonwealth of Australia. (2020). Strengthening and Streamlining Oversight of the Financial Advice Sector, available at: https://ministers.treasury.gov.au/ministers/josh-frydenberg-2018/media-releases/strengthening-and-streamlining-oversight-financial.

[94] FASEA, Financial Planners and Advisers Code of Ethics. (2019). Explanatory Statement, para. 6, available at: https://www.legislation.gov.au/Details/F2019L00117/Explanatory%20Statement/Text.

[95] Taking Action on the Banking, Superannuation & Financial Services Industry Royal Commission—Recommendation 2.10: New financial Adviser Disciplinary System, available at: https://ministers.treasury.gov.au/ministers/jane-hume-2019/media-releases/taking-action-banking-superannuation-financial-services.

is established, it will not displace the role of the State in policing financial misconduct. ASIC retains its powers to investigate contraventions of the Corporations Act 2001, including breaches of section 921E of the Act. ASIC may also suspend or terminate the financial services licence of a relevant provider that is a licensee for a breach of the Code where they do not take reasonable steps to ensure their representatives comply with it.

The Australian Banking Association (ABA), an industry association, has also updated its Banking Code to provide greater oversight of the banking sector more broadly,[96] delineating over 200 new or improved customer rights.[97] It was not, however, established as a mandatory, statutory code; banks voluntarily subscribed to it. Once subscribed, however, it is a set of enforceable standards that Australian banks must live up to. The Code recognises the role and impact of banks in society, promises to build a culture on strong ethical foundations, deliver good customer service, and pledges its members to be accountable and transparent in their dealings.[98] The CEO of the ABA stated that the Association formulated this code because it recognised that it had to play a greater role in living up to social expectations that it would act ethically and in the interests of consumers.[99]

An independent committee, the Banking Code Compliance Committee (BCCC), monitors compliance with the code, investigates violations, makes findings, and takes disciplinary action for breaches of the code.[100] It may require corrective action, seek a review of remediation actions, issue a formal warning, require staff training, name and shame the wrongdoer firm, and report non-compliance to ASIC.[101] It does not offer compensation for complainants; the Australian Financial Complaints Authority (AFCA), formed from three former bodies—the Financial Ombudsman Service (FOS), the Credit and Investments Ombudsman (CIO) and the Superannuation Complaints Tribunal (SCT)—performs this role. The BCCC must detail its activities in its annual report which is published and presented to

---

[96] ABA, The Banking Code, available at: https://www.ausbanking.org.au/banking-code/.

[97] ABA. (2020). Tougher Rules, Back to Basics and the Fixing Culture One Year On, available at: https://www.ausbanking.org.au/wp-content/uploads/2020/01/ABA-Media-Release-One-year-on-from-the-RC.pdf.

[98] ABA. (2020). Banking Code of Practice Setting the standards of practice for banks, their staff and their representatives, available at: https://www.ausbanking.org.au/wp-content/uploads/2021/02/2021-Code-A4-Booklet-with-COVID-19-Special-Note-Web.pdf.

[99] Ibid.

[100] The Banking Code Compliance Committee Charter, available at: https://www.ausbanking.org.au/banking-code/.

[101] The Banking Code Compliance Committee Charter, para. 7.2, available at: https://www.ausbanking.org.au/banking-code/.

the ABA Council.[102] First issued in 1993 and refreshed several times since, the ABA code is not entirely new, and its strengths and weaknesses are well canvassed.[103] It was incorporated into contracts between the customer and the subscribing bank, making it enforceable as a breach of contract and subject to the jurisdiction of what was the Financial Ombudsman Service, and now subject to the jurisdiction of the AFCA.[104] It is significant, however, that ASIC has used its recently acquired approval rights under the Financial Sector Reform (Hayne Royal Commission Response) Act 2020 to approve of the code. The legislation also empowers ASIC to declare provisions of the code to be enforceable at law. Whilst it has not exercised this latter power, it is expected to do so.[105]

Empowering ASIC to recognise an industry code as mandatory and declare its provisions enforceable at law reflects a very significant change in regulatory approach because it shifts the emphasis away from whether providers have subscribed to the code to whether they are important for enforcement purposes. It means that "individuals can rely on these provisions, and allows for judicial decisions to set precedents that can be enforced".[106] Moreover, ASIC may take enforcement action for breaches of an enforceable code provision.[107] The legislation also requires insurers to avoid conflicts of interest, prohibits hawking products that were not requested, gives greater powers to ASIC to take action against superannuation trustees, increases the circumstances when breaches must be reported, and provides a statutory basis for APRA and ASIC to cooperate and share information with each other. The Financial Sector Reform (Hayne Royal Commission Response No. 2) Act 2021 also requires financial services providers to provide greater transparency

---

[102] The Banking Code Compliance Committee Charter, para. 9.3, available at: https://www.ausban king.org.au/banking-code/.

[103] Howell, N. J. (2015). Revisiting the Australian Code of Banking Practice: Is Self-Regulation Still Relevant for Improving Consumer Protection Standards. *University of New South Wales Law Journal*, 38, 544–586.

[104] ABA—Australian Bankers' Association: Code of Banking Practice Works Well for Bank Customers—ABA Responds to Mr Wilkie Independent MP, available at: https://www.marketscreener. com/news/latest/ABA-Australian-Bankers-Association-nbsp-Code-of-Banking-Practice-works-well-for-bank-customers--14466974/. The FOS was superseded by the Australian Financial Complaints Authority (AFCA) in 2018.

[105] ASIC Authorises Variations to the Banking Code of Practice, available at: https://www.gtlaw.com. au/insights/asic-authorises-variations-banking-code-practice.

[106] The Treasury Australian Government. (2019). Enforceability of Financial Services Industry Codes. Taking action on recommendation 1.15 of the Banking, Superannuation and Financial Services Royal Commission Consultation Paper, p. 5, available at: https://treasury.gov.au/sites/default/files/2019-03/cp-c2019-t368566.pdf.

[107] Morris, J. & Charlton, P. (2020). Enforceable Code Provisions Effective 1 January 2021, available at: https://www.nortonrosefulbright.com/en-au/knowledge/publications/1e19156e/enf orceable-code-provisions-effective-january-1-2021.

on the fees they charge, an obligation to declare any conflicts of interest or lack of independence, and stricter rules on charging interest without providing advice.[108]

Reflecting on the initiatives proposed in both the UK and Australia, both jurisdictions propose that banking should embark on a pathway towards professionalisation, with Australia already well on its way to this goal, particularly with respect to financial advisors and planners. The emphasis on education, raising standards, and enforceable codes of ethics is welcome. Reflecting meta-regulatory theory, the State is exercising its influence indirectly by mandating and encouraging industry itself to take greater ownership of the actions of its membership, whilst preserving its ability to exercise regulatory oversight when needed.[109] These developments are designed to create a culture in which financial services professionals are educated to make skilled judgements, serve pro-social purposes, forge an identity in line with its code of ethics, and exercise both informal pressure and formal discipline that favours the internalisation of norms. Though Australia is providing a more thorough legislative basis for these developments, the emphasis is on professionals taking ownership of their own members. Financial services professionals are designing their own codes to reflect industry norms and which reflect standards that the professionals should observe to preserve their sense of identity and standing. These efforts thereby aim to internalise norms of behaviour across the industry.

3.3   Ireland

In Ireland, the public conversation on professionalising banking is less advanced. Various inquiries investigating the banking sector did not consider the benefits of establishing banking as a profession,[110] though some efforts have been made to increase ethical and competency standards in banking,[111]

[108] Financial Sector Reform (Hayne Royal Commission Response No. 2) Act 2021, available at: https://www.legislation.gov.au/Details/C2021A00019.

[109] Grabosky, P. (2017). Meta-Regulation. In Drahos, P., *Regulatory Theory: Foundations and Applications*. ANU Press, 149–162.

[110] Honohan P. (2010). *The Irish Banking Crisis: Regulatory and Financial Stability Policy*. Central Bank of Ireland; Nyberg P. (2011). *Commission of Investigation into the Banking Sector in Ireland*. Government Publications Office; Regling K., & Watson, M. (2010). *A Preliminary Report on the Sources of Ireland's Banking Crisis*. Government Publications Office.

[111] Report of the Joint Committee of Inquiry into The Banking Crisis, January 2016, available at: https://inquiries.oireachtas.ie/banking/wp-content/uploads/2016/01/02106-HOI-BE-Report-Volume1.pdf.

in particular through the implementation of fitness and probity requirements under the Central Bank Reform Act 2010 and implementing measures. Under section 50 of this Act, the CBI has powers to adopt codes setting out standards of fitness and probity. Pursuant to section 50 of this Act, for example, a Fitness and Probity Standards code and Minimum Competency Code (MCC),[112] which sets "minimum professional standards for persons providing certain financial services, in particular when dealing with consumers", have been adopted; associated regulations have also been adopted.[113] The MCC requires individuals falling within its scope to be accredited and complete 15 hours of CPD each year, where at least one hour of training must be completed on ethics. No equivalent specific and detailed qualification/CPD requirements currently apply to more senior staff or board members. The CBI also has in place a Consumer Protection Code (CPC), which sets out principles that financial services providers must observe, including obligations to act "honestly, fairly, and professionally in the best interests of its customers".[114] Furthermore, aggrieved consumers may also make complaints to the Financial Services and Pensions Ombudsman.[115]

In addition, an industry-funded body, the Irish Banking Culture Board (IBCB), has recently been set up in Ireland.[116] In its first annual report, published in 2020, it noted that one in five bank employees reported a dissonance between the banks' stated values and its culture.[117] In a more recent report, summarising surveys conducted in the midst of the Covid 19 crisis, it

---

[112] CBI. (2014). Fitness and Probity Standards, available at: https://www.centralbank.ie/docs/default-source/regulation/how-we-regulate/authorisation/fitness-probity/regulated-financial-service-providers/regulatory-requirements/gns-4-1-1-3-1-1-fitness-and-probity-standards.pdf?sfvrsn=6; CBI. (2017). Minimum Competency Code 2017, available at: https://www.centralbank.ie/docs/default-source/regulation/how-we-regulate/authorisation/minimum-competency/minimum-competency-code-2017.pdf?sfvrsn=4.

[113] Central Bank of Ireland. Minimum Competency Code and Minimum Competency Regulations 2017. https://www.centralbank.ie/regulation/how-we-regulate/authorisation/minimum-competency. See Central Bank (Supervision and Enforcement) Act 2013 (Section 48(1)) Minimum Competency Regulations 2017.

[114] Central Bank of Ireland. Consumer Protection Code 2012. General Principal 2.1, available at: https://www.centralbank.ie/docs/default-source/tns/contact/codes/tns-5-3-consumer-protection-code.pdf?sfvrsn=2. See further: Donnelly, M. (2012). Revisions to the Consumer Protection Code: Expanding the Scope of Financial Services Regulation. *Commercial Law Practitioner*, 19(1), 3–13.

[115] Donnelly, M. (2012). The Financial Services Ombudsman: Asking the Existential Question. *Dublin University Law Journal*, 35, 229–260. The Financial Services Ombudsman was replaced by the Financial Services and Pensions Ombudsman by the Financial Services and Pensions Ombudsman Act 2017.

[116] See: The Irish Banking Culture Board website, available at: https://www.irishbankingcultureboard.ie.

[117] IBCB. (2020). Annual Report 2019–2020, available at: https://www.irishbankingcultureboard.ie/wp-content/uploads/2020/09/IBCB-Annual-Report-2019_2020.pdf?x92768.

found that three quarters of the public agreed that banks had an important role in helping society in a crisis, but that public trust in banking remains low, with four out of ten people stating that their perception of banks had worsened since 2008.[118] Such research suggested that the public believe in the important pro-social role of banking but do not believe that bankers are performing this role in practice. Moreover, not only has the IBCB published surveys of stakeholders and bank employees, it has also launched a potentially promising initiative, the DECIDE ethical decision-making model, which provides a framework for individuals to consider the ethical implications of their decision.[119]

Finally, it is worth noting that the Institute of Banking, which provides education and training in the sector, runs a suite of programmes on banking culture to raise professional standards and develop a consumer-focused culture in financial institutions.[120] These programmes provide bankers at all levels with classes on a range of topics, including organisational culture, decision-making biases, and group dynamics, and students are examined via learning journals that promote self-reflection. This work complements the work of the IBCB which is also educating the public and industry stakeholders about banking culture and its mission. With time, these initiatives may bear significant fruit.

Nevertheless, most of these regulatory requirements and industry initiatives, perhaps with the exception of the Institute of Banking's training programmes, do not indicate substantial progress on the trajectory towards professionalisation. In the first instance, the regulatory requirements in the form of the CBI codes referred to above have not been designed by the banking industry itself. Instead, they were essentially devised by the State, in particular the regulator, following input from a consultation process with industry. Secondly, these regulatory requirements are not self-policed or enforced by the banking community. Thirdly, whilst an ombudsman is valuable in providing opportunities for individuals to make a complaint, it is a dispute resolution service, and not a professional disciplinary mechanism through which the industry regulates itself. Similarly, the IBCB, like its UK equivalent, is not designed to be a self-regulatory body with disciplinary powers.

---

[118] IBCB. (2021). Public Trust in Banking Survey, p. 14, available at: https://603101-1952083-raikfcquaxqncofqfm.stackpathdns.com/wp-content/uploads/2021/05/IBCB-2021-eist-Public-Trust-in-Banking-Survey-ONLINE-v2.pdf.

[119] IBCB. (2020). DECIDE, available at: https://www.irishbankingcultureboard.ie/wp-content/uploads/2021/02/67621-IBCB-Decide-framework-A5-WEB.pdf.

[120] IOB, Developing an Effective Consumer Focused Culture in Financial Services, available at: https://iob.ie/areas/culture.

4   Propelling Banking Further Along the Trajectory to Professionalisation

Previous sections of this monograph analysed the core characteristics of a profession, the extent to which banking mapped onto that framework, and critically evaluated nascent efforts to professionalise the banking sector. In Australia, the journey to professionalisation is well underway with respect to advisors and planners but incomplete more generally in the broader banking community. In the UK, professionalisation has begun. In Ireland, it is not yet discussed to a significant extent. This section critically evaluates the case for further professionalisation, by reference to each of the four characteristics of a profession identified above. It acknowledges that there are significant cultural issues which hinder the further professionalisation of banking and that bankers lack the incentives to fully realise professionalisation on their own. Nevertheless, it argues that the trajectory towards professionalisation holds promise as a means of generating cultural change at the structural level of the financial services industry. It further argues that the banking industry should be more strongly encouraged to take greater control of their own membership and provide a credible and pragmatic model that provides bankers with the conditions to further professionalise. In particular, this model should emphasise industry-generated codes of conduct and an educational formation that champions the pro-social purpose of banking.

There are significant challenges at organisational and individual levels to professionalising the banking sector. Research by Cohn and Maréchal, for example, suggests that the identity of "being a banker" primes people to cheat and be dishonest.[121] They found that, when individuals were primed with materials that emphasised their identities as bankers, they were more likely to cheat to earn a bonus, compared with another group that were not primed in that way. The authors concluded that the identity of the participants as bankers prompted them to engage in unethical behaviour. Commenting on the experiment, Ariely stated, "Bankers do think of themselves as dishonest—not in a conscious way, necessarily, but in an unconscious way. Because otherwise this priming would not work".[122] If banking industry cultures, not merely individuals or firms, produce bad behaviours then it might be hard to argue that bankers see themselves as a community which

---

[121] Cohn, A., Fehr, E., & Maréchal, M. A. (2014). Business Culture and Dishonesty in the Banking Industry. *Nature*, 516(7529), 86–89.

[122] Ariely, D., quoted in Mohan, G. (2014). Banking Industry Culture Primes for Cheating, Study Suggests. *Los Angeles Times* (November 21), available at: https://www.latimes.com/science/sciencenow/la-sci-sn-cheating-bankers-20141119-story.html.

has a higher social purpose beyond making money. A sorting culture exists in which people of similar belief systems convene and cohere together.[123] The expected behaviour of this group produces norms, influences identities, and shapes individuals' choices.[124] Breaching the norms of the group will result in the wrongdoer's peers taking disciplinary action which reinforce identities and decision frameworks. All of this suggests that bad banking cultures are self-perpetuating and that disrupting an embedded culture will be extraordinarily difficult.

4.1   Education and Training

If existing industry-wide networks, norms, and identities that give rise to misconduct are to be disrupted in the longer term, this monograph argues that this must begin with an educational formation that precedes or takes place shortly after any immersion in an organisational environment which champions profit maximisation and prioritises shareholder interests over wider societal interests. Only then will professional training have a chance of bringing bankers' individual decision-making processes outside of the hierarchical structures of their own firms. This process may begin in university.[125]

Nevertheless, recognising qualifying degrees, entrance exams, traineeships, and continuing professional development is necessary but insufficient in itself. Educational expectations, standards, and requirements must change in multiple additional ways. Many bankers, particularly at senior levels, will have completed degrees and gained qualifications from business schools, and may even have completed training on ethics. Business schools, however, have been criticised for perpetuating economic systems that promote market competition, and suppressing personal values and critical perspectives.[126] Zingales, for example, notes that "poorly attended ethics classes" validate the idea that they are "of interest only for the less bright students"; that business schools must teach in all regular classes that pro-social norms are "crucial to the flourishing of a market economy"; and that they should be "much more

[123] Thakor, A. V. (2016). Corporate Culture in Banking. *Economic Policy Review*, 22(1), 5–16.

[124] Akerlof, G. A., & Kranton, R. E. (2010). *Identity Economics: How Our Identities Shape Our Work, Wages, and Well-Being*. Princeton University Press.

[125] Romme, A. G. L. (2019). Revitalizing the Quest for Professionalism in Business and Management: Purpose, Knowledge, Behavior, and Expectation. *International Business Research*, 12(5), 40–52.

[126] Learmonth, M. (2007). Critical Management Education in Action: Personal Tales of Management Unlearning. *Academy of Management Learning & Education*, 6(1), 109–113.

transparent about the negative aspects of the financial industry, from rent-seeking behaviour to captured regulation, from inefficient boards to outright fraud".[127] Others argue that whilst the syllabi may draw on rigorous research, they are insufficiency anchored in the realities of business life and do not provide practical relevance.[128] It is suggested that some professors treat their students like consumers and do not sufficiently challenge them and engage them to think for themselves.[129]

Such shortcomings do not produce reflective bankers.[130] If a shared body of knowledge in banking is to be developed, it must be both academically rigorous and practically relevant.[131] This may be achieved where it is informed by both creative discovery and scientific validation; keeps pace with cutting edge practices which are debated and tested; and where "trading zones" provide opportunities for different professionals to meet and collaborate.[132] These zones are designed to overcome existing criticisms that business scholars do not engage sufficiently with practitioners and that they only write for their own "tribes".

Some initiatives along these lines already exist, where practitioners and universities collaborate to improve educational standards. In Australia, FINSIA, a professional membership body, has developed standards and professional training programmes to educate bankers at different stages of their careers.[133] In Ireland, the Institute of Banking provides various valuable educational programmes, including an innovative qualification that aims to

---

[127] Zingales, L. (2015). Presidential Address: Does Finance Benefit Society? *The Journal of Finance*, 70(4), 1327–1363, 1358–1359.

[128] Bennis, W., & O'Toole, J. (2005). How Business Schools Lost Their Way. *Harvard Business Review*, 83(5), 96–104.

[129] Mintzberg, H. (2004). *Managers, Not MBAs: A Hard Look at the Soft Practice of Managing and Management Development*. Berrett-Koehler Publishers.

[130] De Déa Roglio, K., & Light, G. (2009). Executive MBA Programs: The Development of the Reflective Executive. *Academy of Management Learning & Education*, 8(2), 156–173.

[131] See, for example, the work completed by the Federal Reserve Bank of New York which created the Education and Industry Forum on Financial Services Culture—a committee comprising business school professors and bankers with a shared interest in improving ethics in financial services. It has published six case studies, each of which highlights ethical dilemmas facing junior employees in financial institutions. They are designed for use in the classroom and in firms, available at: https://www.newyorkfed.org/eif/educational-resources.

[132] Georges, A, Romme, L., Avenier, M. J., Denyer, D., Hodgkinson, G. P., Pandza, K., Starkey, K., & Worren, N. (2015). Towards Common Ground and Trading Zones in Management Research and Practice. *British Journal of Management*, 23(4), 544–559.

[133] Whitehead, C., & Gentilin, D. (2021). Professionalism in Australia's Banking & Finance Industry. In Starling Compendium, Culture & Conduct Risk in the Banking Sector. Why It Matters and What Regulators Are Doing to Address It, 185–188, Available at: https://starlingtrust.com/the-starling-compendium/.

embed ethical cultures within financial services organisations.[134] The Chartered Banker: Professional Standards Board in the UK also performs a similar role to promote professionalism in the industry.[135] Similarly, the Federal Reserve Bank of New York established the Education and Industry Forum on Financial Services Culture. It is composed of "business school professors and leaders from financial services firms who are committed to promoting the development of an agile, adaptable, and ethical future workforce in the financial services industry".[136] Banks in Malaysia signed a similar commitment with the Asian Institute of Chartered Bankers (AICB) to enrol key staff, including board directors, on AICB programmes and to complete courses on ethics and professional standards.[137]

These kinds of initiatives are likely to be helpful in educating the industry in respect of ethics and expected norms of behaviour. They often come too late, however, if they are only directed at the existing banking community who have already been immersed in organisational cultures with established ways of thinking that are resistant to change. These initiatives could, however, be a valuable form of CPD, or complement CPD, where students in university have been primed on these issues before starting their professional careers. This monograph argues that CPD should become a mandatory requirement for all bankers. CPD training should be required at all levels of banks, particularly at more senior levels, and cover ethics and expected norms of behaviour. In this regard, one of the recommendations of a 2016 Oireachtas (Irish Parliament) Report into the banking crisis in Ireland was that "all members of bank boards should have requisite financial skill sets and experience and should undergo ongoing compulsory Continuing Professional Development (CPD) appropriate to banking, to include risk and governance".[138] This recommendation has not, to date, been implemented in Ireland. This kind of training gap underscores the need to establish appropriate educational expectations for bankers.

---

[134] Institute of Banking website, available at: https://iob.ie/programme/leading-cultural-change.

[135] Chartered Banker website, available at: https://www.charteredbanker.com/the-institute.html.

[136] See, website of the New York Federal Reserve for information on the Education and Industry Forum on Financial Services Culture, available at: https://www.newyorkfed.org/eif/about.

[137] See, AICB statement, November 2016, available at: https://www.aicb.org.my/announcements/ind ustry-wide-commitment-to-professionalise-the-malaysian-banking-industry-through-chartered-banker-programme/; See also, more generally, Strengthening Conduct and Culture in the Financial Industry, Central Bank of Malaysia, March 2018, available at: https://www.bnm.gov.my/index.php?ch=en_pub lication&pg=en_work_papers&ac=68&bb=file.

[138] Report of the Joint Committee of Inquiry into the Banking Crisis, January 2016, available at: https://inquiries.oireachtas.ie/banking/wp-content/uploads/2016/01/02106-HOI-BE-Report-Volume1.pdf.

4.2   A Common Purpose, a Higher Purpose

Bankers' education and training should also ingrain, from the earliest possible stage in their careers, a sense that banking is a community-based activity that serves society. Professional training may do so when it emphasises "the importance of the interconnection of people and views individuals as members of a larger community, who should strive to bring out what is best in them to achieve common interest; and highlights the importance of one being ethical to act ethically".[139] In a sense, instilling a higher social purpose in bankers should be easy. Banking, of course, already performs important social and economic purposes. In particular, the payments system it provides enables goods and services to be bought and sold easily. It also serves to match lenders with borrowers so that savings can be directed to productive uses. In addition, it enables the management of finances over the longer term so that firms, non-profit entities, and individuals (and governments) can plan their finances.[140] Finance is also positively associated with economic growth and promoting entrepreneurship.[141]

As noted by Thakor, however, their purpose should be defined not in terms of their economic transactions, but in terms of their pro-social contribution.[142] Banking culture, he argues, must be linked with this explicitly higher social purpose, which will generate greater public trust in banks. According to this view, banking can be viewed as something akin to a public utility.[143] Of course, bankers may state that they serve higher social purposes but this is not always manifested in practice. In an inquiry into the causes of the financial crisis in Ireland, for example, Nyberg noted that bankers eschewed the idea that their purposes were strictly profit-driven and stated that they were driven by a higher purpose than money: "A consistent message of the bankers interviewed by the Commission has been that money is only part of their work incentive. For people serious about professional public service, money should

---

[139] Despotidou, L., & Prastacos, G. P. (2012). Professionalism in Business: Insights from Ancient Philosophy. In *Leadership Through the Classics*. Springer, 437–455, 453.

[140] Kay, J. (2016). *Other People's Money: Masters of the Universe or Servants of the People?* Profile Books, 6.

[141] Levine, R. (2005). Finance and Growth: Theory and Evidence. In Aghion, P., & Durlauf, S. N. eds., *Handbook of Economic Growth*. North-Holland Elsevier; Guiso, L., Sapienza, P., & Zingales, L. (2004). Does Local Financial Development Matter? *Quarterly Journal of Economics*, 119, 929–969.

[142] Thakor, A. V. (2019). *The Purpose of Banking: Transforming Banking for Stability and Economic Growth*. Oxford University Press.

[143] Omarova, S. T., & Tahyar, M. E. (2011). That Which We Call a Bank: Revisiting the History of Bank Holding Company Regulations in the United States. *Review of Banking and Financial Law*, 31, 113–198; White, A. M. (2015). Banks as Utilities. *Tulane Law Review*, 90, 1241–1283.

be even less of an incentive".[144] The Report suggested, however, that "professional pride and a desire to catch up with or stay ahead of the competition (i.e. playing to win) also seem to have been important".[145]

This suggests that high-minded ideals may pale in comparison to high rewards. Training may begin in university but it requires the industry itself to maintain this sense of purpose within the profession, including through ongoing CPD and workplace cultures that support it. Nevertheless, Thakor offers hope that this is possible, if banking leaders "clearly articulate a sense of higher purpose for the bank that transcends business goals but also intersects with these goals" where the higher purpose is "consumer-centric, employee-centric, or designed to serve society".[146]

This, however, is only a part of the picture. The higher purpose must be one that gives bankers a sense of meaning so that their personal identity is intertwined with their professional role and activities. They must be able to derive not only extrinsic benefits from their role, like pay, but intrinsic benefits, which may include a sense of personal achievement and a sense of contributing to something bigger than oneself.[147] In the absence of those intrinsic motivations, the work performed is less fused with a sense of identity and just becomes a job.[148] Whilst bankers may derive some intrinsic benefits from cleverly creating or understanding a complex financial arrangement that few others could comprehend,[149] that is not the goal here. The intrinsic benefits must be ethical. Indeed, research has shown that bankers will derive greater meaning from their work where it serves pro-social purposes.[150]

Positive workplace cultures can empower people to embrace their better selves and further inculcate the higher social purpose that was emphasised in their educational formation. As noted by the FCA, "good culture is about more than ensuring good people don't do bad things—it's about enabling

[144] The Commission of Investigation Into the Banking Sector in Ireland. (2011). Misjudging Risk: Causes of the Systemic Banking Crisis in Ireland, p. x.

[145] Ibid., para. 2.3.3.

[146] Thakor, A. V. (2019). *The Purpose of Banking: Transforming Banking for Stability and Economic Growth*. Oxford University Press, p. 83.

[147] Franceschini, C. (2020). The Purpose of Work: Intrinsic Motivations in Banking. In Transforming Culture in Financial Services Driving Purposeful Cultures Discussion Paper DP20/1, pp. 52–59, available at: http://repository.tavistockandportman.ac.uk/1934/1/Menon%20-%20Denial.pdf.

[148] Akerlof, G. A., & Kranton, R. E. (2005). Identity and the Economics of Organizations. *Journal of Economic Perspectives*, 19(1), 9–32.

[149] Ochs, S. (2014). Inside the Banker's Brain: Mental Models in the Financial Services Industry and Implications for Consumers, Practitioners, and Regulators. Monograph, Initiative on Financial Security, The Aspen Institute.

[150] Ashraf, N., & Bandiera, O. (2017). Altruistic Capital. *American Economic Review*, 107(5), 70–75.

good people to do better things".[151] For this to work, firms will have to make this sense of social engagement and higher social purpose more salient to their employees. As noted by Franceschini, firms must clearly communicate to their employees the individual and firm-wide impact of their activities on the community and wider society; listen to and act on the employees' suggestions to achieve pro-social goals; and create channels where employees get direct feedback from external stakeholders so that they see the benefits of their work.[152] Some have argued in favour of a hierarchy of business purposes in which businesses serve society, serve customers, and make profit, in that order.[153] It may not be necessary, however, to have such a hierarchy or to impose this ordering if bankers simply committed to not sacrificing one of these goals (community, customer, shareholder) for the sake of any other. This would emphasise that the pro-social role of banking is compatible with a strong emphasis on profitability. It may also be helpful when banks face conflicts of interest amongst their purposes and must decide which to prioritise.[154]

4.3   Codes of Ethics/Conduct

Codes of ethics and oaths may also play a role in inculcating a higher sense of purpose in the profession. Codes are already common in the financial services sector and are unlikely to be considered problematic. There are numerous examples of financial services industry-generated codes of conduct globally. These include the 2018 Global FX Code,[155] which was developed collaboratively by central banks and industry, and does not include any legally binding norms or enforcement mechanisms. Nevertheless, the Federal Reserve Bank of New York cited it as an example of a partnership between central banks and

---

[151] FCA. (2019). Transforming Culture in Financial Services Driving Purposeful Cultures Discussion Paper DP20/1, pp. 21–23, available at: http://repository.tavistockandportman.ac.uk/1934/1/Menon%20-%20Denial.pdf.

[152] Franceschini, C. (2020). The Purpose of Work: Intrinsic Motivations in Banking. In Transforming Culture in Financial Services Driving Purposeful Cultures Discussion Paper DP20/1, 52–59.

[153] Garner, J. (2020). The Pyramid of Business Purpose. In Transforming Culture in Financial Services Driving Purposeful Cultures Discussion Paper DP20/1, 21–23.

[154] Gandy provides an interesting example of "a bank [which] advertised itself as the Bank Which Likes to Say Yes. That is a good marketing strap line but knowing when to say NO is beneficial to more people". Saying no, in this instance, forgoes the profit that banks might make at the expense of customers who borrow on terms that are unfavourable to them. It may also serve to protect the bank from the customer defaulting on the loan. See: Gandy, A. (2020). Lending and Purpose: Focusing Purpose on Deliverable Technical and Cultural Change. In Transforming Culture in Financial Services Driving Purposeful Cultures Discussion Paper DP20/1, pp. 23–25.

[155] See, Global Foreign Exchange Committee website: https://www.globalfxc.org/fx_global_code.htm.

industry to build ethical norms.[156] Other examples include the Statements of Good Practice of the UK industry body, the Fixed Income, Currencies and Commodities Markets Standards Board.[157]

The UK FCA also has a process for formally recognising certain types of industry codes, with the aim of supporting and encouraging the development of good quality industry codes of conduct.[158] This recognition is of benefit to individuals whose behaviour is in line with a recognised industry code of conduct, as the FCA will consider that this tends to show that the individual has met their regulatory obligation to observe "proper standards of market conduct".[159] Additionally, in Australia, one of the recommendations in the Hayne Report was for the amendment of existing law to extend ASIC powers to approve industry codes of conduct and for breaches of such codes to constitute a breach of the law.[160] This recommendation was adopted in the Financial Sector Reform (Hayne Royal Commission Response) Act 2020, following a process of consultation.[161]

Industry efforts serve a useful purpose in articulating and promoting norms of behaviour to address specific issues in the industry. In the UK, an example of this is the FSCB statement of good practice and supporting guidance in relation to the certification regime and regulatory references.[162] These non-binding industry guidance documents are the product of industry engagement aimed at developing guidance for industry that go beyond minimum regulatory requirements. Whilst narrowly focused, non-binding, non-enforceable codes are insufficient of themselves for self-regulation by the profession, they demonstrate that the foundations already exist for the development of more meaningful industry codes of conduct of wider scope.

The swearing of oaths by individuals in industry also seems to be gaining currency.[163] Some have argued in favour of a Hippocratic style oath for

---

[156] See: https://www.newyorkfed.org/newsevents/events/banking/2020/1019-2020.

[157] See: https://fmsb.com/.

[158] FCA Policy Statement PS 18/18, July 2018, available at: https://www.fca.org.uk/publication/policy/ps18-18.pdf. Also, FCA website: https://www.fca.org.uk/about/recognised-industry-codes.

[159] FCA Policy Statement PS 18/18, July 2018, available at: https://www.fca.org.uk/publication/policy/ps18-18.pdf. Also, FCA website: https://www.fca.org.uk/about/recognised-industry-codes.

[160] Hayne Report, p. 24.

[161] See, Enforceability of Financial Services Industry Codes: Taking Action on Recommendation 1.15 of the Banking, Superannuation and Financial Services Royal Commission, 2019, Consultation Paper, available at: https://treasury.gov.au/sites/default/files/2019-03/cp-c2019-t368566.pdf.

[162] FSCB Publishes Guidance on Regulatory References, 2019, available at: https://financialservicescultureboard.org.uk/bsb-publishes-guidance-on-regulatory-references/.

[163] de Bruin, B. (2016). Pledging Integrity: Oaths as Forms of Business Ethics Management. *Journal of Business Ethics*, 136(1), 23–42; de Bruin, B. (2019). Epistemic Corporate Culture: Knowledge, Common Knowledge, and Professional Oaths. *Seattle University Law Review*, 43, 807–840.

managers.[164] It is thought that such oaths can help to restore the reputation of business leaders in the wake of the financial crisis.[165] Despite their seeming novelty, oaths have a long history in banking. Swearing an oath was an early way of regulating financial activity in the UK in the seventeenth century,

> where the first attempt to regulate financial activity occurred in 1697 when legislation was enacted that required those who worked within the "City of London" to be licensed annually by the Court of Aldermen … The regulatory regime required licensees to take an oath that they would undertake transactions honestly and without fraud.[166]

Whilst perhaps considered quaint by some, oaths are experiencing a resurgence. Since 2015, all bankers in the Netherlands must swear an oath of eight "integrity vows" pledging responsibilities to society. This is an enforceable oath with teeth. Breaches of the oath can result in a fine of up to €25,000 and a three-year ban from the industry. Bankers in Australia may voluntarily swear an oath but it is not enforceable.[167] In the UK, a representative of the British Bankers' Association stated that a banking oath "very well could be part of the answer" to restoring trust in the sector but this approach appears to have been abandoned.[168] Zaring notes, nonetheless, that bankers' oaths, "whilst short and rife with platitudes",[169] "appear to be signalling devices, which are designed to remind bankers of their responsibilities".[170] The question is: do these reminders work?

Though there is considerable scepticism about the value of bankers' oaths,[171] recent research in the behavioural sciences suggests that oaths work

[164] Khurana, R., & Nohria, N. (2008). It's Time to Make Management a True Profession. *Harvard Business Review*, 86(10), 70–77.

[165] Anderson, M. (2009). Why We Created the MBA Oath. *Harvard Business Review*. See also: Anderson, M., & Escher, P. (2010). *The MBA Oath: Setting a Higher Standard for Business Leaders*. Penguin.

[166] Francis, A., & Ryder, N. (1997). Preventing and Intervening in White-Collar Crimes. In Rorie, M., *The Handbook of White-Collar Crime*, 262–278, 263. See further: https://www.british-history.ac.uk/statutes-realm/vol7/pp285-287.

[167] Myer, R. (2019). The Bankers' Oath That Can't Be Enforced and Has Never Rubbed Out a Member. *New Daily* (February 15), available at: https://thenewdaily.com.au/money/finance-news/2019/02/14/the-bankers-oath-that-cant-be-enforced/.

[168] Sky News. (2014). Bankers Should Be Made To Take "Moral Oath", 29 July, available at: https://news.sky.com/story/bankers-should-be-made-to-take-moral-oath-10395032.

[169] Zaring, D. (2017). The International Campaign to Create Ethical Bankers. *Journal of Financial Regulation*, 3(2), 187–209.

[170] Zaring, D. (2019). Regulating Banking Ethics: A Toolkit. *Seattle University Law Review*, 43, 555–578.

[171] de Bruin, B. (2019). Epistemic Corporate Culture: Knowledge, Common Knowledge, and Professional Oaths. *Seattle University Law Review*, 43, 807–840; Loonen, T., & Rutgers, M. (2017).

as behaviourally based regulatory tools that reduce dishonesty and increase mutual trust.[172] Earlier research on this topic produced mixed results. Some experiments suggested that those who signed commitment forms before exams were more likely to cheat.[173] Others found equivalent promises to obey the tax filing requirements did not affect those with strong and stable preferences for cheating, though oaths did improve compliance amongst those with weak preferences for lying.[174]

Pe'er and Feldman, however, conducted an experiment which found a more positive correlation between pledges and honesty. They asked individuals to solve a calculus problem and if they reported that they did so correctly, they received a bonus. Some participants were not required to make an honesty pledge (the control group), some were required to swear this pledge (the pledge-only group), and some were required to swear the pledge but could also be subject to a sanction in the form of a fine for dishonesty (the pledge-and-fine group). This latter group were told that 10% of reports were audited and that if caught cheating, they would lose their bonus. Participants in the pledge-only group reported solving far fewer calculus problems—i.e. they were more honest than those who did not make a pledge. The pledge and sanction group was even more honest. Moreover, Pe'er and Feldman found that the resulting honesty did not diminish with time; one year later, they conducted the experiment again and achieved similar results. In addition, they found that neither previous tendencies to follow rules, nor periodic reminders of the pledge, made a significant difference to the results. They concluded that such pledges could reduce regulatory burdens and increase trust between regulators and the regulated.[175]

4.4   Self-Policing

A greater question is whether bankers should be allowed to self-regulate and police their own members if banking were to be reconceived as a profession. As described above, in the aftermath of the GFC, politicians have

---

Swearing to Be A Good Banker: Perceptions of the Obligatory Banker's Oath in The Netherlands. *Journal of Banking Regulation*, 18(1), 28–47.

[172] Peer, E., & Feldman, Y. (2021). Honesty Pledges for the Behaviorally-Based Regulation of Dishonesty. *Journal of European Public Policy*, 1–21.

[173] Cagala, T., Glogowsky, U., & Rincke, J. (2019). Content Matters: The Effects of Commitment Requests on Truth-Telling, available at: https://papers.ssrn.com/sol3/papers.cfm?abstract_id=3432445.

[174] Jacquemet, N., Luchini, S., Malezieux, A., & Shogren, J. F. (2020). Who'll Stop Lying Under Oath? Empirical Evidence from Tax Evasion Games. *European Economic Review*, 124, 1–14.

[175] Pe'er, E., & Feldman, Y. (2021). Honesty Pledges for the Behavioral Regulation of Dishonesty. *Compliance and Enforcement*, available at: https://wp.nyu.edu/compliance_enforcement/2021/05/07/honesty-pledges-for-the-behavioral-regulation-of-dishonesty/#more-25460.

condemned bankers in the strongest possible rhetorical terms and have called for punitive sanctions to address wrongdoing and irresponsibility in this sector. These demands reflect the political desire to act out punitively for public approval.[176] It seems unlikely that there is sufficient public trust in the banking sector to allow it to police itself in any meaningful way, at least in the near future.[177] Given the precipitous decline in trust and confidence in banking after the GFC, is it possible that the financial services community may recognise that its survival depends on its willingness to control the worst impulses of its own members? Drawing analogies with the nuclear power industry, Omarova argues that the financial services sector might also be recognised as a "community of fate" which exercises self-restraint because its future requires it.[178] Omarova states that industry-wide self-regulation is overlooked in the drive for increased responsibility and argues in favour of embedded self-regulation where profit and risk-generating activities of banking are anchored and limited by broader social values. She notes, however, that the financial services industry lacks the incentives to effectively embrace this form of self-policing framework. In effect, financial markets are too characterised by profit maximisation norms to exercise self-restraint for the public good, and too unwilling to share information with competitors to make peer oversight effective.

Whilst it may well be the case that the financial services industry lacks the incentives to self-regulate effectively at present, it is also clear that bankers want to rebuild confidence and trust in their industry, even if only to forestall further legislative and regulatory interventions. As noted at the outset of this chapter, bankers themselves have called for more stringent professional standards in the sector for at least a century. In the wake of the Great Crash, they lamented the loss of social standing, the failure to observe a higher social purpose, and vowed that they had learned from their failings. They did the same when giving evidence to parliamentary inquiries after the GFC.

In many ways, history appears to be repeating itself and yet bankers still not have embarked far down the trajectory towards professionalisation by

---

[176] McGrath, J. (2019). Regulating White-Collar Crime in Ireland: An Analysis Using the Lens of Governmentality. *Crime, Law, and Social Change*, 72(4), 445–465.

[177] For an overview of recent public surveys, see: Hope Haley, V. (2020). Beyond Regulation—Adopting Purpose for Trust Repair in Financial Institutions, available at: https://www.fca.org.uk/publication/discussion/dp20-1.pdf. She states: "The 2019 Edelman Trust Barometer found the financial services sector continued to be the least-trusted sector it measures. Ipsos Mori found over a third of their respondents disagreed the banking sector shares the same values as the public or behaves responsibly; a third disagreed the banking sector even keeps its promises; and 52% agreed the sector would try to take advantage of them if it could", p. 36.

[178] Omarova, S. T. (2011). Wall Street as Community of Fate: Toward Financial Industry Self-Regulation. *University of Pennsylvania Law Review*, 159(2), 411–492.

themselves. In the UK and Australia, recent (and limited) efforts at professionalisation have been at the spur of official inquiries. It seems that the banking industry is unlikely to fully embrace professionalisation on its own because, whilst there are some incentives to do so, they do not outweigh the disincentives. This is not to say that professionalisation and self-regulation do not confer significant benefits. For one, the financial services industry is likely to expend fewer resources on compliance issues once regulators are satisfied that compliance has improved. For another, the industry will benefit from fewer fines and related costs if cultures of compliance are developed and successfully implemented.

The difficulty with such an approach is, however, that whilst it is in the interests of all to raise standards, it may not be in the interests of individual financial services providers to raise their own standards on a voluntary basis when they cannot be certain that others would follow suit. The difficulty for individual firms is that if they invest significantly in addressing misconduct issues within their firm, prohibiting "sharp" practices, for example, they may be less profitable than others in the wider industry where this is common. Accordingly, they risk putting themselves at a competitive disadvantage in the market. This was described by the staff at the Federal Reserve Bank of New York as a "co-ordination failure" problem. If firms fail to reach a common objective that is in the collective best interests of the industry, firms seeking to reduce misconduct risk face short-term competitive pressures. This will make it difficult for them to make long-term investments in their "cultural capital".[179] For this reason, financial services firms may choose not to take misconduct sufficiently seriously.[180]

Accordingly, significantly greater public debate, involving a range of affected stakeholders, should focus on efforts to encourage a trajectory towards professionalisation in banking. For the reasons already noted, however, it is recognised that this is not without significant challenges. Nevertheless, there is some evidence that nascent efforts at professionalisation in the UK are already increasing public trust and building a new, more ethical identity for bankers. In a survey conducted in 2017, the Chartered Banker Professional Standards Board, a voluntary membership scheme for bankers who identify as professionals, determined that the public has more trust in bankers who meet professional standards, that bankers who are members of a professional body were prouder of their work, and that those who identified

---

[179] Chaly, S., Hennessy, J., Menand, L., Stiroh, K., & Tracy, J. (2017). Misconduct Risk, Culture, and Supervision. Federal Reserve Bank of New York, available at: https://www.newyorkfed.org/med ialibrary/media/governance-and-culture-reform/2017-whitepaper.pdf.
[180] Ibid.

as a professional banker were more likely to say they did what was best for customers and do their work with higher standards of integrity.[181]

In sum, this section has outlined the challenges and opportunities posed by professionalising the financial services community. Banking would benefit from raising educational standards, setting clear training pathways, and by embracing continuing profession education. This will not be sufficient in itself, however, unless the nature of the educational formation also further embraces critical and analytical thinking, combining academic rigour with practical relevance, and anchors banking in pro-social community purposes. Business leaders generally want to make a positive difference to society and many bankers themselves already accept the pro-social purposes of banking, in theory at least, so perhaps the battle is already partly won.[182] The difficulty is, however, that financial rewards can crowd out high-minded ideals. Educational formation, tying personal identity to professional activities, informal peer pressure, formal self-discipline, codes of ethics, and oaths, will all play a part in inculcating a professional identity which exists outside the hierarchical structure of professionals' own firms. Industry self-regulation will not replace, in any way, the powers and functions of the industry regulator to regulate the industry and the individuals within it. Rather, at least in the early stages of professionalisation, there may be scope for an industry body to cajole its members into raising their standards through various forms of engagements. Nevertheless, change will not be achieved overnight. Change will be slow, halting, and inconsistent. Each of the four elements of professionalisation discussed in this chapter may, for example, move at different paces.

Unfortunately, despite discussions stretching back a century, bankers have not sufficiently moved to professionalise themselves. Accordingly, greater efforts by stakeholders (including politicians, the media, and consumer groups) would be appropriate and timely, though enabling legislation for professionalisation may also be required. If the banking industry embraces this process, it should require higher standards than those currently mandated by law, hold itself to those standards, and demonstrate that it understands that effective self-regulation is in its interests to restore public trust and confidence in banking.

---

[181] Chartered Banker Professional Standards Board. Building Professionalism in Banking CB:PSB Research 2012–2017, available at: https://www.charteredbanker.com/static/uploaded/8a3eff7d-02ea-4c1c-80dd8d1b5bcef8a2.pdf.

[182] Grant, A. M., & Berg, J. M. (2012). Prosocial Motivation. In Cameron, K. S. & Spreitzer, G. M. eds., *The Oxford Handbook of Positive Organizational Scholarship*. Oxford University Press, 28–44; Grant, A. M. (2007). Relational Job Design and the Motivation to Make a Prosocial Difference. *Academy of Management Review*, 32(2), 393–417.

5   Conclusion

Self-policing, Ayres and Braithwaite declared, works best in the shadow of the big gun held by the State.[183] As noted by the former Chairman of the SEC, when self-regulation fails, the government keeps the "shotgun, so to speak, behind the door, loaded, well-oiled, cleaned, ready for use but with the hope it would never have to be used".[184] Professionalisation, however, advances an idea which is broader than mere self-regulation. Professionalisation stimulates an environment which is cognisant not only of attitudes to compliance within firms but also champions the broader pro-social goals that the banking community may advance.[185] It challenges the industry to manage its own risks and exercise discipline over its members, thereby de-centring regulation away from the State.[186]

Nevertheless, the State is not displaced. Instead, the State meta-regulates banking, through the approval of codes of ethics, etc., to ensure that regulatory goals and objectives are met.[187] In this system, financial regulation remains subject to government oversight but professionalisation is important because it harnesses private industry to embrace a smarter, more pluralistic regulatory architecture,[188] in which the State's regulatory power is more dispersed and shared with other actors.[189] For it to be successful, however, it will simultaneously require firms to have the appropriate culture and organisational capacity and incentives to support the compliance systems which are put in place, whilst also requiring regulators to possess sufficient skills and industry experience to evaluate firms and the courage and political support to challenge them.[190]

---

[183] Ayres, I., & Braithwaite, J. (1992). *Responsive Regulation: Transcending the Deregulation Debate.* Oxford University Press.

[184] Douglas, W. O. (1940). *Democracy and Finance.* Yale University Press, 82.

[185] Baldwin, R., & Black, J. (2008). Really Responsive Regulation. *The Modern Law Review,* 71(1), 59–94.

[186] Black, J. (2002). Regulatory Conversations. *Journal of Law and Society,* 29(1), 163–196.

[187] Grabosky, P. (2013). Beyond Responsive Regulation: The Expanding Role of Nonstate Actors in the Regulatory Process. *Regulation & Governance,* 7(1), 114–123.

[188] Gunningham, N. (2016). Compliance, Enforcement, and Regulatory Excellence. In Coglianese, C. ed., *Achieving Regulatory Excellence.* Brookings Institution Press.

[189] Black, J. (2001). Decentring Regulation: Understanding the Role of Regulation and Self-Regulation in a 'Post-regulatory' World. *Current Legal Problems* 54, 103–46; Scott, C. (2004). Regulation in the Age of Governance: The Rise of the Post-regulatory State. In Jordana, J., & Levi-Faur, D. eds., *The Politics of Regulation: Institutions and Regulatory Reforms for the Age of Governance.* Edward Elgar, 145–174.

[190] Black, J. (2015). Regulatory Styles and Supervisory Strategies. In Moloney, N., Ferran, E., & Payne, J. eds., *The Oxford Handbook of Financial Regulation.* Oxford University Press, 217–253, 228.

Professionalisation may establish a basis for rebuilding trust in the banking community, provided there are robust institutional structures that support genuine professional integrity on the one hand and discipline wrongdoing on the other.[191] Professionalism will provide "both an increase in competence to undertake the various roles and membership of authoritative professional bodies which set high standards of conduct and to whom their individual members are accountable".[192] Moreover, professionalisation advances the concept of new accountability which de-emphasises sanctions in favour of strategies that promote the internalisation of ethical norms. It is a form of new accountability in which individuals are accountable to their peers. Nevertheless, efforts to establish banking as a profession would not be straightforward. In particular, banking encompasses a very broad spectrum of activities. Retail banking, for example, is very different in many relevant respects to wholesale banking. Also, the nature of banking is changing very fast, due particularly to technological change, giving rise to new industry players, who do not fit the traditional mould of bankers. The new players may see themselves as industry "disruptors" who may not wish to associate with a "profession" of banking.

Accordingly, establishing an industry-wide professional identity, beyond traditional retail banking, may be difficult; it may, for example, involve a number of different banking-related bodies dealing with specific types of activities. Also, developing banking as a profession would not, in any event, be a panacea. There is always the risk that the norms of expected behaviour that are articulated by the financial services industry itself are likely to be met with some scepticism. They may, for example, be criticised as a public relations exercise. There is also the risk that any industry-generated codes either largely duplicate the standards articulated by the financial services regulator or create confusion if they are substantially different. Professionalisation is, however, a concrete structural reform that may instil an ethos within the industry that it has a wider social function and a responsibility to society that goes beyond short-term value-maximisation for shareholders.

Coalescing as a profession can generate peer pressure, which has been known to regulate banking behaviour.[193] Groups, as Ellemers argues, are our moral anchors; we define what is right and wrong by what others

[191] O'Neill, O. (2014). Trust, Trustworthiness, and Accountability. In Morris, N., & Vines, V. eds., *Capital Failure: Rebuilding Trust in Financial Services*. Oxford University Press, 172–189, 188.

[192] Brener, A. (2019). Developing the Senior Managers Regime. In Russo, C. A., Lastra, R. M., & Blair, W. eds. *Research Handbook on Law and Ethics in Banking and Finance*. Edward Elgar Publishing, 274–301, 300.

[193] DNB. (2015). Supervision of Behaviour and Culture: Foundations, Practice & Future Developments, available at: https://www.dnb.nl/media/1gmkp1vk/supervision-of-behaviour-and-culture_t cm46-380398-1.pdf.

around us consider to be right and wrong.[194] Individuals typically wish to fit in with and belong to the group with which they identify.[195] As social beings, the influence of others can shape our moral climate, affect our judgements, and influence our behaviours.[196] Individuals belong by conforming to the norms of that group. This can have negative effects where an individual can rationalise unethical behaviours on the basis that "everyone's doing it".[197] The same dynamic can, however, give rise to positive effects where there is clear evidence of ethical behaviour by the group.[198] Professionalisation has the potential to generate the industry-wide normalisation of good behaviours because when behaviours are common in a group, they become moral norms.[199] These norms can signal positive, desirable behaviours which banking professions observe and replicate to maintain their membership in the group, creating mental shortcuts or heuristics that maintain social connections and a sense of belonging through acquiescence.[200]

For this peer pressure to have the desired effect, these standards must be clearly articulated by senior leadership.[201] Moreover, they must be commonly known and understood amongst the membership, particularly because people may have very different understanding of what integrity means in specific circumstances.[202] These understandings must also be continuously reinforced to reduce unwanted variations or "noise" in personal judgements.[203] In addition, the specified standards of behaviour must be higher than the minimum standards set by the regulator. This system will work best when the profession

---

[194] Ellemers, N. (2017). *Morality and the Regulation of Social Behaviour: Groups as Moral Anchors*. Psychology Press.

[195] Ellemers, N. (2012). The Group Self. *Science*, 336(6083), 848–852.

[196] Moore, C., & Gino, F. (2013). Ethically Adrift: How Others Pull Our Moral Compass from True North, and How We Can Fix It. *Research in Organizational Behavior*, 33, 53–77.

[197] Sykes, G. M., & Matza, D. (1957). Techniques of Neutralization: A Theory of Delinquency. *American Sociological Review*, 22(6), 664–670; McGrath, J. (2020). Why Do Good People Do Bad Things? A Multi-level Analysis of Individual, Organizational, and Structural Causes of White-Collar Crime. *Seattle University Law Review*, 43, 525–553, 525.

[198] Ellemers, N. (2012). The Group Self. *Science*, 336(6083), 848–852.

[199] Lindström, B., Jangard, S., Selbing, I., & Olsson, A. (2018). The Role of a "Common Is Moral" Heuristic in the Stability and Change of Moral Norms. *Journal of Experimental Psychology: General*, 147(2), 228–242.

[200] Ariely, D. (2008). *Predictably Irrational: The Hidden Forces That Shape Our Decisions*. Harper Perennial.

[201] UK Finance/Ashurst. (2019). SMCR: Evolution and Reform, available at: https://www.ukfinance.org.uk/system/files/SMCR%20-%20Evolution%20and%20Reform.pdf. Industry engagement to develop standards is important, as is guidance from the regulator on those standards.

[202] de Bruin, B. (2020). Epistemic Corporate Culture: Knowledge, Common Knowledge, and Professional Oaths. *University of Seattle Law Review*, 807–840, 836.

[203] Kahneman, D., Sibony, O., & Sunstein, C. S. (2021). *Noise: A Flaw in Human Judgment*. William Collins.

stays close to its members and when it does not lose the "self" in self-regulation and duplicate or resemble governmental regulatory agencies.[204] Professionalism, when properly harnessed, however, can help propel banking:

> toward a more sustainable and ethical culture by leveraging the work of industry bodies that are dedicated to bank culture. Only with collective effort, and perhaps undertaken through third parties, can the banking services industry develop an ethical esprit de corps—a reimagined professionalism in banking.[205]

In the absence of professionalisation, bankers may not have a separate professional identity in the same way as a lawyer would have, for example, as an officer of the court.[206] Accordingly, their ethical reasoning will likely be very strongly guided by their perception of the culture of the firm in which they are immersed.[207] In the absence of an educational formation that precedes admission to practice and which emphasises the pro-social professional ethos of banking, this will likely be affected by their perceptions of the interests of the firm's shareholders, so that unethical conduct may be perpetrated or tolerated if it is in the perceived interests of shareholder value maximisation. In particular, as argued by Awrey et al., where conflicts arise between value generation and ethical objectives, the latter are likely to be subordinated, especially when shareholders are powerful and there is a corporate objective that prioritises their interests.[208] For an individual in the organisation who has a separate professional identity, however, it may be that the ethical norms of that profession have a countervailing influence on the individual, making it more difficult for the individual to rationalise unethical conduct whilst maintaining a self-image as ethical.[209]

---

[204] Birdthistle, W. A., & Henderson, M. T. (2013). Becoming a Fifth Branch. *Cornell Law Review*, 99, 1–70.

[205] Skinner, C. (2021). An Evolving Legal Literature on "Misconduct Risk" and Bank Culture. In Starling Compendium, Culture & Conduct Risk in the Banking Sector/ Why It Matters and What Regulators Are Doing to Address It, 46–47, available at: https://starlingtrust.com/the-starling-compendium/.

[206] Held, M. (2017). Worthy of Trust? Law, Ethics, and Culture in Banking Blog Series, UK Banking Standards Board, p. 5, available at: https://financialservicescultureboard.org.uk/wp-content/uploads/2017/12/Worthy-of-trust-Nov17.pdf.

[207] McGrath, J. (2021). Self-Deception as a Technique of Neutralisation: An Analysis of the Subjective Account of a White-Collar Criminal. *Crime, Law and Social Change*, 75, 415–432; McGrath, J. (2020). Walk Softly and Carry No Stick: Culture, Opportunity, and Irresponsible Risk-Taking in the Irish Banking Sector. *European Journal of Criminology*, 17(1), 86–105.

[208] Awrey, D., Blair, W., & Kershaw, D. (2013). Between Law and Markets: Is There a Role for Culture and Ethics in Financial Regulation. *Delaware Journal of Corporate Law*, 38, 191–245.

[209] McGrath, J. (2021). Self-Deception as a Technique of Neutralisation: An Analysis of the Subjective Account of a White-Collar Criminal. *Crime, Law and Social Change*, 75, 415-432.

Educational requirements which emphasise the pro-social function of banking and a code of ethics, where they are deeply embedded in the industry and intertwined with the identity of the professional, may afford bankers the ability to exercise skilled independent decisions, even whilst fitting into an organisation.[210] This may inculcate a sense of commitment to stakeholders that extends beyond the shareholders of the individual's firm. When banks pursue pro-social goals that are not profit maximising, they make "important contributions and although costly in the short term will build trust and begin perhaps to restore the reputation of the banks".[211] The goal is to make bankers recognise for themselves that they are a crucial part of a broader socio-economic architecture, and do not stand apart from it.[212]

---

[210] Held, M. (2017). Worthy of Trust? Law, Ethics, and Culture in Banking Blog Series, May, UK Banking Standards Board, p. 5, available at: https://bankingstandardsboard.org.uk/wp-content/uploads/2017/12/Worthy-of-trust-Nov17.pdf.

[211] Clarke, B. (2020). Cultural Reforms in Irish Banks. Walking the Walk During the Covid-19 Crisis. In Gortsos, C., & Ringe, W.-G. eds., *Pandemic Crisis and Financial Stability*. European Banking Institute, 127–154, 143.

[212] Hollensbe, E., Wookey, C., Hickey, L., George, G., & Nichols, C. V. (2014). Organizations with Purpose. *The Academy of Management Journal*, 57(5), 1227–1234.

7

New Accountability in Financial Services: Concluding Thoughts

This monograph uses "new accountability" as a lens to describe an emphasis on measures that promote ethical cultures and the internalisation of good governance norms, rather than an approach that emphasises blame, sanctions, and punishments. It argues in favour of a trajectory towards professionalising banking, as a form of new accountability in which bankers recognise that they owe obligations to society, not merely to their firms and shareholders. It also de-emphasises a command and control, sanctioning approach to regulating the financial services sector in favour of a compliance-oriented model, in which the banking community takes more ownership for ensuring ethical standards amongst its members, albeit with state oversight, in which sanctions for wrongdoing are usually a last resort.

The emphasis on industry-wide ownership for ensuring ethical standards amongst its members is important. Recent financial scandals suggest that wrongdoing in the financial services sector is rarely the result of the actions of a few bad apples. Widespread instances of misconduct in the financial services sectors in the UK, Ireland, and Australia, much like the widespread practice of corporate irresponsibility leading to the global financial crisis more generally, suggests that the problem is not confined to a small number of individuals or a single institution. The problem is systemic and persistent; changing culture and banking behaviours across the industry is therefore crucial.

The issue that now arises is how best to ensure that banking culture, and the culture of the financial services industry more broadly, does not continue

© The Author(s), under exclusive license to Springer Nature Switzerland AG 2022
J. McGrath and C. Walker, *New Accountability in Financial Services*, Palgrave Socio-Legal Studies, https://doi.org/10.1007/978-3-030-88715-5_7

to give rise to excessive risk-taking, and sharp practices. Criminal and civil sanctions can play crucial roles in punishing and deterring wrongdoing, but sometimes they are merely a form of damage limitation after the fact. They do not preclude making preventative strategies a priority and cultural change a necessity.

In the aftermath of the global financial crisis (GFC), the limitations of criminal and civil sanctions to address misconduct are particularly apparent. There have been significant difficulties in holding senior individuals to account for wrongdoing in the financial services industry, especially where they have managed to close their eyes to wrongdoing, claim ignorance, or hide behind collective decision-making.

Accordingly, the individual accountability regimes (IARs) discussed in detail in the preceding chapters have recently been adopted by various jurisdictions to address misconduct. The leading regime is the Senior Managers and Certification Regime (SMCR) in the UK, first introduced in March 2016. It inspired the introduction of similar regimes in other jurisdictions. In Australia, a new Banking Executive Accountability Regime (BEAR) was adopted in February 2018. It is expected to be reformed and expanded in scope as the Financial Accountability Regime (FAR), to be implemented in 2022. In Ireland, in July 2021, the government published a General Scheme of a Central Bank (Individual Accountability Framework) Bill that is aimed at introducing in Ireland an IAR along the lines of the SMCR.

The exact nature of these regimes differs in each jurisdiction. In general, however, these IARs charge banks and other financial services firms with the obligation to document the specific areas of the firm's business for which each senior manager is individually accountable and map them across the organisation, ensuring that the lines of individual senior manager accountability and internal governance are clear in all of the main aspects of a firm's business. The emphasis on individual accountability is clear. The framework makes it easier to identify which senior manager is responsible for failing to address wrongdoing within their area of activity and influence.

This addresses the problem of wilful blindness by senior managers to misconduct, forcing them to take responsibility for their own actions and those of the persons they oversee. If there is information relating to potential misconduct that they could and should know and investigate further, it is no longer a defence for the senior manager to choose not to know. Potential wrongdoing within a firm becomes a specific, named senior manager's personal responsibility to address. This has the potential to lead to positive change in the tone at the top of an organisation regarding ethical conduct, which should influence the rest of the organisation. Senior managers who do not properly discharge their responsibilities face potential sanctions, depending on the jurisdiction. This framework is designed to improve internal governance and drive cultural change so that bankers and other financial services providers will treat their customers better, act ethically and embed good governance in their corporate cultures.

The new IARs are important and valuable tools which may address individual decision-making frameworks and organisational cultures. They are not, however, designed to address broader structural issues in the financial services sector that inform organisational cultures and which influence the individuals that work within them.

Research in the behavioural sciences suggests that generating ethical, industry-wide norms are important because the values inherent in an industry may bring out the best or the worst in its membership. When people form groups, they share objectives and ambitions that may allow them to transcend personal motivations and individual differences to achieve collective and social goals. Group dynamics inform the social conditions which shape individual cognitive understanding of problems and solutions. These ties may help to guide the decision-making processes of individual members, who feel committed to a group, to act in accordance with the common purpose and the collective interests of that group.

The banking community may also be a moral anchor for its members. By embarking on a trajectory towards professionalisation, bankers can reinforce a common sense of right and wrong and emphasise that bankers owe broader obligations to society that go beyond short-term profit-maximisation for their shareholders. This equally applies, of course, to all other sectors of the financial services industry. Much of the discussion in this monograph has related to banking simply because most of the main official reports into misconduct in financial services in the three jurisdictions relate largely to banking (and retail banking in particular).

Proceeding with a trajectory towards professionalisation may involve, for example, an educational formation that primes bankers with ethical identities from an early point in their careers, and inculcates a common pro-social purpose in bankers. It would also be important to have in place continuing professional development expectations, including in relation to ethical norms, that go beyond any minimum requirements imposed by regulation. These expectations should be met by bankers at all levels within the firms, including the most senior, not just customer-facing staff (which is currently predominantly the case). Industry-designed codes of ethics could support this trajectory. A professional structure provides a group identity that helps its members articulate norms of acceptable and unacceptable behaviour within the group. When these understandings and practices are common, they become moral norms and members of the group are likely to observe them to fit in with their peers. Individuals may invest in this professional identity so that breaching industry-wide, pro-social, ethical norms is to betray an important part of one's own sense of self.

There are, of course, significant challenges with increasing professionalisation. These would include, for example, how the banking industry could be encouraged in practice to raise its standards above those that can be enforced by regulation. Considerations also include whether there is a need for legislation to facilitate this; the role of industry-funded bodies, such as the UK Financial Services Culture Board and Irish banking Culture Board; and the effectiveness or otherwise of industry-wide guidance and direction. These challenges would need to be examined in further detail in due course.

Furthermore, a trajectory towards professionalisation does not equate with self-regulation and certainly not, in the foreseeable future, the extent of self-regulation that exists in well-established professions such as law and medicine. Rather, it provides more opportunities for constructive industry engagement to achieve high standards of individual behaviour in the industry. A trajectory towards professionalisation would advance meta-regulatory strategies over self-regulatory ones to achieve regulatory objectives, de-centring regulation but without displacing the role of the state which retains its full regulatory powers.

The goal must ultimately be to make bankers, along with others in the financial services industry, internalise ethical norms so that they obey the law because they recognise that it is both the right thing to do and, in their interests, though sanctioning misconduct will always be a necessary strategy to have available when they do not obey the law.

Index

© The Editor(s) (if applicable) and The Author(s), under exclusive
license to Springer Nature Switzerland AG 2022
J. McGrath and C. Walker, *New Accountability in Financial Services*,
Palgrave Socio-Legal Studies,
https://doi.org/10.1007/978-3-030-88715-5

Printed by Printforce, the Netherlands